The Industrial Revolution

Recent Titles in Crossroads in World History

The Enlightenment: History, Documents, and Key Questions
William E. Burns

The Rise of Christianity: History, Documents, and Key Questions
Kevin W. Kaatz

The Rise of Fascism: History, Documents, and Key Questions
Patrick G. Zander

The Industrial Revolution

HISTORY, DOCUMENTS, AND KEY QUESTIONS

Jeff Horn

Crossroads in World History

 ABC-CLIO™

An Imprint of ABC-CLIO, LLC
Santa Barbara, California • Denver, Colorado

Library of Congress Cataloging-in-Publication Data

Names: Horn, Jeff (Historian)
Title: The industrial revolution : history, documents, and key questions / Jeff Horn.
Description: Santa Barbara : ABC-CLIO, 2016. | Series: Crossroads in world history | Includes bibliographical references and index.
Identifiers: LCCN 2016020574 (print) | LCCN 2016022008 (ebook) | ISBN 9781610698849 (alk. paper) | ISBN 9781610698856 (ebook)
Subjects: LCSH: Industrial revolution—History. | Industrialization—History. | Social history.
Classification: LCC HD2321 .H67 2016 (print) | LCC HD2321 (ebook) | DDC 330.9/034—dc23
LC record available at https://lccn.loc.gov/2016020574

ISBN: 978-1-61069-884-9
EISBN: 978-1-61069-885-6

20 19 18 17 16   1 2 3 4 5

This book is also available as an eBook.

ABC-CLIO
An Imprint of ABC-CLIO, LLC

ABC-CLIO, LLC
130 Cremona Drive, P.O. Box 1911
Santa Barbara, California 93116-1911
www.abc-clio.com

Contents

Alphabetical List of Entries

Topical List of Entries

KEY PEOPLE

Arkwright, Richard
Bridgewater, Duke of
Brunel, Isambard Kingdom
Cartwright, Edmund
Chaptal, Jean-Antoine
Cockerill, William
Fitch, John
Hargreaves, James
Jacquard, Joseph-Marie
Liebig, Justus von
Owen, Robert
Slater, Samuel
Watt, James
Wedgwood, Josiah
Whitney, Eli

EVENTS

Agricultural Revolution
Consumer Revolution
Crystal Palace
Enlightenment
Factory Acts
Luddites
Second Industrial Revolution

INSTITUTIONS

Colonialism
Credit
Mercantilism
Patent(s)
Royal Society of Arts
Tariffs and Excise Taxes
Transportation by Water
Workforce

PROCESSES

American System of Manufactures
Armory Practice
Discipline
Division of Labor
Domestic Industry
Education
Factory System
"Industrious Revolution"
Interchangeable Parts
Pollution, Health, and Environment
Productivity
Role of the State
Socialism
Standard of Living
Waltham System

RAW MATERIALS AND INVENTIONS

Coal
Cotton
Interchangeable Parts
Iron and Steel
Railroad
Steam Engine

How to Use This Book

Throughout the course of history various events have forever changed the world. Some, like the assassination of Julius Caesar, happened centuries ago and took place quickly. Others, such as the rise of Christianity or the Enlightenment, occurred over an extended period of time and reshaped worldviews. These pivotal events, or crossroads, were departures from the established social order and pointed to new directions and opportunities. The paths leading to these crossroads in world history were often circuitous, and the routes branching off from them led to developments both anticipated and unexpected. This series helps students understand the causes and consequences of these historical turning points.

Each book in this series explores a particular crossroad in world history. Some of these events are from the ancient world and continue to reverberate today through our various political, cultural, and social institutions; others are from the modern era and have markedly changed society through their immediacy and the force of technology. While the books help students discover what happened, they also help readers understand the causes and effects linked to each event.

Each volume in the series begins with a timeline charting the essential elements of the event in capsule form. An overview essay comes next, providing a narrative history of what happened. This is followed by approximately 50 alphabetically arranged reference entries on people, places, themes, movements, and other topics central to an understanding of the historical crossroad. These entries provide essential information about their topics and close with cross-references and suggestions for further reading. A selection of 10 to 15 primary source documents follows the reference entries. Each document is accompanied by an introductory paragraph discussing the background and significance of the text. Because of their critical nature, the events covered in these volumes have generated a wide range of opinions and arguments. A section of original essays presents responses to key questions concerning the events, with each essay writer offering a different perspective on a particular topic. An annotated bibliography of print and electronic resources concludes the volume. Users can locate specific information through an alphabetical list of entries and a list of entries grouped in topical categories, as well as through a detailed index.

The various elements of each book are designed to work together to promote greater understanding of a crossroad in world history. The timeline and introductory essay overview the event, the reference entries offer easy access to essential information about key topics, the primary source documents give students first-hand accounts of the historical event, and the original argumentative essays encourage students to consider different views related to the events and to appreciate the complex nature of world history. Through its combination of background material, primary source documents, and argumentative essays, the series helps students gain insight into historical causation as they learn about the pivotal events that changed the course of history.

Preface

The Industrial Revolution changed the world. In economic terms, it gave rise to the modern era. It took centuries to develop the institutional structures, technological capacity, and global markets while accumulating enough capital to enable industrialization to occur. Centered in Great Britain in the century between 1750 and 1850, but with competition initially from France and the Austrian Netherlands (later Belgium) and then the United States and the German lands, the Industrial Revolution took advantage of European colonialism in the Atlantic world and trade ties with Asia. The Industrial Revolution also facilitated the later spurt of 19th- and 20th-century imperialism. The gap between the industrial "haves" and "have nots" widened dramatically. Unprecedented growth in manufacturing output resulting from the Industrial Revolution accelerated the elaboration of European global hegemony, forcing states that hoped to compete to seek to jumpstart their own industrial revolutions. Those that did not, or could not, found themselves relegated to providing resources and markets for increasingly dominant industrialized or industrializing powers.

This extraordinary economic transition did not come cheap. A significant proportion of the wealth, resources, and markets that underlay the Industrial Revolution were generated by the Atlantic slave trade and slavery. But the emerging working classes put in tremendously long hours laboring on dangerous machines in terrible conditions as more productive means of manufacturing goods were developed. Given this situation, it is not surprising that a huge percentage of the laborers in the first factories were there because they had no choice. Evidence for the declining standard of living for the first generations of industrial workers is overwhelming and incontrovertible. The Industrial Revolution was simply not beneficial to those who provided the raw materials or made the goods that streamed in increasing numbers from Britain's, then the West's factories, mills, and workshops. Only after 1830 did improvements in living standards trickle down to England's workers and slowly reach the working classes in other industrialized countries.

How did—how could—such a system emerge? Socioeconomic elites developed progressively more powerful state structures capable of enforcing their control over recalcitrant populations that did not want to work such long hours, in dangerous and polluted places tied to machines, especially for so little money. With the population growing and opportunities for emigration to the colonies as an outlet, beginning in the 17th century, the rulers of Britain identified the interests of the state with those of entrepreneurs ever more tightly. The British state implemented a legal framework conducive to protecting property owners, supported financial institutions like the Bank of England to provide cheap and plentiful credit, and fought wars both to defend and to acquire economic assets. Acts of Parliament to aid certain industries and particular entrepreneurs with money or monopolistic control were supplemented by the deployment of troops, police spies, and the entire military apparatus of the British state to prevent the working classes from effectively resisting their domination with force. Despite the prevalence of the myth that laissez-faire underlay its economic policies, government action was essential to British leadership of the Industrial Revolution. States that sought to follow in Britain's footsteps had to be even more active in fostering and protecting industrial society.

The key to the economic breakthrough known as the Industrial Revolution was making labor more productive through investments of capital. Human ingenuity responded to the challenge with mechanization; the replacement of human and animal power by wind, water, and coal; building factories, canals, steamships, and railroads; all while increasing the division of labor and management's oversight of the production process. This was no supply-side process; entrepreneurs and states invested their time and energy in response to clear signs of rapidly accelerating demand for a myriad of goods. One of the chief reasons for the success of industrialization was the seemingly unquenchable desire of people up and down the social scale and throughout the western world for ever more material possessions that first manifested itself in the late 17th century and shows no sign of coming to a halt.

The Industrial Revolution is studied most effectively using an inter- and cross-disciplinary perspective. History establishes the narrative and provides the evidence. An historical understanding, however, should be enriched by insights from business, political science, gender studies, sociology, and especially economics. At the same time, this book seeks to correct assumptions or misinterpretations about the Industrial Revolution that are based too much on theoretical constructs rather than on the historical record. That major thinkers on economics from Karl Marx to Paul Krugman have devoted so much attention to the age of the Industrial Revolution reminds us that this ground-breaking transition is not some irrelevant past event that can be easily or safely ignored. The Industrial Revolution still has lessons for today's policymakers, politicians, and pundits, especially those concerned with the developing world.

Following the guidelines of the series, Crossroads in World History, this book is divided into several sections for ease of use. A timeline begins the volume to structure and show the relationship between and among events. A broad yet deep essay exploring the Industrial Revolution follows to provide a narrative that introduces and contextualizes the material to come in a comprehensible framework. A section of encyclopedia entries examines the people, places, events, and processes essential to understanding a transformation as complex as the Industrial Revolution. These synthetic entries are trailed by excerpts from primary source accounts that seek to provide a flavor of the period and the issues that motivated the people who lived through these turbulent times. Many of these accounts offer conflicting interpretations of what was going on to allow readers to make their own decisions about which accounts are more convincing. Having been introduced to the central issues and considered what contemporaries had to say about them, a Key Questions section examines three issues of vital import to scholars and students from contrasting viewpoints to provide alternative interpretations to provide pathways to deeper reflection on the meaning and import of the Industrial Revolution. An annotated bibliography guides readers to the most useful and appropriate sources for further research along those pathways. Through these features, this volume provides a concise and clear means of understanding one of the most important and most enduring changes in world history.

Timeline

1771	Richard Arkwright's mechanized factory at Cromford is powered entirely by waterwheels.
1772	The Duke of Bridgewater's canal connects Manchester and Liverpool.
1773	Opening of the London Stock Exchange.
1774	Samuel Crompton begins work on the spinning mule, which combines spinning and weaving into one machine.
1776	Adam Smith publishes *The Wealth of Nations*.
1776	James Watt's main patent for an improved steam engine.
1776	United States Declaration of Independence.
1779	Samuel Crompton patents the spinning mule.
1781	Watt adapts his steam engine from a reciprocal to a rotary motion.
1783	United States becomes independent.
1783	Marquis Claude de Jouffroy builds the first steamboat on the Saône River in France.
1784	Englishman Henry Cort develops the puddling process for wrought iron.
1784	Frenchman Claude Berthollet develops a method for chemical bleaching.
1785	Edmund Cartwright invents the power-loom in England, which is patented in stages over the next three years.
1785	Henry Cort invents highly successful iron refining techniques in England.
1785	Frenchman Honoré Blanc demonstrates fully interchangeable gunlocks.
1786	Anglo-French Commercial Treaty lowers tariff rates dramatically.
1789	Outbreak of the French Revolution.
1790	Establishment of U.S. patent system in law.
1791	John Fitch receives both U.S. and French patents for a steamboat.
1793	American Eli Whitney develops the cotton gin.
1794	The first telegraph line is set up between Paris and Lille for military information.
1794	Creation of the Polytechnic and the National Institute in Paris.
1798	Englishman Edward Jenner introduces vaccination against smallpox.
1799	Englishman Charles Tennant creates bleaching powder for use on textiles by combining chlorine with lime.
1799–1800	Combination Acts make it illegal in England for workers to unionize in order to bargain for higher pay or better working conditions.

1799	Napoleon Bonaparte becomes the ruler of France.
1800	Englishman Richard Trevithick constructs a new model steam engine based on higher steam pressures.
1802	Health and Morals of Apprentices Act passes in the United Kingdom.
1803	The term *socialism* first appears in print, in Italian.
1804	Frenchman Joseph-Marie Jacquard patents a loom capable of weaving complex patterns using punch cards.
1807	American Robert Fulton's steamboat the *Clermont* completes a five-day roundtrip voyage from New York City to Albany.
1809	Frenchman Nicolas Appert develops canning to preserve food.
1811	Luddites begin breaking machines; this lasts until 1817.
1812	Parliament passes law making it illegal on penalty of death to destroy industrial machines.
1812	War of 1812 begins between the United States and the United Kingdom. It lasts until 1815.
1813	Waltham System is inaugurated by Francis Cabot Lowell.
1815	Napoleon Bonaparte is exiled for good to Saint Helena.
1815	The English Corn Laws are reformulated to provide higher profits to landowners.
1819	Cotton Mills and Factories Act passes in the United Kingdom.
1821	First iron steamboat launches in the United Kingdom.
1822	Boston Manufacturing Company founds a mill town named Lowell.
1823	Mechanics Institutes is founded in London and Glasgow to provide mechanical training to artisans and the working classes.
1824	John Hancock Hall achieves gun interchangeability at the U.S. Harpers Ferry Armory.
1825	George Stephenson develops an effective steam locomotive from his first prototype of 1814. He is commissioned to construct a 30-mile-long railway from Liverpool to Manchester.
1825	Richard Roberts patents the self-acting mule.
1825	Justus Liebig sets up the first research laboratory at the University of Giessen in Hesse.
1825	Utopian socialist community is established at New Harmony, Indiana. Robert Owen is a major influence.
1825	Erie Canal connecting Hudson River and Lake Erie is completed.
1829–1832	Captain Swing riots rock rural England.
1830	The Liverpool and Manchester Railway is the first commercial rail service.

1832	Sadler Committee investigates child labor in factories and issues report to Parliament.
1833	Slavery is abolished in Britain's colonies (completed in 1838).
1833	The Factory Act regulates child labor in textile factories.
1834	Poor Law creates "poorhouses" for the destitute.
1838	The steamship S.S. *Great Western* designed by Isambard Kingdom Brunel is launched.
1841	Great Western Railway linking London and Bristol is completed by Isambard Kingdom Brunel.
1842	Publication of the Children's Employment Commission (Mines) Report.
1842	Plug Plots led by Staffordshire miners conclude the era of machine-breaking in Britain.
1846	End of the English Corn Laws.
1847	Ten Hours Act for women and children's labor passes in the United Kingdom.
1848	British government sets up the General Board of Health to investigate sanitary conditions, setting up local boards to ensure safe water in cities.
1848	Karl Marx and Friedrich Engels publish *The Communist Manifesto.*
1848	Slavery is outlawed in the French empire.
1851	The international Exhibition featuring the Crystal Palace opens in London.
1860	Anglo-French free trade treaty is signed.
1870	Second Industrial Revolution begins.

Historical Overview

The Industrial Revolution transformed European and ultimately world society. It gave birth to the modern economy and provided the context for equally revolutionary political and social changes. Although the foundations began to be laid more than a century earlier, the transition to a fundamentally new type of industrial production emerged around 1780 in Great Britain and in other places in northwestern Europe and then spread later to North America. The initial stages of industrial transformation lasted until about 1850, which marked the height of British industrial dominance. After a few generations and based on the suffering of tens of millions of workers and slaves, the Industrial Revolution allowed Europe and later North America to improve the standard of living of the vast majority of the population and to develop the power required to maintain and then increase the West's domination of the world economy.

T. S. Ashton provided the most widely accepted definition of this revolutionary economic transformation. He identified five characteristics to differentiate an industrial "revolution" from other, less significant, forms of economic growth: increased population; the application of science to industry; a more intensive and extensive use of capital; the conversion of rural to urban communities; and the rise of new social classes. Demographic developments appear to be the essential factor, yet many historians and economists focus on Ashton's depiction of the development of a "wave of gadgets that swept Britain" during the Industrial Revolution, thereby overemphasizing the role of technological change at the expense of the role of the state and the importance of empire. Arguments that the Industrial Revolution resulted from an increasing supply of goods, both consumer and capital, available at ever-cheaper prices, are insufficiently based on the historical record. Instead, the new forms of production that made the Industrial Revolution must be understood as a means of coping with growing demand. This demand stemmed from rapid population growth and an influx of wealth siphoned off from other parts of the world. Taken together, these two massive sources of increased demand for various sorts of industrial products pushed innovators to find novel ways of giving the people what they needed, wanted, and desired.

The Industrial Revolution gave rise to a new organization of society—the emergence of new classes, urbanization, and a vastly more powerful state. Industrialization made possible rates of economic growth that overcame demographic pressures for the foreseeable future. This achievement was and is enormously important in its own right, but the Industrial Revolution also led eventually to dramatic and long-lasting improvements in the standard of living that underpin the affluence of the contemporary industrialized world. These two achievements explain why the process of industrialization in the late 18th and 19th centuries was so "revolutionary."

The Industrial Revolution was fostered effectively first by the British government and then by those states that followed in England's wake. During the early-modern era, official direction of the economy is generally associated with a group of policies collectively known as mercantilism. From 1651, Britain closely oversaw trade through a series of Navigation Acts and tight control over tariff policies to create and then maintain maritime supremacy by enabling British merchants and landowners to earn large profits. The British also gave certain mercantile associations charters to explore, colonize, and trade with specific areas. Several companies became "states within states" ruling vast territories and generating enormous profits for investors. These companies tied the global economy together, expanding world trade for the benefit of Europe. By developing institutions like the Bank of England to allow it to borrow money at low rates, the British state obtained what proved to be a decisive military advantage in the series of eight wars fought against France between 1688 and 1815. The British state used its legal system and violence to protect property and the authority of elites to encourage investment and guarantee the domination of employers over workers. Law and order enforced by the state were essential components of the British industrial advantage. The government also provided monetary incentives, tax breaks, and monopolies to entrepreneurs. Parliament passed laws to create patents to support invention while also investing in improvements to ships, docks, harbors, and weapons. Without the thoroughgoing intervention of the state, Britain would not have pioneered the Industrial Revolution.

Although the Industrial Revolution in Great Britain has been studied thoroughly, the partial nature of available statistics make it difficult for scholars to agree on the pace, scope, or timing of the emergence of high levels of economic growth. The most convincing estimates of the percentages of annual growth in the rate of real output from manufacturing range from 1.24 to 2.61 for the period 1760–1780, from 2.7 to 4.4 for the era 1800–1830, and from 2.9 to 3.1 for 1830–1870. Newly industrialized sectors accounted for nearly two-thirds of productivity growth in the British economy between 1780 and 1860. By the middle of the 19th century, Great Britain dominated the global market for the products of "modern" industry. For a generation during the middle of the 19th century, Britain produced two-thirds of world output of "new technology" products. Britain furnished half the planet's iron and cotton textiles and mined two-thirds of its coal. Discounting for inflation, Britain's gross national product (GNP) increased fourfold between 1780 and 1850. The British share of world industrial production rose from 2 percent in 1750 to 4.3 percent in 1800 to 9.5 percent in 1830 and to nearly 20 percent in 1860. Thanks to the Industrial Revolution, a relatively small island nation became the "workshop of the world," achieving a level of global economic dominance never seen before or since.

National and global economic statistics obscure the sectoral and regional character of industrialization. Certain key industries like cotton textiles and machine building grew at stunning rates thanks to technological changes that boosted labor productivity. In the key growth sector—cotton textiles—output increased more than fivefold while prices fell 50 percent in the generation from 1815 to 1841. The value of British cotton textile production skyrocketed from £600,000 in 1770 to £48.6 million in 1851 and then to £104.9 million in 1871, of which about 60 percent was exported. This phenomenal expansion was centered in the county of Lancashire, which produced between 55 and 70 percent of Britain's cotton goods. Textiles contributed a whopping 46 percent of the value added by British industry both in 1770 and in 1831. Cotton's share grew from 2.6 percent to 22.1 percent and wool fell from 30.5 percent to 14.1 percent. The woolen textile–producing region of the West Riding in Yorkshire and the iron foundries and machine shops of the West Midlands, known as the "Black Country" to contemporaries because of the heavy concentration of coal use, along with the Scottish Lowlands were the other key districts that pioneered the British Industrial Revolution. An extremely high percentage of Britain's modern industries were situated in these four regions. In 1831, Lancashire and the West Riding possessed a stunning 55 percent of all manufacturing employment in the United Kingdom, demonstrating the revolutionary character of these regions' industrial growth.

This economic development was made possible by and took advantage of rapid population growth. Britain grew from approximately 6.3 million people in 1761 to 15.9 million in 1841. This expansion was most rapid from 1791 to 1831. Britain's population growth was even more impressive because heavy emigration to the colonies and the United States as well as long years of war punctuated this era. Declining mortality played an important role, particularly among infants and young children, but increasing fertility was a greater factor. Rising fertility resulted from falling mean age of marriage and the space between births, while the proportion of women who married grew and married women became more likely to have children. These factors overcame the harsh living and working conditions, health hazards, and poor nutrition that characterized the period. These factors combined with skyrocketing urbanization to lower average life expectancy in Britain from 41.3 years in 1826 to 39.5 years in 1850. The simultaneous drop in infant and child death rates and the absence of major wars suggests both how sharp the decline in adult mortality was during the Industrial Revolution and the dramatic increases in British fertility that surmounted it.

The British Industrial Revolution was based on a number of economic, social, and political developments that began in the late 15th century and accelerated during the 17th century. These developments provided the capital and infrastructure that made industrialization feasible and profitable. Increased crop yields significant enough to be described as an "Agricultural Revolution" complemented dramatic expansion of commercial interaction both within Europe and between Europe and the rest of the world, especially the Americas. Goods from Europe's colonies in the western hemisphere were exchanged for luxury goods from Asia and human beings from Africa who were brought to the Americas to work as slaves in farms, mines, and homes. It was only once the Industrial Revolution was well underway that European manufactures could compete in many key markets around the world. The emergence of a true world economic system in the 18th century was vital to Europe's ability to industrialize. New goods, new experiences, and increased interaction with other peoples and places supported fresh ways of thinking associated with the Scientific Revolution and the Enlightenment. In their quest to understand the natural world, these movements encouraged tinkering and experimentation, which sometimes led (usually indirectly) to improvements in production.

The critical technological developments that permitted a transformation of the manufacturing process took place in England during the second half of the 18th century, but were continually refined and improved on until superseded after 1850. In almost every case, new machines and/or production processes responded to specific problems that slowed down manufacturing. In this sense, innovation was driven by economic "demand" rather than scientific or technological "supply." The decisive industry was textiles, particularly cotton, which was both stronger and easier to work than wool, linen, or silk, facilitating the switch to machine production. Cotton was also lighter, washable, and could be grown in many places around the world. Therefore, cotton textiles had an enormous potential market, greater than any other textile.

The first "blockage" to expanding production was to manufacture enough thread. This problem was resolved by Richard Arkwright's water frame (1769), James Hargreaves's spinning jenny (1770), and Samuel Crompton's spinning mule (1779). Arkwright and Hargreaves applied principles developed in woolens to the new fiber, using water and hand power respectively. Crompton's machine combined both power sources in impressive fashion; a spinning mule did 200–300 times the work of a spinning wheel. This mechanization put pressure on weavers to make use of the increased amount of available thread. Edmund Cartwright developed the power-loom (1785–1788) in response. Although for several decades the power-loom did not work any faster than a weaver, one worker could run first two, and then many looms, increasing output exponentially. American Eli Whitney patented the cotton gin in 1793 to get the seeds and dirt out of raw cotton. Finished yarn could be bleached with chlorine using a process invented by French chemist Claude-Louis Berthollet in 1784. Fifteen years later, Englishman Charles Tennant greatly improved on Berthollet's discovery by combining chlorine with lime to make bleaching powder, which was easier, more effective, and cheaper to use.

These advances permitted the British cotton industry to grow rapidly. Although wool remained the largest textile sector throughout the 18th century, the cotton industry expanded much more quickly. British cotton production increased approximately tenfold between 1760 and 1800, and accelerated even more rapidly in the 19th century. By 1830, cotton goods constituted half of all British exports.

Improvements in iron production made the rapid mechanization of industry feasible. The key to British predominance in iron making stemmed from the use of coal in smelting rather than charcoal. Iron makers preferred charcoal because, as a vegetable fuel, it did not pass on impurities to the smelted iron. However, in 18th-century England, wood shortages made charcoal expensive, encouraging the English to use coal as a replacement fuel. A great deal of British iron production shifted to the 13 North American colonies where wood was plentiful. The loss of these colonies in the War of American Independence accelerated the cost incentive to replace charcoal. Iron masters experimented until they discovered how to apply heat indirectly using a reverberatory furnace that kept coal from direct contact with iron. Englishman Henry Cort (1740–1800) developed this process, known as "puddling," in 1783–1784 and improved it in the 1790s. Rapid expansion of iron production began in the late 1790s and skyrocketed in the first decades of the

19th century as machines made from metal became ever more crucial to economic development.

The experience of artisans and iron makers with using coal as fuel and experimenting with machines stimulated British technological creativity. The most important example was the steam engine. First developed in the late 17th century and improved frequently over the course of the 18th century, the steam engine, powered by coal, put almost unlimited power at humanity's disposal, superseding the limitations of human or animal power. Early steam engines were highly inefficient at turning steam pressure into motive power. Some of Britain's best engineers, led by James Watt (1736–1819), an instrument maker from Glasgow, sought to increase its efficiency. Watt solved several technical problems, which saved a huge amount of coal and permitted the engine to be moved, making a vast array of industrial machinery possible. Watt's patented steam engine was essential to mechanization and the emergence of the factory system, but it was too large and did not produce enough pressure to run a steam-powered vehicle. Only after another Englishman, Richard Trevithick, developed such an engine in 1800 did it become possible to build steamboats and railroads, the era's most vital advances in transportation.

The question of why Great Britain was able to undertake an industrial revolution has been hotly debated since the first signs of industrialization became visible in the late 18th century. Other countries—notably France, the Netherlands, and what became Belgium—had many of the same social, economic, and technological preconditions for industrialization, so what made Britain unique? The issue remains important today because it affects national economic policies in the nonwestern world.

Britain enjoyed a number of important advantages for industrialization. Rapid population growth provided a surplus of workers forced to labor for low wages while generating a burgeoning demand for manufactured goods. In terms of natural resources, Britain had a productive agricultural sector, and large, high-quality deposits of iron and coal. Britain had myriad rivers and streams to power machines and to provide cheaper transportation. No place in Britain is more than 70 miles from the sea or more than 30 miles from a navigable waterway. The surrounding seas protected the British Isles from invasion and the damage associated with events like the Revolutionary and Napoleonic wars (1792–1815) that devastated the continent. Colonies and overseas commerce furnished needed raw materials and lucrative markets. Centuries as a leading mercantile nation had generated significant capital and fostered institutions capable of managing the national economy, like the Bank of England, that facilitated industrialization. However, by themselves, these advantages do not explain the process of industrialization or how Britain was able to lead the way to a new economy.

The labor force explains why Britain was able to lead an industrial revolution more effectively than any other factor. As a group, British workers were relatively well educated and possessed many craft skills. Perhaps more importantly, British laborers were thoroughly disciplined. They adopted innovations in technology and in the organization of production far more systematically than their brethren on the other side of the Channel. The British also adapted to the time-clock and the demands of the machine while their counterparts were distracted by political and military diversions during the upheavals of the French Revolution and Napoleon. These characteristics resulted from a combination of greater control by British elites and by heightened desperation on the part of laborers on the margins. The willingness of entrepreneurs to invest in machines and the financial need of enough laborers to accept mechanized work, which they despised, were the twin bases of Britain's major advantage in the process of early industrialization: labor productivity. This "domestication" of labor permitted the successful implementation of the factory system.

The term *domestication* has a double meaning because the rudimentary machines found in early factories required the entire family to enter the factory together, recreating the division of labor found on many farms. In general, fathers did the heavy manual labor, women undertook tasks requiring greater dexterity, and children cleaned, fetched raw materials, or tended difficult-to-reach parts of the machine. Despite the dangers to life and limb from unsafe machinery; rickety, crowded factories; and toxic materials essential to production, children and their parents worked 12- to 17-hour days, six days a week in order to earn a living wage. Only the continual improvement of machines in the 19th century made it possible for the family unit to be replaced by individuals and, later, for men to be supplanted by women or children. The ease of finding families, and subsequently children, to perform these onerous tasks reminds us of how difficult economic conditions were, and why socialist doctrines highlighting the inequality of profits created by industrialization coming at the expense of enormous human suffering by the working classes ultimately found such a large audience.

Factories concentrated workers at one site rather than in the home while mechanized production increased the division of labor and enforced hierarchical management. The use of machinery imposed geographical constraints—factories required a nearby power source, either water or coal. Thus, industrialization was regional more than national, clustering around rivers and coal deposits. This new form of production lowered costs, not only permitting greater profits but also allowing prices to be reduced, bringing manufacturing goods within the purchasing reach of more people, dramatically increasing potential demand. The creation and spread of the modern factory system within the confines of the British textile industry during the late 18th century was essential to the Industrial Revolution.

The British pioneered the factory system, and it spread most rapidly there. As a result, manufactured goods produced in the British Isles tended to be cheaper and in many cases better (thanks to the mechanization of many operations) than the same products made in other countries. British industrial dominance was founded on relatively inexpensive goods made with machinery and a high level of division of labor by workers with unique craft skills in economic sectors with highly elastic demand. Changes in the production process, the development of other countries' industrial sectors, and the evolution of consumer demand eventually sounded the death knell for Britain's advantages, but not until after 1870.

The Industrial Revolution: A to Z

AGRICULTURAL REVOLUTION Between 1600 and 1750, an "Agricultural Revolution" in Great Britain, the Dutch Republic, and parts of northern France dramatically increased crop yields. The Agricultural Revolution was an essential precondition for the Industrial Revolution, and, before the 19th century, this transformation affected the daily lives of more people than industrialization.

The Agricultural Revolution employed and spread existing knowledge, changing technique rather than applying new technology. The methods put into practice to increase crop yields had been known for centuries, but only came into widespread use in northwestern Europe in the 17th and 18th centuries. Executed most thoroughly in the Dutch Republic and England, implementation stemmed from population pressure and the desire of elites to earn higher profits from their landholdings.

Explicit production for the market, usually termed "commercial agriculture," replaced subsistence farming thanks to a host of factors such as irrigation; greater use of draft animals; different crop rotations that included grasses and clover to permit land to recover from growing grain that also provided fodder to feed larger herds of animals; more thorough breeding of animals; the systematic use of fertilizer; the enclosure of common land; the consolidation of plots; and the clearing of new land. These improvements provided incentives to consolidate holdings, creating larger farms that increased efficiency, maximized the income of landowners, allowed a significant number of people to eat better, and increased the available quantity of agricultural commodities.

The Agricultural Revolution had remarkable economic consequences. The production of more grain allowed urban areas to grow. Improved techniques meant that less labor was needed for agriculture: a greater percentage of the population could labor at other tasks such as manufacturing or mining. By increasing yields, farmers made more money, which enabled them to purchase manufactured goods, increasing demand overall and to new areas. The production of more food let prices fall despite the increasing population. Declining food prices meant people could eat more. The decline in the number of stillborn children and in infant mortality is powerful evidence of improved nutrition. Escalating profits for landowners generated by commercial agriculture could be invested in industry. In short, without the capital and other improvements provided by the Agricultural Revolution, the Industrial Revolution would not have taken place when or where it did.

British agriculture represented an enormous and continuing comparative advantage. At the dawn of the industrial age, the output per worker of British agriculture was one-third greater than France's and twice that of Russia while Europe enjoyed double the productivity of any other part of the world. By 1851, British output per worker was twice that of any contemporary European state. Not only did high agricultural productivity foster effective work habits throughout the population, but it also released labor. This labor could be employed in industry, but the path does not seem to have been direct. Instead, high wages or employment opportunities attracted rural labor to migrate within the "internal empire" of Ireland and Scotland, to the cities, or abroad. This migration fostered urbanization and the expansion of more sophisticated and dense markets that steadily increased demand for industrial products. In addition, agricultural productivity encouraged population growth, which stimulated the development of the market for manufactured goods. Current explanations for this agricultural productivity in Britain generally focus on the role of the state in fostering a system of land tenure based on a distinctive and profoundly inegalitarian system of property rights that increasingly favored the formation of more efficient, large estates.

Most of the efficiency gains from the Agricultural Revolution were realized by 1750. It preceded and permitted the onset of industrialization. During the Industrial Revolution, although total output and labor productivity continued to improve, the increments were far less than in the period from 1600 to 1750. Despite the best efforts of agricultural reformers like English agronomist Arthur Young or French author François Quesnay, after the mid-18th century, the majority of the growth in agricultural output in areas undergoing industrialization stemmed from increases of the area of land under cultivation. Nor did agriculture provide a vital market for manufactures, generate new capital, or release labor in different fashion than before 1750. The finding that the benefits of agricultural transformation did not continue during the Industrial Revolution is the result of recent research. The significance of these findings stems first from the fact that it shows a continuous process of economic transformation operating in northwestern Europe beginning in the 17th century, and second refocuses attention on demand rather than supply as the primary cause for the emergence of the Industrial Revolution. The spread of the techniques associated with the Agricultural Revolution outside of western Europe during the 19th century along with the development of new technologies that improved agricultural productivity, combined with the enormous expansion of farmland devoted to commercial agriculture in other parts of the world, contributed greatly to increasing global commodity output and facilitating the spread of industrialization beyond northwestern Europe.

See also: Standard of Living; Workforce; Document: "The State of the Poor"

Further Reading

Broadberry, Stephen, and Kevin O'Rourke, eds. *The Cambridge Economic History of Modern Europe*, vol. 1, *1700–1870*. Cambridge: Cambridge University Press, 2010.

Clark, Gregory. "The Agricultural Revolution and the Industrial Revolution: England, 1500–1912." 2002. Available online at http://faculty.econ.ucdavis.edu /faculty/gclark/papers/prod2002.pdf.

King, Steven, and Geoffrey Timmins. *Making Sense of the Industrial Revolution: English Economy and Society 1700–1850*. Manchester: Manchester University Press, 2001.

Overton, Mark. *Agricultural Revolution in England: The Transformation of the Agrarian Economy 1500–1850*. Cambridge: Cambridge University Press, 1996.

AMERICAN SYSTEM OF MANUFACTURES   The American System of Manufactures refers to a method developed during the middle third of the 19th century of making metal goods through careful division of labor and mechanization using specially designed, single-purpose machines. Often these machines were powered by water or steam. It allowed high-quality goods to be made in quantity and to replace more easily skilled workers with semiskilled laborers to give management far more control over the production process. The American System of Manufactures built on armory practice and was an important step on the road to true mass production in the 20th century.

Only the financial support of the federal government made the American System possible. Eli Whitney's abortive industrial efforts attracted the government's interest from 1798. The arsenals at Springfield, Massachusetts, and Harpers Ferry, Virginia, were commanded to make weapons with interchangeable parts. Despite some success in 1826, it took until 1840 for the arsenals to make guns with reliably interchangeable parts. Nor did that interchangeability survive a change in design. When a new weapon was introduced in 1842, it took seven years to develop the precision machine tools to mimic the same results. The hand-filing of parts was succeeded by the invention of machines that automatically made identical parts to a specified pattern. Weapons with interchangeable parts were considerably more expensive than handmade weapons, but they were easier to repair. It was at the 1851 Crystal Palace Exhibition in London that the "American System of Manufactures" received its name from impressed observers.

Once developed, the American System was used to manufacture sewing machines and then bicycles in addition to ever-more-lethal weapons. From bicycles, the American System diffused to the automobile industry. The success of this system came from the design and use of machine tools, which could fashion exactly alike metal parts for products ranging from clocks, to cash registers, to typewriters, to reapers, to locomotives, and finally to automobiles. Many of these products were not internationally competitive on price or quality, but U.S. manufacturers were able to survive by selling to the vast and growing American market while high tariffs kept out foreign rivals. Only after a long period of constant improvement did U.S. manufacturers become truly competitive in the world market in the last decades of the 19th century. Simultaneous improvements in steel making along with U.S. expertise in machine building permitted the factory assembly line to be created. The assembly line must be seen as the culmination of a century-long process through which genuine mass production emerged out of the American System of Manufactures.

See also: Armory Practice; Crystal Palace; Interchangeable Parts; Iron and Steel; Role of the State; Second Industrial Revolution; Tariffs and Excise Taxes; Whitney, Eli

Further Reading

Hoke, Donald R. *Ingenious Yankees: The Rise of the American System of Manufactures in the Private Sector*. New York: Columbia University Press, 1990.

Hounshell, David A. *From the American System to Mass Production, 1800–1932: The Development of Manufacturing Technology in the United States*. Baltimore: Johns Hopkins University Press, 1984.

Mayr, Otto, and Robert C. Post, eds. *Yankee Enterprise: The Rise of the American System of Manufactures*. Washington, DC: Smithsonian Press, 1981.

Meyer, David R. "The Roots of American Industrialization, 1790–1860." Available online at https://eh.net/encyclopedia/the-roots-of-american-industrialization-1790–1860/.

Smith, Merritt Roe. *Harpers Ferry Armory and the New Technology: The Challenge of Change*. Ithaca, NY: Cornell University Press, 1977.

ARKWRIGHT, RICHARD   Richard Arkwright developed the water frame to spin thread for use in the manufacture of textiles in 1767 (patented in 1769). This machine transformed the production process and gave a major boost to the nascent cotton textile industry. He also established the first modern factory at Cromford in Derbyshire, England, in 1771.

Arkwright (1732–1792) was a barber and wigmaker with no experience in making textiles when he devised the water frame or throstle with the help of a clockmaker. This relatively simple wooden machine was about 32 inches high. A wheel was connected to four pairs of rollers that stretched the roved cotton, which was then twisted and wound on spindles placed vertically on the machine. The coarse yarn produced by a water frame was strong and tightly twisted; it was suitable for hosiery and the warp for cotton goods. Arkwright intended to use horses to power his machine, but water was swiftly found to be far more economical and gave the device its name. The water-frame conceived of by Arkwright differed little from several others developed over the previous 30 years.

If the technology of Arkwright's machine did not represent a breakthrough, his implementation of this device was nothing short of revolutionary. At first, Arkwright set up a horse-powered workshop in 1769 to make cotton textiles in Nottingham not far from James Hargreaves's mill. It was clear that this enterprise did not have sufficient capital to set up the manufacture as efficiently as possible, which led Arkwright to form an association with two rich hosiers, Jebediah Strutt and Samuel Need, to create Cromford. When this factory opened in 1771, it had space for a complete set of machines and was purpose-built to be lit by candle for night work. The machines were run by large waterwheels. By 1773, the three partners had set up a weaving workshop to make England's first all-cotton calicoes in imitation of goods imported from India. Their technical and financial achievements enabled Arkwright, Strutt, and Need to lobby the government successfully in 1774 to eliminate the tariff on imports of raw cotton. Arkwright's most persuasive argument was that "The said manufacture, if not crushed by so heavy a duty, will rapidly increase and find new and effectual employment for many thousand British poor, and increase the revenue of the kingdom."

Cromford became the model for many other establishments. It swiftly grew to house several thousand spindles and 300 workers. In 1776, there were 140 Arkwright-type water-powered mills spinning cotton. By 1800, England housed 900 cotton-spinning factories of which 300 were large mills patterned on Arkwright's that employed more than 50 workers apiece.

Initially, few unemployed, even unskilled, workers sought jobs at Cromford because the rural site was picked for maximizing water power potential, not for convenience or ease of access for the labor force. (Unskilled workers were preferred because they did not have to unlearn other techniques, they did not mind the closer supervision demanded by factory labor, and they were willing to be trained to work the machines.) Arkwright solved the labor problem by accepting a huge number of youthful apprentices from Poor Houses all over Britain. Apprentices who were children or teenagers lived at the mill and were bound legally to work for Arkwright either until they were 18 or for seven years, whichever was longer!

To address an ongoing shortage of labor, Arkwright set up several mills in Lancashire in association with different groups of limited partners, becoming Europe's first cotton baron. The mills got bigger and bigger. The factory at Chorley was the biggest in Great Britain with 500 workers. In Manchester, Arkwright engaged 600 workers and built a multistory mill with weavers established on the premises instead of in a separate building. In the 1780s, Arkwright greatly upgraded earlier carding machines that combed and straightened the raw cotton. It hardly mattered that Arkwright's patent to this machine was revoked in 1785. The British government ruled that he had stolen the idea that made his fortune. Stolen or not, Arkwright's water frame was the foundation of the factory system inaugurated in Britain's cotton textile industry.

See also: Cotton; Discipline; Division of Labor; Domestic Industry; Factory System; Hargreaves, James; Lancashire; Patent(s); Productivity; Role of the State; Document: "The State of the Poor"

Further Reading
"The Arkwright Family in Cromford." Available online at http://www.cromfordvil lage.co.uk/arkwrights.html.

Hills, Richard L. "Sir Richard Arkwright and His Patent Granted in 1769." *Notes and Records of the Royal Society of London* 24, no. 2 (1970): 254–60.

MacLeod, Christine. *Heroes of Invention: Technology, Liberalism and British Identity 1750–1914*. Cambridge: Cambridge University Press, 2007.

Mokyr, Joel. *The Enlightened Economy: An Economic History of Britain 1700–1850*. New Haven, CT: Yale University Press, 2009.

ARMORY PRACTICE   The term *armory practice* refers to manufacturing innovations that occurred in U.S. military arsenals starting around 1800 in Springfield, Massachusetts. Overseers deliberately sought to diminish the power of artisanal skill by substituting division of labor and mechanization. The willingness of the U.S. government to pay a much higher price for guns made with interchangeable parts subsidized this effort. Armory practice was a major step in disciplining independent-minded American workers, especially in metalworking, to accept factory labor. The habits inculcated in the armories spread throughout the machine shops scattered across the Northeast.

Behind high tariff walls, the U.S. government supported industrial competitiveness by paying high prices for technologically advanced goods and supporting entrepreneurs seeking to overcome the unwillingness of many artisan-trained workers to diminish the role of skill or submit to industrial discipline. The United States competed most successfully in products that required the use of machine tools. The federal government—inadvertently—fostered American specialization in machine tools and precision production. Around 1800, in imitation of French practice, the federal armory at Springfield, Massachusetts, began to break down the tasks that went into the manufacture of guns. This division of labor proceeded rapidly. By 1815, 36 separate tasks had been identified and, by 1825, about a hundred. In 1855, there were more than 400 different operations involved in making a gun with interchangeable parts at the Springfield armory. Production reached 20,000–30,000 muskets annually in the 1840s, and, at the height of the U.S. Civil War, the Springfield Armory produced a mind-boggling 276,000 muskets in a single year. As in Europe, workers did not like to see their skills discounted or turned into tasks that anyone could accomplish. Nor did they appreciate the labor discipline that the managers of the armory insisted on. Worker resistance was, however, successfully overcome in the 1820s and 1830s. Thanks to the armory's example, the factory discipline developed at such enormous cost in Great Britain became standard operating procedure in the machine shops of New England with relative ease despite the vastly different economic environments.

If the division of labor was one key to armory production, mechanization was its twin. Over the course of 35 years, mechanics adapted or invented a large number of special-purpose machines to produce precision parts either in wood or metal. These machines undermined the influence of skilled workers, allowed significant labor cost savings, and permitted greater quality control. Mechanization was facilitated by the general familiarity of Americans with machines. Thanks to the federal government's willingness to pay a premium for weapons with interchangeable parts, and the introduction of inspectors to insure that only correctly made parts were used, machine tools were continually invented, improved, and used to manufacture a wide variety of parts. Although the weapons made at the Springfield and Harpers Ferry, Virginia, armories were more expensive than those without interchangeable parts, the federal government accepted the added cost. At the same time, federal superintendents inculcated a different attitude toward the work process, division of labor, and mechanization that, taken together, was called "armory practice."

These production methods, like the acceptance of factory discipline, spread from the armories to other machine shops throughout the country and then to the manufacture of other products. Armory practice was the other essential foundation of the American system of production, but it did not lead directly to true mass production that only became possible thanks to a new wave of technological developments at the tail end of the 19th century.

See also: American System of Manufactures; Discipline; Division of Labor; Factory System; Interchangeable Parts; Productivity; Role of the State; Tariffs and Excise Taxes; Document: "Lowell Mill Girls"

Further Reading

Hounshell, David A. *From the American System to Mass Production, 1800–1932: The Development of Manufacturing Technology in the United States.* Baltimore: Johns Hopkins University Press, 1984.

"The Industrialization of the Springfield Armory, 1812–1865." Available online at http://www.forgeofinnovation.org/Springfield_Armory_1812-1865/index.html.

Shackel, Paul. *Culture Change and the New Technology: An Archaeology of the Early American Industrial Era.* New York: Plenum, 1996.

Smith, Merritt Roe. *Harpers Ferry Armory and the New Technology: The Challenge of Change.* Ithaca, NY: Cornell University Press, 1977.

Thompson, Ross. *Structures of Change in the Mechanical Age: Technological Innovation in the United States 1790–1865.* Baltimore: Johns Hopkins University Press, 2009.

BRIDGEWATER, DUKE OF   Francis Egerton, third Duke of Bridgewater, was an Enlightened English aristocrat who sought to increase the profits earned from the large coal deposits on his vast estates in Lancashire. Getting the coal to market was the stumbling block. Despite the daunting technical difficulties, Bridgewater successfully built a canal from his lands to Manchester. He then developed a canal linkage between Liverpool and Manchester. By lowering transportation costs on raw materials and finished goods, canal builders like the Duke of Bridgewater contributed to a major British competitive advantage.

As a 17-year-old, Francis Egerton (1736–1803), third Duke of Bridgewater, visited the European continent to complete his education. While on this Grand Tour, he saw the Canal du Midi in France that linked the Atlantic and Mediterranean Seas. Inspired by this great feat of engineering, Egerton decided in 1758 to construct a seven-mile-long canal from his estate at Worsley to the city of Manchester. The investment was potentially profitable because of the staggering 9–10 shillings a ton cost of transporting coal to Manchester. Transportation priced Worsley coal out of the market. After consulting two noted engineers—James Gilbert, who drew up the plans, and James Brindley, who oversaw construction—Bridgewater also decided to improve the drainage in his mines, which would increase production. That growth in output would be sold in Manchester via the canal he envisioned.

The technical difficulties involved were enormous. The directors of an existing canal, the Mersey & Irwell, made them worse by obstructing the project. A significant portion of the canal had to be constructed underground. The canal also had to cross the Mersey & Irwell which they addressed by building an aqueduct 38 feet above the existing canal. Needless to say, this proposal was widely ridiculed by contemporaries. Despite the staggering cost of about "10,000 guineas [each worth 21 shillings or 1.05 pounds] a mile," the section of the canal running from Worsley to Castlefield in Manchester was completed in 1761. Canal boats drawn by horses operated until the late 19th century. Once Worsley coal began to reach Manchester by water, the price of coal in the city fell by half.

In 1762, Egerton embarked on a major expansion of the canal to link Manchester and Liverpool. It took more than a decade to complete this section because the marshy ground was hard to stabilize. Ultimately about 47 miles of underground canal were constructed at four different levels as links between the various segments of Egerton's canal. Other waterways were constructed to form a more effective and efficient transportation network throughout the rapidly growing region. Building these additions nearly bankrupted Egerton, but, by the end of the century, he had recouped his investment and begun to make substantial profits. Known as the "Canal Duke," Egerton remained an enthusiastic supporter of canals and canal building throughout his life. His heirs sold the canal network in the 1870s for a huge profit and the canals remained in commercial operation until 1974.

The Duke of Bridgewater inspired two vitally important groups of people. The duke's determination to profit from his landholdings by selling coal attracted the attention of nobles and other large landowners who had largely been aloof from the industrial economy. His audacious and ultimately profitable canal-building schemes motivated others to seek similar opportunities by developing improved communications. British elites modeled their actions after successful pioneers like the Duke of Bridgewater to lead the Industrial Revolution.

See also: Coal; Lancashire; Transportation by Water

Further Reading

"The Bridgewater Canal." Available online at http://www.bridgewatercanal.co.uk /history/.

"The Bridgewater Canal: The Duke's Cut." Available online at http://www.canalar chive.org.uk/stories/storycontents.php?enum=TE133.

"Bridgewater Estates Collection." Available online at http://discovery.nationalar chives.gov.uk/details/rd/51a53e3d-9afe-4975-a94b-653841a57e3c.

"Duke of Bridgewater's Underground Canal at Worsley." Available online at http:// web.archive.org/web/20060924230857/http://www.d.lane.btinternet.co.uk /canal.html.

Malet, Hugh. *Bridgewater: The Canal Duke, 1736–1803*. Manchester: Hendon Press, 1977.

BRUNEL, ISAMBARD KINGDOM   Isambard Kingdom Brunel was a mid-19th-century British engineer who realized many of the potentialities of the Industrial Revolution in transportation and infrastructure. Between 1826 and his death in 1859, Brunel built 25 railroad lines, more than 100 bridges, several dock complexes, the first tunnel underneath a navigable river, and the S.S. *Great Britain*, the first ocean-going, propeller-driven, iron steamship. Brunel's innovative designs laid the foundations for modern engineering practice.

Brunel (1806–1859) was born into the engineering profession. His French-born father Marc fled the Revolution to become the chief engineer of New York City. After inventing a new machine to manufacture ship's blocks, Brunel moved to Great Britain where he became a productive inventor of industrial machinery and an engineer charged with designing a pedestrian tunnel under the Thames River. Marc Brunel made sure that Isambard got the best mathematical training available, which meant going to France. When Isambard returned in 1822, he worked for his father as resident engineer on the Thames Tunnel.

Brunel made his name by winning a contest to design a bridge over the Avon Gorge outside Bristol in 1831. Only two years later, he was appointed the chief engineer of the Great Western Railway linking London and the busy port of Bristol. He successfully convinced the directors that by using a broader gauge track (7 feet, 0.25 inches vs. the standard 4 feet, 8.5 inches), locomotives could almost double their speed to 60 miles per hour. After careful surveying, construction began in 1837. The route required the construction of several viaducts, bridges, and tunnels, including the two-mile-long Box Tunnel. Completed in 1841 at a cost of £6.5 million, double the original estimate, Brunel shifted attention to the stations at either end. First Brunel designed and built the Temple Meads station in Bristol and then was tasked with rebuilding Paddington Station, the London terminus, in preparation for the 1851 Crystal Palace Exhibition. Paddington Station was built by the same contractors in the same style as the exhibition building, of wrought iron and plate glass.

In Brunel's all-encompassing transportation plan, the Great Western Railway should and could extend across the Atlantic Ocean. Launched in 1838, the S.S. *Great Western*, a wooden paddle steamer that was the longest ship in the world, missed being the first steamship to cross the Atlantic by a mere three hours, despite leaving four days after the ultimate winner. The S.S. *Great Western* ran regularly between Bristol and New York, demonstrating the commercial viability of transatlantic steamship service. Brunel followed up by designing and building the S.S. *Great Britain*, an iron steamship driven by a six-bladed propeller. Widely considered the first modern ship, the *Great Britain* first crossed from Liverpool to New York in 1845, but soon was shifted to other routes. Its owner went bankrupt. The third ship Brunel was commissioned to build was intended to take passengers to India and Australia. At almost 700 feet long, the S.S. *Great Eastern* was the largest ship built before the 20th century. It could carry up to 4,000 passengers in luxury and was supposed to be able to cruise nonstop from London to Sydney and back. Brunel resolved many of the technical problems associated with large-scale, propeller-driven, all-metal steamships, but only at huge cost. He lived to see the *Great Eastern* make its shakedown cruise in 1859, but not its first transatlantic voyage the following year. Like the *Great Britain*, the *Great Eastern* was a technical success but a financial failure in large measure because his designs and vision of transportation were too far ahead of their time.

In addition to many railroad lines, bridges and docks, both in England and abroad in India, Australia, and Italy, Brunel is known for building a prefabricated hospital of wood and canvas that could be broken down and reassembled where it was needed, in this case near the facility in Constantinople (modern-day Istanbul) overseen by Florence Nightingale to care for British military personnel fighting in the Crimean War. In five months, Brunel designed, built, and shipped 18 prefabricated buildings based on the most up-to-date knowledge of hygiene and sanitation, each able to handle 50 patients at a time. The hospital complex was established at Renkioi.

Brunel brought a can-do attitude to resolving technical problems. His amazing capacity to oversee and complete several complex projects at once involving very different types of engineering issues both inspired and daunted. Brunel's career coincided with and brought to fruition many of the greatest engineering achievements of the Industrial Revolution as Britain ploughed some of its great wealth into the next phase of transportation and infrastructure improvements. Many of Brunel's bridges and viaducts are still in use today. He built for the long haul.

See also: Crystal Palace; Education; Iron and Steel; Railroads; Role of the State; Transportation by Water

Further Reading

"Brunel 200." Available online at http://www.brunel200.com/.
"Isambard Kingdom Brunel: Design Engineer (1806–1859)." Available online at
    http://design.designmuseum.org/design/isambard-kingdom-brunel.html.
Landes, David. *The Unbound Prometheus: Technological Change and Industrial Devel-
    opment in Western Europe from 1750 to the Present.* Cambridge: Cambridge Uni-
    versity Press, 1969.
MacLeod, Christine. *Heroes of Invention: Technology, Liberalism and British Identity
    1750–1914.* Cambridge: Cambridge University Press, 2007.
Pugsley, Alfred, ed., *The Works of Isambard Kingdom Brunel.* Cambridge: Cambridge
    University Press, 1980.

CARTWRIGHT, EDMUND   The Reverend Edmund Cartwright was a
self-taught inventor from Nottingham, England, who was responsible for developing the power-loom (in 1785) and a wool-combing machine (in 1790)
among other patents. Although his inventions clearly responded to important
blockages in production, their implementation took decades, primarily because of determined resistance from workers and the slow improvement of
the machine's mechanics.

Cartwright (1743–1823) was the son of well-to-do landowners and gradu-
ated from Oxford University to become a clergyman in the Church of England. Active and well educated, Cartwright was profoundly interested in
helping the rural population he served, teaching them the newest fever remedies and latest agricultural methods. Cartwright applied this same energy to
a major industrial problem when he learned about the relative oversupply of
thread as a result of Richard Arkwright's and Samuel Crompton's inventions.
Although he had never even seen a handloom before, Cartwright believed he
could invent a power-loom to take advantage of the growing supply of cotton
thread. With the help of a carpenter and a blacksmith, Cartwright developed
a machine that ran, though not very well or for very long. He patented this
machine in 1785 and made several major improvements over the next two
years. The power-loom worked no faster than a skilled handloom adult
weaver, but an unskilled apprentice could oversee first two and eventually far
greater numbers of power-looms.

Cartwright sought to take advantage of his invention. He set up a factory
in Doncaster, Yorkshire, with 20 looms powered first by horses and then,
after 1789, by a Watt steam engine. The factory was badly run and failed. In
partnership with Manchester manufacturer Robert Grimshaw, Cartwright
erected a large factory in 1791 that would eventually have hundreds of his
looms, but with only the first 30 in place, handloom weavers, fearing for their

livelihoods, burned the factory to the ground in 1792. Cartwright lost his entire investment and, because no other manufacturer thought that the rewards were worth the risks, was unable to find other partners. Cartwright was forced to turn his patent over to trustees while he dealt with his debts. While the invention languished, the number of home-based handloom weavers expanded greatly from 75,000 in 1795 to 225,000 in 1811.

Cartwright did not stop inventing. He made a wool-combing machine in 1790 and took out several other patents related to textile manufacture. Diffusion of the wool-combing machine was also slowed dramatically by opposition from wool-combers who recognized the threat to their high wages based on a unique skill. Although a few entrepreneurs were able to make the investment in power-looms profitable, especially after a number of Stockport manufacturers made major improvements in the device, widespread implementation of Cartwright's invention did not come until the mid-1820s. The wool-combing machine came into wide usage in the same era.

By 1825, a power-loom could weave 7.5 times as much as a cottage artisan in domestic manufacture, and a boy could supervise two looms. From 2,400 looms in 1813 and 14,150 in 1820, the number of looms expanded to 100,000 in 1833 and 250,000 by midcentury. Cartwright did not live to see the success of his inventions; he needed a grant of £10,000 from the Parliament of the United Kingdom in 1809 to get rid of his last creditors from his entrepreneurial endeavors. In 1821, he was elected a fellow of the Royal Society. Cartwright's inventions solved two major industrial blockages, yet he was unable to profit from them in large measure because of the organized opposition of workers, which highlights the gap between invention and implementation.

See also: Arkwright, Richard; Cotton; Division of Labor; Domestic Industry; Education; Factory System; Luddites; Patent(s); Royal Society of Arts; Steam Engine; Workforce; Document: "Defending the Factory System"

Further Reading

"Edmund Cartwright." Available online at http://lemelson.mit.edu/resources/edmund-cartwright.

MacLeod, Christine. *Heroes of Invention: Technology, Liberalism and British Identity 1750–1914.* Cambridge: Cambridge University Press, 2007.

Mantoux, Paul *The Industrial Revolution in the Eighteenth Century: An Outline of the Beginnings of the Modern Factory System in England,* rev. ed. New York: Harper & Row, 1961.

Mokyr, Joel. *The Lever of Riches: Technological Creativity and Economic Progress.* Oxford: Oxford University Press, 1991.

CHAPTAL, JEAN-ANTOINE Jean-Antoine Chaptal was the architect of the French path to industrial society. A noted chemist and a wildly successful manufacturer of chemical products, Chaptal was Napoleon Bonaparte's most influential minister of the interior (1800–1804). It was thanks to his leadership that the French abandoned their hope to imitate the British and fashioned their own approach to industrial development. Continental governments played an essential role in British industrialization because the demands imposed by being forced to play "catch up" compelled the state to take over many essential economic functions directly. The manner of state direction of the manufacturing economy inaugurated by Chaptal remained characteristic of the French industrial landscape throughout the 19th century and beyond.

Born into a bourgeois family in Montpellier, Chaptal (1756–1832) studied medicine and chemistry in Paris. His reputation in chemistry was based on solving practical problems. He wrote important treatises that detailed how to improve production of wine, butter, and cheese as well as a well-regarded chemical textbook. Ennobled in 1788, Chaptal was imprisoned during the Reign of Terror for his political moderation. Late in 1793, he was released and charged with overseeing the production of gunpowder, a difficult task because of the lack of raw materials. Chaptal became professor of chemistry at the elite Paris Polytechnic in 1798. Under Bonaparte, Chaptal was named a councilor of state and charged with improving public education. Napoleon soon appointed Chaptal minister of the interior in 1800, a job he kept until 1804. Upon leaving the ministry, Chaptal entered the Senate and became Count of Chanteloup in 1808.

According to Chaptal, who built on Adam Smith's views, the 19th-century government's role in managing industry had three basic components. First, the state had to mend the damage done by the prerevolutionary administration. By depriving those involved in the production and distribution of goods of their proper place in society, the prerevolutionary Bourbon regime had damaged French "public spirit" and alienated potential entrepreneurs. Only active state sponsorship of the social value of commerce and industry could repair centuries of contempt. Second, Chaptal asserted, with regard to industry, "The actions of government ought to be limited to facilitating supplies, guaranteeing property, opening markets to manufactured goods and to leaving industry to enjoy a most profound liberty. One can rely on the producer to pay attention to all the rest." Third, Chaptal recognized that, in reality, the government could not be quite so "hands-off." To ensure that all French citizens could find gainful employment and to guarantee that the revolutionary ideal of equality under the law existed in economic practice, the state must intervene. Chaptal contrasted the French emphasis on equality with Great

Britain, where "private interest directs all actions." To Chaptal, the public good required state mediation of the myriad of private interests.

Chaptal founded, revived, or sponsored a host of institutions such as Chambers of Commerce, Consultative Chambers of Manufacturing, Arts, and Crafts, industrial expositions, Councils of Agriculture, Arts, and Commerce as well as Schools of Arts and Crafts, the Society for the Encouragement of the National Industry, Museums of Arts and Crafts, and free spinning schools for women. This list is not exclusive and demonstrates both Chaptal's commitment to state intervention in the economy and how wide open the field was for institutional innovation.

Chaptal was not just a bureaucrat or a theoretical chemist. He was also an entrepreneur. He created three large-scale chemical workshops around Paris. On his vast estate, he became vitally concerned—both scientifically and commercially—with improving the process of distilling sugar from grapes and naturalizing the sugar beet and merino sheep in France. In 1819, Louis XVIII named Chaptal a peer of the realm. That same year, Chaptal published one of the first accounts of the nascent industrial revolution in France. For the rest of his life, Chaptal actively promoted educational reform to improve interaction between theoretical and applied science while employing his precepts to increase his personal fortune. Chaptal's career shows that with the support of the state, economic rationality and market orientation often led in different directions on the continent than in Britain.

See also: Education; Mercantilism; Role of the State; Document: "Adam Smith on the Division of Labor"

Further Reading

Bolado, Elsa, and Lluis Argemí. "Jean Antoine Chaptal: From Chemistry to Political Economy." *European Journal of the History of Economic Thought* 12, no. 2 (2005): 15–39.

Horn, Jeff. *The Path Not Taken: French Industrialization in the Age of Revolution, 1750–1830.* Cambridge, MA: MIT Press, 2006.

Jacob, Margaret C. *Scientific Culture and the Making of the Industrial West.* Oxford: Oxford University Press, 1997.

Paul, Harry W. *Science, Vine and Wine in Modern France.* Cambridge: Cambridge University Press, 2002.

Smith, John G. *The Origins and Early Development of the Heavy Chemical Industry in France.* Oxford: Oxford University Press, 1979.

COAL   Coal, more than any other source of fuel, powered the Industrial Revolution. Water, wind, and animals all contributed mightily to the energy used in industrialization, but without question, coal took pride of place, especially in Great Britain. With wood increasingly expensive, England began relying heavily on coal both for domestic heating and for industrial purposes in the 16th century. Coal played the largest part in the radical transformation from organic (human and animal) to inorganic (water, wind, and coal) energy that permitted large-scale industrialization. Britain's lead in switching primarily to coal was a major reason for its ability to have an industrial revolution.

Coal became vital on the British Isles because wood was a relatively scarce resource as early as the 16th century. Britain was blessed with large supplies of high-quality coal that also happened to be conveniently located. The three great coal fields—in Northumberland, Lancashire, and south Wales—were all found within a few miles of access to the sea, encouraging Britons to make use of this precious natural resource.

Europeans had mined coal for hundreds of years, but pits were small and not very productive: many were open cast mines (just big holes dug in the surface). Tunneling to find richer coal seams was both difficult and dangerous, especially because of the threat of drowning when water flooded the shaft. Necessity led British miners to become expert at sinking mine shafts, extracting ore, and transporting it. More importantly, British artisans, mechanics, tinkerers, and scientists became accustomed to using coal as a fuel source. Early dependence on coal gave the British essential craft knowledge, based on trial and error, of coal's properties and the best practices of using it. Coal provided much more energy than wood and could be used in myriad ways. Thanks to this experience with coal, British metallurgy and machine building became among the best and most economical in Europe. A great deal of process-oriented innovation resulted from the search for ways to use coal as fuel.

Such knowledge was a major national advantage when technological change and increasingly scarce charcoal also forced Britain's competitors to switch over to coal at various points in the 19th century. A lack of familiarity with using coal as fuel made it harder to transfer British technology to other nations, heightening the island nation's industrial advantage. British coal production reached 3 million tons annually in 1700, already a high level. From there, British output skyrocketed, attaining almost 9 million tons by 1775 at the dawn of the Industrial Revolution. By 1815, British coal production was 22 million tons, tripling to almost 67 million tons annually at the end of the 1850s, which represented a staggering two-thirds of global output. In the next 50 years, production tripled once more as the Industrial Revolution expanded more broadly and the transition to inorganic sources of fuel was completed.

Britain's coal was mined by up to 200,000 men, women, and children. During the age of the Industrial Revolution, coal ore was cut from rock by hand with pickaxes. As the demand for coal grew and pits grew deeper, steam engines were used to pump water out of the mines, but the tunnels that reached the coal faces were rarely very large, forcing miners to contort themselves into uncomfortable positions to get at the coal. Women and girls were usually responsible for pushing tubs of ore often weighing more than they did to a collection point. Children as young as five were employed to get into tight places. Flooding and fire-damp (the combustion of explosive gases in enclosed spaces with a spark) were daily dangers as were the collapse of mine shafts or accidents with explosives used to blast tunnels in hard rock. In the 19th century, these threats killed hundreds of British miners annually. Long hours inhaling coal dust while getting alternately soaked with cold water or baked by humid heat led many miners to develop respiratory and joint problems, most notably coal workers' pneumoconiosis, also known as black lung disease or black lung; bronchitis; and rheumatism.

The reforms that improved working conditions in factories took longer to apply to mines. As in the case of textiles, British elites claimed that they could not take better care of miners or improve safety without undermining profits or losing jobs to overseas competition. These unfounded claims—as the massive increases in production during the 19th century demonstrated—were allowed to stand unchallenged for most of the era of the Industrial Revolution. Only after the same reformers who tackled child labor in the factories led by Lord Anthony Ashley-Cooper, the seventh Earl of Shaftesbury, turned their attention to the mines did the British state take action. The publication of the shocking Children's Employment Commission (Mines) Report in 1842 detailing the horrible working conditions in the mines led directly to the parliamentary passage of a Mines and Collieries Act, which outlawed women and children under age 10 from working underground. Because no means of enforcing the bill's provisions were included, several pieces of follow-up legislation in the 1850s and 1860s were needed to keep women and children out of the mines. In Britain, government-mandated improvements to safety and working conditions took place only in subsequent decades, long after the end of the first Industrial Revolution.

Outside Britain, coal also played a transformative role in industrial development. France's coal reserves were hard to get to and not as high quality as Britain's. As a result, France used coal only when necessary and focused more on water power. This was a rational, though not quite as profitable, strategy given that nation's natural resource endowment. The United States' almost inexhaustible supplies of wood along with easy access to water power retarded development of the coal industry until the needs of iron makers amplified demand after 1840. In succeeding decades, the United States' rapidly expanding population required steamboats, railroads, and many other machines and consumer products especially in the growing cities, which necessitated ever more coal. Like Britain, Belgium and the German lands had also used coal for centuries. When incorporated into Revolutionary and Napoleonic France between 1795 and 1814, these areas had boomed by supplying coal and iron to the vast French market. After Napoleon's second defeat in 1815, these areas, with thoroughgoing support from their governments, began to develop coal mining and iron making on the English model, often using British workers and entrepreneurs to jumpstart the process. After 1830, Belgium and the German lands also experienced rapid growth in coal output that was essential to the onset of full-scale industrialization. The heavy hand of the state helped coal and iron production expand rapidly enough to begin catching up to Britain both in efficiency and, in the case of Germany, in total output. Differing factor endowments and industrial strategies affected the intertwined roles of coal and iron in the process of industrialization, but the shift to coal as a major source of energy in manufacturing was essential to the Industrial Revolution, in Britain and in its closest competitors alike.

Rising demand for coal came from many sources. As the population increased, so did the domestic market. The growing towns needed coal for heating and manufacture as wood was depleted nearby. More and more industries from iron makers to brewers and bakers adopted coal as it became cheaper and more cost effective. Around 1800, British cities began to install coal-powered gas lamps; 52 urban areas had gaslight networks by 1823. The burgeoning demand for industrial machines and products made from iron also required copious amounts of coal for smelting. Steam engines devoured coal at a rapid pace. Once railroads began to be built after 1830, demand for coal accelerated further. Some historians and economists believe that steam engines built of iron and powered by coal were the critical combination that, more than any other factor, created the Industrial Revolution.

See also: Factory Acts; Factory System; Iron and Steel; Pollution, Health, and Environment; Productivity; Railroads; Role of the State; Steam Engine; Transportation by Water; Workforce; Document: "Conditions in the Mines"; Document: "Living and Working in Manchester"

Further Reading

Adams, Sean Patrick. "The US Coal Industry in the Nineteenth Century." Available online at http://eh.net/encyclopedia/the-us-coal-industry-in-the-nineteenth -century/.

Burt, Roger. "The Extractive Industries." In *The Cambridge Economic History of Modern Britain*, ed. Roderick Floud and Paul Johnson. Cambridge: Cambridge University Press, 2004.

Landes, David. *The Unbound Prometheus: Technological Change and Industrial Development in Western Europe from 1750 to the Present*. Cambridge: Cambridge University Press, 1969.

Testimony Gathered by Ashley's Mines Commission. Available online at http://www.victorianweb.org/history/ashley.html.

Wrigley, E. A. *Energy and the English Industrial Revolution*. Cambridge: Cambridge University Press, 2010.

COCKERILL, WILLIAM   English mechanic William Cockerill emigrated to Belgium early in the 19th century. Over the next 40 years, he and his family established metallurgical enterprises there and in western Germany that paired continental natural resources and markets with English technologies and craft knowledge. The experiences of Cockerill and his firm demonstrate the workings of personal technology transfer so common in the nations following in Britain's industrial wake as well as the difficulties of entrepreneurship during the early Industrial Revolution.

William Cockerill (1759–1832) emigrated from England to Verviers in French-held Belgium in 1798 to take advantage of the opportunities afforded by his specialized craft knowledge to set up his own firm. He swiftly built five mechanized mills to spin wool, beginning a rapid modernization of the moribund woolens industry in that region. The first firm to invest in innovation remained the largest single producer for the rest of the 19th century. Flush with success, Cockerill, his three sons William Jr., John, and James, along with his son-in-law James Hodson, established a workshop in 1805 to build machines in Liège. The demand for textile machines spawned a host of orders, and the quality of Cockerill construction guaranteed sales. A supplemental workshop was established in Paris to supply the French market, and Cockerill spinning machines also equipped the woolens industries of Prussia and Saxony. In the hothouse atmosphere created by the protectionism of Napoleon's Continental System, the Cockerill establishment swiftly became a vertically integrated enterprise comprising coal and later iron mining, iron smelting, pig-iron processing, metal fabrication, and machine building.

After 1815, the Cockerills introduced puddling and the blast-furnace to the continent and built the first locomotives and iron steamships outside of Britain, all with the direct financial support of King William I of the Netherlands. In engineering and metallurgy, the Cockerill enterprises now centered at Seraing (a mansion bought from the king for a pittance) were among the largest and most productive in the world. At their height, the machine-building shops alone employed 2,700 workers and helped to naturalize high-pressure steam-engine construction in the region. Woolens weaving was mechanized after 1814, again with machines built by the Cockerills.

John moved to Berlin where he set up a wool-spinning factory, established a satellite machine-building shop, and bought and refurbished three other woolens spinning mills. William Jr. remained in Berlin. James built a machine-building workshop in Aachen. This spurt of metallurgical development spurred complementary growth in several districts in Belgium and western Germany as local entrepreneurs, often paired with English engineers or technicians, rushed to open coal mines, modern blast furnaces, puddling plants, and machine shops in hopes of exploiting the same deep vein of demand tapped by the Cockerills.

These two generations of entrepreneurs also revealed the limits of personal involvement in managing a far-flung and diverse enterprise. The Cockerills failed to establish a business structure capable of weathering recessions and the waning of their initial technological advantages. By the late 1840s, the industrial empire built by the Cockerills had largely passed into the hands of others, demonstrating the growing importance of business organization to long-term industrial success by a family firm.

See also: Coal; Iron and Steel; Role of the State; Transportation by Water

Further Reading

Heckscher, Eli. *The Continental System: An Economic Interpretation*. Oxford: Clarendon Press, 1922.

Henderson, William O. *The Industrial Revolution in Europe, 1815–1914*. Chicago: Quadrangle Books, 1968.

"Industrial History: Belgium." Available online at http://www.erih.net/industrial-history/belgium.html.

Teich, Mikuláš, and Roy Porter, eds. *The Industrial Revolution in National Context: Europe and the USA*. Cambridge: Cambridge University Press, 1996.

COLONIALISM   European states began establishing colonies to the south and west in the 14th century, reviving earlier patterns of territorial expansion. From the late 15th century, the Spanish and Portuguese militarily controlled access by water to the wealth of Asia, sub-Saharan Africa, and the Americas. To break or sidestep the putative monopoly of the Iberian powers, the Dutch, English, and French attempted to conquer Spanish and Portuguese trading stations, forts, and settlements and founded communities in less desirable, unoccupied areas to create their own spheres of influence. Colonial conquest and commercial exploitation rapidly became a free-for-all in which every power preyed on the others as well as on native populations. The acquisition and development of overseas territories is known as colonialism and was an essential part of a long series of wars fought by European powers across the globe.

In the 16th century, Spain and Portugal developed and maintained vast empires. Spain dominated the coastline of the western hemisphere from Florida to the straits of Magellan with the exception of Portuguese Brazil. Portugal set up trading stations and forts to protect the route to the East Indies. Only in the 17th century did the Dutch wrest control of much of Portugal's Asian empire while also acquiring South Africa and a handful of territories in and around the Caribbean. The French managed to establish footholds in Canada, throughout the Caribbean, and in strategic spots in western Africa and India while the British acquired most of the eastern half of the continent of North America, a host of possessions in the Caribbean led by Jamaica, trading stations on the coast of Africa, and scattered outposts on the subcontinent of India, especially Bengal, among other territories and spheres of interest spread out across the globe. These colonies provided markets and raw materials that generated truly enormous wealth essential to industrialization.

For Europeans, the twin poles of economic attraction were the Americas and Asia. Although they eventually established political and economic control of vast swaths of territory in Asia, European settlement was always limited, especially during the age of the Industrial Revolution. European settlement and political control in Africa was even more restrained. Both areas were able to defend themselves relatively effectively, and disease constrained the ability of Europeans to settle in many tropical areas of India and west and central Africa. In the western hemisphere, the introduction of European diseases like measles so drastically decimated the native population—from about 54 million in 1492 to approximately 13.5 million in 1570, a decline of 75 percent—that Europeans were able to seize the best land and resources much more easily and cheaply than they could anywhere else on the globe. To take advantage of this temporary relative strength, 17th and 18th century European colonialism focused on the western hemisphere.

Atlantic trade made outsize contributions to European profits, especially for Great Britain and France. The average annual value of Britain's Atlantic commerce (exports, re-exports, imports, and services) increased from £20,084,000 in 1651–1670 to £105,546,000 in 1781–1800 to an amazing £231,046,000 in 1848–1850. African labor, both in Africa and in the Americas, generated most of the wealth that financed this burgeoning trade. European exports made up a little less than 40 percent of these totals. Historian Joseph Inikori estimated that Africans produced no less than 69 percent (in 1651–1670 and in 1848–1850) and up to 83 percent (in 1761–1780) of the value of British Atlantic commerce. For Britain, whose economy made up about one-third of the Atlantic total, the rate of increase in Atlantic trade was far superior to that for other regions. Whereas total British foreign trade doubled over the course of the 18th century, British Atlantic trade increased by a factor of 12 in that same period!

Atlantic trade was founded on the conquest and expropriation of native supplies of precious metals. Once ready stocks of gold and silver had been seized and sent back to Europe, Europeans began to exploit American ores using native and then African labor. The exhaustion of most of these mines in the 17th century set the stage for the development of plantations by a host of European states. These plantations grew tropical and semitropical commodities such as tobacco, then sugar, cotton, chocolate, coffee, and rice. Plantations furthered the development of an economy in the western hemisphere that was focused on furnishing raw materials to Europe either for its own consumption or to pass along to Asia. The labor demands of mining and plantation agriculture spurred the rapid increase in the acquisition of millions of human slaves from Africa. Thus, two trade triangles emerged. First, gold and silver from the Americas went to Asia passing through European intermediaries in exchange for "oriental" goods that were consumed in Europe. Second, manufactured goods were sent from Europe or re-exported from Asia to Africa where they were exchanged for human beings, who were then brought to the Americas to mine precious metals for trade with Asia or grow agricultural commodities for consumption in Europe. Europeans were the chief (though not the sole) "winners" of this system and enslaved Africans along with enslaved and/or dispossessed native Americans were the primary "losers."

The dramatic expansion of trade on this scale had a multitude of effects. British manufactured products were sold in protected markets even if they enjoyed no competitive advantage other than a legal monopoly. Commercial expansion spurred the development and application of new technologies. The wide range of territories that became tied into this global trading network required different trading goods, thereby promoting commercial and industrial diversification. In addition, the size of the domestic market no longer determined the scale of potential demand, a factor that was of critical importance in newly emerging industrial sectors like cotton textiles.

Colonialism spawned huge profits that could be and were reinvested in industry. Different forms of business practice such as joint-stock companies and commercial institutions like stock markets had to be created to deal with the enormous capital invested. New, exciting, and sometimes addictive products were now available to many more Europeans, which encouraged and, in some cases, forced them to work harder and for longer hours to get their "fix."

Britain's merchant fleet grew spectacularly to deal with the expansion of trade. From a total tonnage of 323,000 in 1700, the merchant marine reached over a million tons in 1788. The British state also extracted tax revenues from colonial trade that amounted to a quarter of its revenues. In short, the Commercial Revolution based in the Atlantic was the means by which Britain developed the legal, financial, and commercial institutions and expertise that supported the Industrial Revolution.

Although Atlantic trade dwarfed commercial interaction with Asia until the late 19th century, it was desire for "oriental" (Asian) goods—spices, especially pepper; cotton and silk textiles; tea and coffee—that encouraged the "take off" of European long-distance trade. European demand for these goods was exceptionally strong, but was not matched by an equivalent Asian desire for European products. Europeans had to pay for pepper, cottons, and silks with hard currency—gold and silver—that they did not have, thus constraining trade. What enabled Europeans to increase their consumption of Asian goods was the exploitation of the Americas. The specie Europeans spent in Asia came overwhelmingly from the Americas. In the 16th century, Spain and Portugal initiated huge transfers of bullion, first by expropriation and then from mining, that were then succeeded by the plantation economies developed in and around the Caribbean Sea.

The exploitation of Africans, both in Africa or in the western hemisphere, enabled Europe to industrialize. Inikori's important findings are complemented by Kenneth Pomeranz's provocative comparison of China and Europe. Pomeranz contends that what enabled Europe to industrialize before China was privileged access to the resources and markets of the Americas. Thus, colonialism centered on the western hemisphere was of world historical significance because of its essential role in permitting the industrialization of Europe.

More effectively than its rivals, Britain developed a colonial empire populated by Europeans centered on the Atlantic world that contributed enormously to the Industrial Revolution. Thanks to the effectiveness of mercantilist trade policies like the Acts of Trade and the Navigation Acts, Britain also profited more thoroughly from its expanding empire than rival European powers. An estimate of the scale of annual profit for the era leading up to the American Declaration of Independence in 1776 was £2.64 million out of an official total of British imports and exports from the 13 North American colonies valued at £9.5 million (28 percent). Although significant, this trade was dwarfed by the annual profits on the trade in human beings, which constituted almost 40 percent of the sum total of all British commercial and industrial investment. Colonial trade comprised 15 percent of British commerce in the 1698 and one-third by 1774. The protected colonial market for staple manufactured goods like woolens and for "new" products like cottons eased the rivalry between the two industries and facilitated a rapid and continued growth of exports. The new industrial goods went overwhelmingly to the colonies, thereby increasing demand and permitting continuous improvements in economies of scale. State regulation also suppressed potential competition from the 13 North American colonies in such key products as woolens and iron, diverting colonial manufacture to less profitable, less essential, supplemental areas. All colonial production was supposed to benefit the home country, but, of course, it did not always work that way.

Colonialism also affected Ireland, which was treated as a colony until 1801, although conditions improved after 1779 because Britain feared that the struggle in North America would touch off a renewed push for independence. The Irish were encouraged to raise sheep and gather raw wool, but that wool had to be exported to England. It could not be used by Irish industry. This measure effectively destroyed the manufacture of woolens, which had been Ireland's most important export. Throughout the 18th century and well into the 19th, efforts to develop Irish industry were crushed with deliberation. English goods were sold at a loss if necessary. Irish cattle, butter, and cheese were barred from the English market, but Ireland was not permitted to do the same to English goods. As compensation, Irish linen (whose manufacture was concentrated among the Protestants of Ulster) was protected and encouraged. It should not surprise, however, that such an unequal economic relationship led the Irish to become expert smugglers. Through conquest and mercantilism, the Hanoverian state created political conditions in Ireland and the rest of the Empire that greatly favored British manufactured goods. The scale and scope of this colonial trade was vital to Britain's ability to inaugurate an industrial revolution.

See also: Consumer Revolution; Cotton; Credit; "Industrious Revolution"; Mercantilism; Role of the State; Tariffs and Excise Taxes; Transportation by Water; Workforce; Document: "Child on Interest, Trade, and Money"

Further Reading

Broadberry, Stephen, and Kevin H. O'Rourke. *The Cambridge Economic History of Modern Europe*, vol. 1, *1700–1870*. Cambridge: Cambridge University Press, 2010.

"Colonialism." Available online at http://plato.stanford.edu/entries/colonialism/.

Inikori, Joseph E. *Africans and the Industrial Revolution in England: A Study in International Trade and Economic Development*. Cambridge: Cambridge University Press, 2002.

Landes, David. *The Wealth and Poverty of Nations: Why Some Are So Rich and Some So Poor*. New York: W. W. Norton, 1998.

Pomeranz, Kenneth. *The Great Divergence: China, Europe, and the Making of the Modern World Economy*. Princeton, NJ: Princeton University Press, 2000.

Stuchtey, Benedikt. "Colonialism and Imperialism, 1450–1950." Available online at http://ieg-ego.eu/en/threads/backgrounds/colonialism-and-imperialism/benedikt -stuchtey-colonialism-and-imperialism-1450–1950.

CONSUMER REVOLUTION   The Consumer Revolution describes a demand-driven desire for a vast array of new, innovative, or previously scarce goods that drove the Atlantic economy in the 18th and early 19th centuries. Centered in northwestern Europe, especially in England, the Netherlands, and northern France, but also encompassing 13 of Britain's North American colonies, the Consumer Revolution was noted by contemporaries in the early 18th century and picked up steam across the decades as it spread to new areas and further down on the socioeconomic scale. Seemingly insatiable demand for luxury goods (many coming from Asia), colonial commodities, and novelties propelled the vast expansion of world and especially Atlantic and intra-European trade that marked this critical era.

In light of powerful domestic and European demand for Asian, especially Chinese and Indian, luxury goods and that they had little other than specie to offer in return, Europeans became even more dependent on the exploitation of their colonies and trade links in the Atlantic world to provide the goods and precious metals necessary to facilitate trade with Asia. On the broad, straining backs of slaves and the slave trade, the Atlantic world furnished agricultural commodities, markets, and profits that supported the Consumer Revolution and facilitated the emergence of a true global economy.

The British proved to be masters at taking advances in science and technology to develop innovative products to capture new markets and satisfy consumer demand. Product creativity by British entrepreneurs was essential to supplying the consumer demand unleashed by economic growth. In a host of industries from pottery to metalwork, to textiles, to glass, manufacturers embraced innovations in quality, product variety, and price as means of attracting the consumer. Taste and aesthetics were explored and cultivated through creative uses of publicity. Imitations of foreign (especially Asian and French) luxury goods were developed using British technological expertise. Improvements to the supply of products for sale in European markets as well as import substitution responded to ongoing and increasing consumer demand.

Although the passion for fashionable goods and products was most easily observed among elites and the growing middle classes, swelling consumer demand also extended to the laboring classes, especially in larger cities like London, Paris, and Amsterdam. Successful workers, artisans, shopkeepers, or farmers sought to emulate their economic betters; they too wanted to be "fashionable" and "in style." One of the most changeable of consumer goods is clothing, where fashionable shifts in texture, pattern, color, and stitching were eagerly bought, particularly as prices fell thanks to innovation. By the 18th century, even the laboring classes could afford stylish cloaks and shirts and began to wear muffs, nightclothes, and underwear, often modeled on or in the style of luxury goods imported from France, India, or China. A major aim of 18th-century technological innovators and merchants was to render goods that had been luxuries into products that could be marketed to much wider audiences. This shift toward a wider market even within the luxury trade was a key link in the chain connecting demand and supply, but it deserves reiteration that most members of the popular classes, even in the richest countries and regions, could not afford such goods: their purchasing power focused on subsistence. For some people outside the elite, the desire to emulate, to consume was so great that they were willing to work longer hours or to send their wives or children to work for wages in what has been termed the "Industrious Revolution."

To encourage these trends and to allow people to distinguish or differentiate themselves from others through their taste or style, entrepreneurs engaged in constant product innovation to attract the wandering eyes of fickle consumers. The ability to implement these innovations marked a major divergence from the market environment of earlier eras where reliably made versions of standardized products, either by region or by a known manufacturer, were sold all over the globe. Speedier and more reliable modes of transportation, the reduction of transfer costs, and improved credit facilities enabled the spread of "fashionable" goods. So too did innovative means of reaching the public. From traveling salesmen to showrooms in the capitals to printed catalogues and advertising in the growing number of "fashion" magazines that appeared in the 1770s throughout western Europe, merchants and manufacturers attempted to influence public taste. Entrepreneurs also developed goods like medallions and plates that combined fashion (although not always good taste!) with trendiness. A growing vogue for shopping developed: to be seen looking at what was for sale was part of the experience. The role of women in the desire for distinction and in the rise of shopping as a social activity has been hotly debated. Women certainly were thoroughly engaged in the process of social differentiation, but men were also deeply involved in shopping. Women were a fundamental part of the development of taste, fashion, style, and luxury, but both genders were responsible for the emergence of consumer capitalism.

An important division emerged between the upper and middle classes whose interest in the new, the fashionable, and in taste extended to all categories of available goods, and the lower classes who focused more (though far from exclusively) on commodities they could consume. These goods included tea, coffee, chocolate, tobacco, and sugar, but beer and spirits also were consumed in increasing quantities. The addictive properties of these commodities made many laboring families willing to work longer and harder to get their cup of tea, chocolate fix, or tobacco product of choice. As Scottish economist

James Steuart put it in 1767, "Men are forced to labour now because they are slaves to their own wants." Thus, as with the Agricultural Revolution, both the "Industrious Revolution" and the Consumer Revolution predated the onset of revolutionary industrial transformation. The similarity of these preconditions once again demonstrates the central importance of demand in calling forth innovative organizational and technological means of meeting potent consumer demand.

See also: Agricultural Revolution; Colonialism; Cotton; Credit; "Industrious Revolution"; Standard of Living; Wedgwood, Josiah

Further Reading

Benson, John. "Consumption and the Consumer Revolution." Available online at http://www.ehs.org.uk/dotAsset/b75cb989-ca95–4860-bb14–846183dec190 .pdf.

Berg, Maxine. *Luxury & Pleasure in Eighteenth-Century Britain*. Oxford: Oxford University Press, 2005.

Breen, T. H. *The Marketplace of Revolution: How Consumer Politics Shaped American Independence*. New York: Oxford University Press, 2004.

Brewer, John, and Roy Porter, eds. *Consumption and the World of Goods*. London: Routledge, 1994.

"The Consumer Revolution." Available online at http://www.history.org/history /teaching/enewsletter/volume5/december06/consumer_rev.cfm.

McKendrick, Neil, John Brewer, and J. H. Plumb. *The Birth of a Consumer Society: The Commercialization of Eighteenth-Century England*. Bloomington: Indiana University Press, 1982.

COTTON The Industrial Revolution began in one key sector: cotton textiles. New machines and new processes were developed to cope with specific problems that had previously slowed down production. To compete with, much less displace, Indian cottons from European, American, and African markets, the manufacture of cotton textiles in Europe required massive improvement in industrial methods. Innovation in technologies, organization of production, labor oversight, management, and marketing in the manufacture of cotton textiles provided a model for a transformation that led the way to an industrial revolution.

As a new sector engaged in import substitution, this industry was independent of guild controls; such independence was vital to the ability of this sector to innovate. Until the 18th century, cotton goods were available from India and were generally brought in by monopolistic chartered companies. Early European attempts to surpass or even successfully imitate Indian cotton goods were thoroughly unsuccessful. Many European governments supported domestic-made goods by banning the import of cotton goods from India, Persia, and China. In Great Britain, an initial ban passed in 1700 was extended and made more wide-ranging in 1719 thanks to pressure from woolens manufacturers who feared both the competition from and the ever-growing demand for cotton textiles.

Cotton played such an important role because of its unique qualities. Thread spun from cotton is both stronger and easier to manipulate than wool, linen, or silk. These properties make it suitable for machine-based production. Bleaching or dyeing both last longer and are more effective on cotton than on other natural fibers. Cotton fabric is also lighter and more washable than these other mainstay textile fabrics. The potential market for cotton, in Europe and overseas, was therefore greater than for any other textile.

To produce a bolt of cotton fabric, the raw cotton had to be combed to remove seeds, dirt, and other impurities. Then the raw cotton had to be spun into thread on a spinning wheel, twisted into yarn, and woven into cloth on a loom. To this basic process, other steps could be added to improve the quality or attractiveness of the cloth. Roving twisted the threads to increase their strength. Cloth could be cleaned and the weave shrunken and thickened by dunking it in a mix of hot water and fuller's earth (or some other cleanser) and then beating it with wooden mallets in a process called fulling. Dyeing or bleaching could help sell the cloth by making it more fashionable or attractive. Treating the fabric in other ways softened it. The process could be sped up by inventing new machines to save labor or by adding an additional source of power to run more than one machine at a time.

At the dawn of the industrial age, weaving was more technologically advanced than the other parts of the production process. In 1733, John Kay invented the flying shuttle, which eliminated the limitation of an "arm's length" to the width of a cloth. The loom's shuttle was fitted with small wheels set in a wooden groove to allow it to move without interfering with the alternating rise and fall of the warp. This simple device both removed a limiting factor and sped up weaving considerably.

As a domestic industry in cotton goods emerged in Lancashire, entrepreneurs and workers identified a series of mechanical bottlenecks as they tried to help spinning catch up to weaving. To find a workable solution, they tinkered with various machines. Over the course of decades, practical men found practical solutions to bottlenecks that held back production. These solutions transformed the industry and began the Industrial Revolution. The same process was going on in several regions of Europe, but the English developed more efficient solutions than their competitors.

The key steps toward mechanizing the manufacture of textiles were taken in the late 1760s. In 1764, James Hargreaves invented the spinning jenny, and in 1767, Richard Arkwright developed the water frame. Both began to be used in 1768. Arkwright's patent dates from the following year, Hargreaves's from the year after. Hargreaves's invention saved considerable labor, but did not fundamentally alter the production process. Arkwright's machine did. With his spinning or jenny-mule (1779), Samuel Crompton, also from Lancashire, vastly increased the utility of both Arkwright's and Hargreaves's machines. As the name suggests, this is a hybrid machine that was soon able to do 200–300 times the work of a spinning wheel.

Crompton's jenny-mule permitted an enormous increase in the quality and quantity of cotton goods produced. For the first time, a European producer could match the quality and undercut the cost of Indian cotton textiles. A measure of how efficient a labor-saving device the jenny-mule was can be seen in a comparison of the hours needed to process 100 pounds of cotton. At the end of the 18th century, it took Indian hand spinners more than 50,000 hours, but with Crompton's machine, it took only 2,000 hours. Mechanics, tinkerers, and workers who actually used the machines continuously made further small refinements that, taken together, rapidly improved the initial machines dramatically, thereby increasing their productivity.

Additional breakthrough machines followed, including the power-loom developed by Reverend Edmund Cartwright in 1786. Although a power-loom was no faster than a hand-weaver for several decades, a single worker could run first two and then several looms, which sped up production considerably. Frenchman Joseph-Marie Jacquard invented a draw loom capable of imprinting designs and figures on the fabric through the use of punch cards. Developed for use with silk in 1801, the Jacquard loom was applied to all fabrics in the second quarter of the 19th century. Richard Roberts applied power to reversing and turning the spindles at varying speeds to create a mule that did not have to be "run" by a human being. He patented the "self-acting" mule in 1825 and improved it greatly five years later. Thanks to these innovative machines, what had taken 2,000 hours in the late 18th century dwindled to only 135 hours in 1825. This first major bottleneck to expanding production—spinning—was swept aside. These machines saved such prodigious quantities of labor that prices could fall, profits could rise, and demand could be satisfied simultaneously.

Other technological developments that eliminated bottlenecks facilitated the skyrocketing growth of the cotton industry. American mechanic Eli Whitney developed the cotton gin in 1793 to remove the seeds and dirt from raw cotton. In the 1780s, Arkwright greatly upgraded earlier carding machines that combed and straightened the raw cotton. Finished yarn could be bleached a brilliant white with chlorine using a process developed by French chemist Claude Berthollet in 1784. However, in what would become a frequent occurrence, in 1799, British chemist Charles Tennant made this continental European's discovery more practical and profitable by creating bleaching powder. These advances permitted the cotton industry to grow rapidly. Although wool remained the largest European textile industry throughout the 18th century, the cotton industry expanded much more quickly. British cotton production increased approximately tenfold between 1760 and 1800 before spurting in the 19th century. By 1830, textiles made of cotton constituted half of all British exports, which fueled the Industrial Revolution.

See also: Cartwright, Edmund; Consumer Revolution; Division of Labor; Domestic Industry; Factory System; Hargreaves, James; Jacquard, Joseph-Marie; Lancashire; Patent(s); Productivity; Steam Engine; Tariffs and Excise Taxes; Whitney, Eli; Workforce; Document: "Robert Owen on Education and the Evils of Child Labor"

Further Reading

Beckert, Sven. *Empire of Cotton: A Global History*. New York: Vintage, 2014.
"Brief History of the Cotton Industry." Available online at http://www.saburchill .com/history/chapters/IR/014.html.
Landes, David. *The Unbound Prometheus: Technological Change and Industrial Development in Western Europe from 1750 to the Present*. Cambridge: Cambridge University Press, 1969.
Riello, Giorgio. *Cotton: The Fabric That Made the Modern World*. Cambridge: Cambridge University Press, 2013.
"Spinning the Web: The Story of the Cotton Industry." Available online at http:// www.spinningtheweb.org.uk/.

CREDIT   Industrialization cost money. Even wealthy entrepreneurs rarely chose to finance their businesses with cash: instead they borrowed money to establish or expand their workshops, mills, and factories. Industrialists needed more than long-term credit; they also needed substantial working capital to pay laborers and purchase raw materials while waiting for customers to buy their goods. Building transportation networks also required vast sums beyond what an individual or even a small group of investors could provide. Sometimes this capital was supplied or guaranteed by the state, especially on the continent, in the colonies, or in North America. The state itself also required enormous amounts of money to wage war and also to develop the military, judicial, and other institutions vital to industrialization. The availability of credit at low rates of interest determined whether certain places would industrialize ahead of their competitors. Britain's development of reliable credit institutions was an important factor in its leadership of the first Industrial Revolution.

During the early stages of the Industrial Revolution, a typical firm had less than one-quarter of its assets in fixed goods like buildings, machines, and tools. About 20 percent was in raw materials and stock while the remaining capital—the bulk of the company's assets—was in trade debt: goods that had been shipped, but not yet paid for. These percentages take on even greater weight when the sums involved are considered. Jedediah Strutt established a cotton-spinning factory at Belper in 1793: it cost £5,000 to erect the building, another £5,000 for various machines (including but not restricted to Arkwright water frames), and another £5,000 for stocks of raw materials. In total, Strutt needed about £60,000 in working capital to get his business off the ground, demonstrating the high financial barrier to industrial entrepreneurship. As machines got bigger and more expensive, the start-up costs and capital requirements increased proportionately.

Credit was available from a variety of sources. Once established, many firms made use of bills of exchange from other businesses, which specified that a certain sum would be paid at a later date, often two or three months in the future. The same mechanism was also utilized to allow storekeepers to stock a manufacturer's goods. A select few entrepreneurs, often inventors or those seeking to achieve import substitution, received funding or loans directly from the state. Banks, however, were the most common source of credit for industry, especially in Great Britain. They provided capital in exchange for mortgages on buildings and machinery. It deserves emphasis that banks and capital markets were regulated (more or less successfully) by the state, usually to ensure its own access to credit.

Banks run by individuals or families and usually licensed by the government had provided credit to industrial enterprises for centuries. In the 17th century, as the financial center of Europe shifted from Amsterdam to London, English banks benefited from the emergence of a sophisticated mortgage market for land that contributed to the availability of capital for productive purposes. The stability of the mercantilist English government, the profits of the empire, and the continuing growth of trade combined with institutional development of the nascent banking system to lower interest rates dramatically. In 1700, annual interest rates were about 6 percent, but this already low figure fell to 3.5 percent a year around midcentury. Between 1714 and 1832, the English government prohibited commercial interest rates above 5 percent a year. In France, Britain's chief industrial competitor, interest rates never dipped below 5 percent and even relatively safe investments in certain regions were required to pay a great deal more than that. Thus, Britons enjoyed the cheapest and most plentiful credit in the world.

The chief means by which Britain became the financial capital of Europe was the Bank of England. Founded in 1694 to assist the government to manage and consolidate its debt while lowering the rate of interest, the Bank was focused on commerce and state finance. The emergence of private or country banks in the early 18th century filled some of the void. These banks were founded by those who were involved in a variety of endeavors (goldsmiths, merchants, manufacturers) and provided much-needed credit due to investments from those wishing to take advantage of the booming industrial economy. When the Bank of England intermittently tightened credit because of government demands between 1772 and 1825, many of these banks failed. Thus, even in the country with the lowest borrowing rates and greatest availability of credit, industry was squeezed for capital and could not expand as fast as it might have. Only after 1825 was the British and then the European banking system organized more effectively, first by the Bank of England and then by other state-run banks, to distribute capital to areas where it was needed and drawing it from areas with a surplus.

The emergence of a more coherent, government-supervised banking system after 1825 helped protect the British industrial achievement while generating profits that would sustain the island economy long after its manufacturers were no longer as competitive. At the same time, government-sponsored banks played major roles in helping continental nations catch up to the British. In France, Belgium, and the German lands, banks furnished credit for strategic purposes to build up the industrial economy rather than strictly from a short-term profit and loss cost accounting. Credit was the grease that made the Industrial Revolution run.

See also: Colonialism; Mercantilism; Railroads; Role of the State; Transportation by Water; Document: "Child on Interest, Trade, and Money"; Document: "Adam Smith on the Division of Labor"

Further Reading

Hudson, Pat. *The Genesis of Industrial Capital: A Study of the West Riding Wool Textile Industry, c. 1750–1850.* Cambridge: Cambridge University Press, 1986.

Kindleberger, Charles P. *A Financial History of Western Europe*, 2nd ed. Oxford: Oxford University Press, 1993.

King, Steven, and Geoffrey Timmins. *Making Sense of the Industrial Revolution: English Economy and Society 1700–1850.* Manchester: Manchester University Press, 2001.

Mokyr, Joel. "The Institutional Origins of the Industrial Revolution." Available online at http://faculty.wcas.northwestern.edu/~jmokyr/Institutional-Origins-4.pdf.

Quinn, Stephen. "Money, Finance and Capital Markets." In *The Cambridge Economic History of Modern Britain*, ed. Roderick Floud and Paul Johnson. Cambridge: Cambridge University Press, 2004.

CRYSTAL PALACE   "The Great Exhibition of the Works of Industry of all Nations" or "The Great Exhibition" was organized by the Society of Arts and held in a purpose-built structure usually referred to as the Crystal Palace erected in Hyde Park, London, between May 1 and October 11, 1851. The Crystal Palace displayed the United Kingdom's technological prowess and taste for innovation at the height of its economic power. At the same time, the exhibits demonstrated that other countries were beginning to catch up to the first industrial nation.

The Crystal Palace was designed and built by Sir Joseph Paxton (he was knighted for successfully erecting his design on time). It was constructed specifically for the event from cast iron and 900 tons of a newly developed form of plate glass that let in natural light, hence the reference to crystal. The building was more than one-third of a mile in length and, at 128 feet high, tall enough to cover the park's majestic trees. Over 14,000 exhibits were on display in the Palace's nearly 1 million square feet of interior space. The Crystal Palace was also the first British building to have public toilets. It would have been impossible to build the structure a mere 20 years before, highlighting the rapid progress of technological capabilities to be able to manufacture building materials of greater strength. A wide-ranging and enormous assortment of goods from all over the world lured more than 6 million British people to visit the Crystal Palace (usually by train), equivalent to nearly 30 percent of the population. Initially, admittance cost £3 for men and £2 for women for a season pass or £1 for a single visit, but the price was soon lowered to a shilling for everyone. The event's substantial profits were used to found London's Victoria and Albert Museum, the Science Museum, and the National History Museum. The innovative building was moved in 1852 to Sydenham Hill outside London with parts incorporated into a new, larger building that housed exhibits and displays of all types until it burned down in 1936.

The Crystal Palace marked the height of Britain's scientific, technological, and economic domination. Britain dominated the age of the Industrial Revolution as no other relatively small country ever had before. By 1841, nearly 50 percent of the British population worked in industry and by 1860, these workers produced an astonishing 20 percent of the world's industrial goods, up from 2 percent in 1750. This small island nation furnished half the planet's iron and cotton textiles and mined two-thirds of its coal. Discounting for inflation, Britain's gross national product increased fourfold between 1780 and 1850. Great Britain emerged as the "workshop of the world." As measured by consumption, the standard of living increased about 75 percent in the same period, which seems paltry, until British population growth is taken into account. Despite heavy emigration and natural disasters like the Irish

Potato Famine of the 1840s, the population of the British Isles grew from 9 million in 1780 to 21 million in 1851. The Crystal Palace was the symbol of that extraordinary growth in national and individual wealth.

Yet, by 1851, change was already in the air. Many British visitors at the Crystal Palace were startled by the high quality and reasonable prices of manufactured goods and luxury items from the continent and even from the United States. Other countries began to industrialize, some on the British model, but all recognized the importance of advanced scientific knowledge and technological ability to economic development.

The United States' industrial "coming of age" took place at the Crystal Palace Exhibition. Although the American exhibit was quite small, the quality was impressive. Cyrus Hall McCormick's mechanical reaper, Charles Goodyear's India rubber life-raft, and Samuel Colt's six-shot pistol all won prestigious medals, and Europeans publicly took notice of American technology and metal-working skills. Success in the world of sport even played a role in winning favorable publicity: the yacht *America* defeated the pride of Great Britain, the S.S. *Titania*, in a race that has been perpetuated as the America's Cup. The *Liverpool Times* fretted, "The Yankees are no longer to be ridiculed, much less despised. The new world is bursting into greatness—walking past the old world, as the Americans did to the yachts . . . America, in her own phrase, is 'going ahead' and will assuredly pass us unless we accelerate our speed." From humble beginnings, it was clear that by 1850 the Industrial Revolution in North America had reached a point that some U.S. manufactured goods could compete on the world market. The Crystal Palace marked both the zenith of British industrial might and possibilities of new industrial rivalries on the horizon.

See also: American System of Manufactures; Armory Practice; Consumer Revolution; Cotton; Factory System; Iron and Steel; Productivity; Role of the State; Royal Society of Arts; Standard of Living; Waltham System

Further Reading
Auerbach, Jeffrey A. *The Great Exhibition of 1851: A Nation on Display.* New Haven, CT: Yale University Press, 1999.
"Crystal Palace: A History." Available online at http://www.bbc.co.uk/london/content/articles/2004/07/27/history_feature.shtml.
Hobhouse, Hermione. *The Crystal Palace and the Great Exhibition: Science, Art and Productive Industry: The History of the Royal Commission for the Exhibition of 1851.* London: Bloomsbury Academic Press, 2002.
Johnson, Ben. "The Great Exhibition of 1851." Available online at http://www.historic-uk.com/HistoryUK/HistoryofEngland/Great-Exhibition-of-1851/.

Picard, Liza. "The Great Exhibition." Available online at http://www.bl.uk/victorian -britain/articles/the-great-exhibition.

DISCIPLINE   Labor discipline made extraordinary contributions to man-ufacturing's profitability. Getting workers to perform the tasks that their mas-ters, managers, and foremen wanted them to do, when and how they wanted them done, was the chief managerial accomplishment of the Industrial Revo-lution. The efforts of British entrepreneurs were powerfully supported by the state, which ensured that their persons and property were safe from all threats—domestic or foreign—while providing legal tools and economic in-struments capable of subordinating the working classes to industrial disci-pline. Workers often accepted this discipline, usually because they had no other choice, but many did not. Laboring men and women recognized their oppression, which goaded them to push for reform. When changes came too slowly or too timidly for their liking, laborers sought more radical solutions. Deeply entrenched labor discipline slowed the pace of worker demands for their rights, but could not stop it. Emigration was often the last resort of mistreated or impotent workers.

The British labor force played a key role in industrialization. As a group, they were relatively well educated and possessed many useful craft skills. Yet, just as or even more importantly, British laborers were more thoroughly dis-ciplined than their continental counterparts. They accepted innovations in technology and in the organization of production far more systematically than their brethren on the other side of the Channel. The British also adapted to the time-clock and to the demands of the machine while their counterparts were distracted by political and military diversions that surfaced during the era of the French Revolution and Napoleon (1789–1815). This situation can be understood both as greater control by British elites and as heightened des-peration on the part of the laborers. Elite willingness to invest in machines and the financial need of enough laborers to undertake mechanized work was the basis for Britain's major advantage in the process of early industrialization: labor productivity. This "domestication" of labor underlay the successful im-plementation of the factory system.

Management sought to increase the productivity of labor in pursuit of profits. Improved discipline was essential to boosting labor productivity. Although oversight in a factory was not as thorough as in a small workshop, an important duty of full-time overseers and managers was to ensure that laborers did not simply punch the clock, but worked as hard as they could throughout their shift. This was a frustrating task. As a whole, entrepreneurs were dissatisfied with their employees' work habits because, as a wool clothier in England's West Country put it, workers "will never work any more time in general than is necessary just to live and support their weekly debauches." To the greatest degree possible, managers wanted laborers to match the regularity and stamina of the machines they tended. Managers resorted to a variety of disciplinary measures that ranged from docking the pay of workers who did not give their best effort to heavy doses of corporal punishment, applied mostly to women and children.

British owners, managers, and foremen attempted to train children to act the way they wanted. Their methods were not gentle. In a study of 609 examples of enforcing discipline or modifying the behavior of factory children undertaken in 1833, nearly 95 percent of all the tactics used were negative, with dismissal being the norm (58 percent), and fines (17 percent), corporal punishment (9 percent), and threats (8 percent) also being common. A reward was given only 23 times (4 percent), a promotion or raise 9 times (1 percent), and kindness twice. Corporal punishment was considered necessary to make "lazy" children work a 12- or 14-hour day, six days a week. In 1832, a slave owner testified before the House of Commons: "I have always thought myself disgraced by being the owner of slaves, but we never in the West Indies thought it possible for any human being to be so cruel as to require a child of nine years to work twelve and a half hours a day, and that, you acknowledge, is your regular practice."

Another aspect of the mounting effort to discipline the workforce focused on getting workers to show up on time, every day, and to remain at their stations the entire day. This was not as easy as it sounded as customary practice ran contrary. Another problem was that when workers labored six days a week, their day of "rest"—Sunday—was often punctuated by blowing off a little steam, often by drinking to excess. "Saint Monday" was the term used when workers failed to come to work after a binge. Even Tuesday was a slow day for those recovering from a particularly intense drunk. Managers also wanted to cut down drastically on the number of holidays, religious or otherwise, both paid and unpaid, to keep the machines humming. When the non-factory workday usually ran from dawn to dusk and clocks and watches were not yet common possessions, it was difficult to ensure punctuality, especially for early morning shifts.

From the perspective of a manager or entrepreneur, discipline also implied an individual relationship between master and man. In other words, managers did not want any kind of union, coalition, or association to unite workers to contest or resist their demands. As individuals, unskilled workers had little bargaining power; their strength rested solely in numbers. So managers attacked workers' organizations, breaking them whenever and however possible. They also took aim at customary work practices that, to their way of thinking, prevented innovation and reduced efficiency. Managers resented attempts by groups of workers to influence hiring and firing practices or work-floor rules and regulations that limited their control in any way. During the Industrial Revolution, managers insisted that their workers function as a blank slate upon which they could impose their own standards, practices, and expectations.

Industrial pioneers like Richard Arkwright found the task of "training human beings to renounce their desultory habits of work and identify themselves with the unvarying regularity of the complex automaton" a difficult proposition at best. When workers complained, the burgeoning population meant that unskilled laborers could be replaced with impunity. When and where that proved to be difficult, laborers were imported from poorer areas such as Ireland or the Highlands of Scotland to fill jobs no local person would take. During the first two or three generations trained to the factory, the new industrial discipline was imposed, in many cases, on workers who were not free to dispose of their own labor; modern notions of discipline were not accepted passively. The frequent resort to violence—judicial and military—on the part of the state to enforce industrial discipline or to protect innovating entrepreneurs demonstrates how deeply changes in customary work practice were resented by laborers whose defiance threatened the entire social order.

The British state enabled entrepreneurs to discipline their workers. By providing a high degree of protection from both domestic and foreign challenges while guaranteeing stability and order, the state contributed mightily to instituting labor discipline. Britain borrowed and spent vast sums to fight its wars, acquire colonies, and control its people. Despite its belligerency and far-flung imperial commitments, more than half of British military expenditure was dedicated to preserving internal order. Scots, Irish, workers, farm laborers, religious dissenters, political reformers, and the poor were all subject to thoroughgoing military rule whose oppressiveness increased over time to eliminate the unruliness of "an ungovernable people." The government made heavy-handed use of spies and informers, and, in the early 19th century, 155 military barracks were constructed in industrial districts to oversee the laboring classes.

The British state enforced discipline through a variety of means. During the age of the French Revolution and Napoleon, the average British person lost many of their customary rights and protections while new repressive laws were enacted to restrict individual liberties and prevent any sort of collective activity by laborers. The transmutation of machine-breaking into a felony carrying the death penalty in 1812 during the Luddite movement (1811–1817) demonstrates the impunity with which British elites utilized the legal system to protect their economic interests by disciplining the working classes.

Extensive legal, military, and political oppression had dramatic economic consequences. Given how dangerous and tightly disciplined the early factories were, entrepreneurs during the first few decades of the Industrial Revolution relied on apprentices, indentures, Irish, Scots, women, and children for a significant proportion of their labor force. It was not simply a matter of economy; it was also an expression of the domination of these groups by the elite. What requires emphasis is that those who went into the factory generally did so out of desperation or hunger. Higher wages were usually insufficient to convince these people to submit to factory life. Thanks to state repression and a lack of other options, this domination of the working classes was widely accepted. The toleration by the working classes of a level of repression that would have sparked a revolution on the continent was the cornerstone of British labor discipline.

See also: Arkwright, Richard; Coal; Cotton; Division of Labor; Domestic Industry; Factory Acts; Factory System; Hargreaves, James; Lancashire; Luddites; Productivity; Role of the State; Socialism; Waltham System; Wedgwood, Josiah; Workforce; Document: "The State of the Poor"; Document: "Defending the Factory System"; Document: "Living and Working in Manchester"; Document: "Resisting Mechanization: The Luddites"

Further Reading

Archer, John E. *Social Unrest and Popular Protest in England 1780–1840.* Cambridge: Cambridge University Press, 2000.

Hobsbawm, Eric. *Industry and Empire: The Birth of the Industrial Revolution.* London: Penguin, 1969.

Horn, Jeff, Leonard N. Rosenband, and Merritt Roe Smith, eds. *Reconceptualizing the Industrial Revolution.* Cambridge, MA: MIT Press, 2010.

"Labor History Links." Available online at http://www.laborhistorylinks.org/index.html.

Thompson, E. P. *The Making of the English Working Class.* New York: Vintage Press, 1966 (1963).

DIVISION OF LABOR   The division of labor refers to breaking down the process of manufacturing into as many simple, easily repeated separate tasks as possible. Each step would be performed by a different person who would become faster and more reliable through repetition. Division of labor facilitated mechanization and expedited the establishment of the factory system. This approach was fundamentally different than artisanal production in which one person made something from start to finish. Division of labor was an important means of increasing the productivity of labor, but it also undermined workers' independence of thought and action, as both Adam Smith and Karl Marx emphasized. Substituting unskilled for skilled labor lowered the costs of production. Increasing the division of labor was a vital component of the economic transformation that supported the Industrial Revolution.

Smith coined the phrase and articulated the benefits and drawbacks of the division of labor in *The Wealth of Nations* published in 1776. His famous example was pin making, which could be broken down into 18 different operations allowing workers to become increasingly efficient at their limited assignments. Labor was also saved because workers did not have to switch tools or move when they shifted from task to task. Division of labor allowed and allows growing economic interdependence as larger populations spread over wider geographic areas could and can contribute to the manufacture of complex goods. It also facilitated and facilitates specialization in the widest possible sense of the term. At the same time, Smith noted that while increasing the division of labor is more efficient, it is also more stultifying. As a worker's "whole life is spent in performing a few simple operations . . . [h]e naturally loses, therefore becomes as stupid and ignorant as it is possible for a human creature to become." Instead of being valued for their knowledge and skill, workers were expected to perform like machines and steadily lost the opportunity to take advantage of their understanding of the production process to become entrepreneurs themselves.

Marx focused on the fact that the division of labor alienated workers from the product of their labor by removing the role of skill and making workers responsible for only one discrete part of manufacturing a product. Since the laboring classes' value to society was defined in terms of what they produced and how they produced it, this alienation diminished their worth and enabled the value of what they produced to be appropriated from them. Thus, for Marx, the division of labor was the starting point for class conflict as well as the basis of the system of capitalism.

More generally, division of labor can and has taken place between genders and nations and among ages and regions. As Smith and Marx made clear, there are significant consequences, both positive and negative, to increasing the division of labor. U.S. "armory practice" relied on increasing the division of labor as did the American system of production and the birth of true mass production with the assembly line during the Second Industrial Revolution.

See also: American System of Manufactures; Armory Practice; Discipline; Factory System; Productivity; Second Industrial Revolution; Socialism; Wedgwood, Josiah; Workforce; Document: "Lowell Mill Girls"; Document: "Adam Smith on the Division of Labor"

Further Reading

Burnette, Joyce. *Gender, Work and Wages in Industrial Revolution Britain*. Cambridge: Cambridge University Press, 2008.

Daunton, Martin J. *Progress and Poverty: An Economic and Social History of Britain 1700–1850*. Oxford: Oxford University Press, 1995.

Hendrickson Kenneth E. III, ed. *The Encyclopedia of the Industrial Revolution in World History*, vol. 3. Lanham, MD: Lexington Books, 2014.

Munger, Michael, "Division of Labor." Available online at http://www.econlib.org /library/Enc/DivisionofLabor.html.

DOMESTIC INDUSTRY   "Domestic industry" refers to the manufacture of goods—most often textiles—in the home, usually but not always in rural areas. "Cottage industry" made use of local materials such as wool or linen to produce cloth for household consumption as well as for the market. This type of labor was generally either seasonal or part-time and complemented agricultural work. From the late medieval era, domestic industry was commonplace in northwestern Europe with its concentrated network of markets, dense population, and long winters. In the late 17th century, and lasting well into the 20th century, domestic industry expanded to include what became known as the "putting out" system by which entrepreneurs sold raw materials to a family that then resold the finished products either to the original merchant or on the market. Reliance on domestic industry to survive was a sign of the financial pressures on the agricultural population in this era and demonstrated that industrial output could be expanded greatly without resorting to implementing a factory system.

Many rural families engaged in domestic industry because the effects of population growth outstripped the gains of the Agricultural Revolution, at least in the short term. Put another way, there were too many people trying to earn a living by working too little land. Rural overpopulation forced farming families to do additional labor to survive if they wanted to remain on the land. For many families, domestic industry filled the slack winter months when there were relatively few agricultural tasks to perform. It was a supplement rather than a replacement for full-time agricultural work.

In families more closely tied to the emerging market economy and without other options, women and children devoted their efforts to industry while males worked either on their own farm or for others. Only in a few places was domestic industry a full-time, year-round occupation. Some liked the ability to work on their own schedule, enjoying a few days off for a festival following the completion of an order. In general, spinning was women's work and weaving was a male pursuit; children helped out wherever they were needed.

The putting out system had tremendous productive potential and played a major role in accelerating the interaction of the rural populace with local, national, and international markets. A prosperous shopkeeper or affluent farmer required only a limited amount of capital to begin finding client families. The profitability of the system was based on the low wages given to rural workers, who accepted a pittance because they needed only to augment their agricultural income. Rural wages were at least 20 percent and up to 50 percent lower than their urban equivalents. Yet careful and thrifty workers could and did better themselves. Especially on the continent, domestic industry allowed significant numbers of poor or marginal agricultural laborers or smallholders to remain on the land far longer than would otherwise have been possible.

Eventually, putting out came to dominate whole regions of Europe and contributed substantially to total industrial output. From Ireland to Prussia, dense networks of rural outworkers numbering in the hundreds of thousands and stretching up to 80 kilometers in a given direction surrounded many large mercantile cities that shipped goods abroad. This phenomenon has sometimes been termed "proto-industrialization." In the Austrian Netherlands (modern-day Belgium), a quarter of the working population toiled in domestic industry in the middle of the 18th century. In addition to textiles, goods that were put out included gloves, lace, ribbons, stockings, hats, boots, shoes, pins, nails, and cutlery, as well as other hardware. At the end of the 18th century, the putting out system accounted for 43 percent of all manufactured goods in the German-speaking lands. By increasing textile production, spreading spinning and weaving skills to the rural population and introducing a market mentality into the day-to-day lives of many Europeans, the putting out system paved the way for industrialization based on the factory system. As a form of production, rural industry lasted alongside newer means of production until the 1930s.

Domestic industry and especially the putting out system also responded to the limitations and lack of flexibility inherent in the output of urban guilds with monopolies on the manufacture and often sale of certain types of goods. With demand outstripping supply, mercantilist governments dedicated to self-sufficiency and import substitution wanted to provide work and dominate the domestic market. Because communities of guilds were unwilling or unable to produce the kinds, qualities, and quantities of goods demanded by other continents as well as by the burgeoning European population, different methods of satisfying these markets had to be developed. To sidestep guild restrictions on urban production, entrepreneurs, including merchants, nobles, and even state officials either funded or allowed the massive expansion of domestic industry into northwestern Europe's large-scale putting out system.

Domestic industry and the putting out system responded to growing consumer demand and the restrictions of the existing productive environment. Rural labor engaged in this poorly paid work in order to remain on the land or, far more rarely, to afford to buy luxuries like coffee, chocolate, or even a fashionable shirt. Although production could be increased relatively easily through this system and the low wages paid to laborers made this approach competitive in some ways, machine-based production was of finer quality and could take advantage of greater economies of scale. Domestic industry lasted into the 20th century in several regions, but its heyday was 1680–1830. It enabled and led to industrialization.

See also: Agricultural Revolution; Consumer Revolution; Cotton; Discipline; Factory System; "Industrious Revolution"; Mercantilism; Productivity; Standard of Living; Workforce; Document: "The State of the Poor"

Further Reading

Daunton, Martin J. *Progress and Poverty: An Economic and Social History of Britain 1700–1850.* Oxford: Oxford University Press, 1995.

Hudson, Pat. "Proto-Industrialisation." Available online at http://www.ehs.org.uk /dotAsset/1d40418e-b981–4076–8974-b81686a9d042.pdf.

Kisch, Herbert. *From Domestic Manufacture to Industrial Revolution: The Case of the Rhineland Textile Districts.* Oxford: Oxford University Press, 1989.

Ogilvie, Sheilagh C., and Markus Cerman, eds. *European Proto-industrialization.* Cambridge: Cambridge University Press, 1996 [1994].

EDUCATION   Education played an indirect role in supporting the initial phases of the Industrial Revolution. That role centered on empowering curiosity, encouraging tinkering, and diffusing existing knowledge. Scientific and technological education enjoyed a greater function in supporting the "catch up" efforts of the second wave of industrializing nations on the continent. A major element of the Enlightenment's agenda was education. Over the course of the 18th century, literacy jumped dramatically. In the Protestant areas of Europe, the trend was most marked, but even in Catholic France, nearly half the male population and over a quarter of the females were literate by the end of the century. In eastern Europe, literacy rates increased, although not as impressively as in western Europe. Scientific or technological training, however, was quite limited in both availability and quality. Universities in Protestant countries did teach mathematics and advance medical knowledge, but the power of organized religion limited both what could be taught and access to higher education. In most of western Europe, the best training in scientific matters came from private institutions like the Dissenting Academies in England, which provided a practical education in modern languages and mathematics to non-Anglican Protestants, not the classical curriculum still in vogue at the universities. In Great Britain, the creation of new state and private institutions expedited the exchange of scientific information. State-sponsored academies and informal private salons successfully spread knowledge of the techniques of scientific agriculture and broadened interest in scientific and technological developments. In addition, the English developed institutions focused on the application of science to manufacturing.

The Royal Society of Arts established in London in 1754 had a decidedly practical orientation. Similar institutions were created throughout the country, with the Lunar Society in Birmingham being the most important. Such learned societies were composed not only of important scientists like Joseph Priestley, but also counted inventors like James Watt, who dramatically improved the steam engine, and industrial entrepreneurs including Matthew Boulton, who manufactured and marketed Watt's steam engine among its members. A close interaction between laboratory and workshop was common among the "Lunatics" and differentiated the practice of science in Great Britain from the continent. The spread of the scientific knowledge by itinerant lecturers and the high level of literacy in Great Britain meant that by the late 18th century, an understanding of some basic scientific principles, most notably mechanics, was more widely disseminated among the British population than anywhere else in Europe.

It was in scientific method that 18th-century education broke most decisively with the past. During the age of Enlightenment, rather than accept the teachings of organized religion and deduce information from known principles, many Europeans and their colonists preferred to investigate nature and natural phenomena. They used rigorous observational and experimental approaches to explain what happened even if they did not yet understand why something occurred. As a result of this interest, a startlingly large number of individual Europeans of all social classes observed the heavens, experimented with machines, and classified plant and animal species. This willingness to investigate, this ability to apply the scientific method, and an emphasis on "what" rather than "why" were all attitudes that expedited the technological breakthroughs of the Industrial Revolution. Although the educational developments of the 17th and 18th centuries encouraged and permitted tinkerers to function, there was no direct link between the scientific advances associated with the Scientific Revolution and the technology that made the Industrial Revolution.

To catch up with Great Britain and to develop or protect productive specialties of their own, the French and later other countries needed to acquire and spread various kinds of specialized craft, scientific, and technological knowledge.

Although financial incentives for innovation and the enticement of skilled workers from abroad played important roles in this process, education was at the heart of the long-term French approach to becoming competitive.

Educational institutions were to facilitate the application of French predominance in basic science, especially in chemistry, mathematics, and medicine to the problems of production. French education also aimed to spread mechanical knowledge more widely and deeply among the laboring classes. These educational efforts began during the Revolution with the creation of the National Institute and the Polytechnic in 1794, which were staffed by some of the best scientific minds alive. These elite institutions were supposed to provide expert training and to reorient theoretically minded French elites toward practical problems of industry and engineering. It was hoped that their effects would trickle down the French educational system. Thanks to Jean-Antoine Chaptal, students at specialized training schools for mining and civil engineers also began to spend part of each year in the field learning about the practical problems they would someday face. The thorough reform of the university system undertaken by Emperor Napoleon I in 1808 supported these goals. To bridge the gap between the elite and the rest of the population, the French opened two Schools of Arts and Crafts (1803, 1811) where skilled workers, foremen, engineers, and scientists melded scientific theory and hands-on practice with machines. According to their founding statutes, these schools were to "train petty officers for industry."

Chaptal and his collaborators also sought to institutionalize the type of interaction of scientists, innovators, entrepreneurs, and bureaucrats that took place in the London Society of Arts and the Lunar Society of Birmingham. These educational efforts helped France develop expertise in areas where they could compete successfully with the British, strongly supporting French industrialization throughout the 19th century.

See also: Chaptal, Jean-Antoine; Enlightenment; Role of the State; Royal Society of Arts; Second Industrial Revolution; Watt, James; Document: "The Enlightenment's Focus on Education and the Usefulness of Knowledge"; Document: "Robert Owen on Education and the Evils of Child Labor"

Further Reading

Horn, Jeff. *The Path Not Taken: French Industrialization in the Age of Enlightenment, 1750–1830.* Cambridge, MA: MIT Press, 2006.

Jacob, Margaret C. *Scientific Culture and the Making of the Industrial West.* Oxford: Oxford University Press, 1997.

Mitch, David. "Education and Economic Growth in Historical Perspective." Available online at https://eh.net/encyclopedia/education-and-economic-growth-in-historical-perspective/.

Mokyr, Joel. *The Gifts of Athena: Historical Origins of the Knowledge Economy.* Princeton, NJ: Princeton University Press, 2004.

ENLIGHTENMENT   The Enlightenment, a fundamentally new way of thinking, made the Industrial Revolution possible. To undermine the claims to exclusive and universal knowledge by the Roman Catholic Church and the absolutist French monarchy under Louis XIV (1638–1715), the most powerful institutions of late 17th and early 18th century Europe, Europeans (most notably in France, Great Britain, and the Netherlands) inaugurated an ever-more-comprehensive investigation of nature and the natural world using new methodologies based on the achievements of the Scientific Revolution. The Enlightenment spawned not only a different conception of the universe, but also shifted perceptions of what humans could accomplish.

In the 18th century, the ideal of comprehending nature that impelled the Scientific Revolution expanded into new areas as the consequences and ramifications of the discoveries of the Scientific Revolution were explored and demonstrated conclusively. During the Enlightenment, the goal of searching out new knowledge was wedded firmly to a generalized ambition to spread existing knowledge as widely as possible. The ultimate goal of those men and women generally referred to as *philosophes* (lovers of knowledge or wisdom) who contributed to the project of Enlightenment was to improve the human condition by elevating their ability to understand and control the natural environment. This combination of objectives not only helped to make the Enlightenment an important period in western intellectual development, but also lay the foundations for greater interaction between science and technology that later became an important element of the Industrial Revolution.

The Enlightenment drew crucial support for its attack on exclusive claims to knowledge from the breakthroughs of Englishman Isaac Newton (1643–1727). Newton and German Gottfried Leibniz (1646–1716) earned the disdain of generations of students by simultaneously developing calculus, a branch of mathematics that was an essential tool to explaining the physics of the universe. In his major work, published in 1687, Newton reconfigured European understandings of celestial mechanics (the movement of heavenly bodies) and explained his three laws of motion. For those with the mathematical skills to decipher the formulas—not to mention the ungrammatical Latin Newton wrote in—this work definitively obliterated the dominant religious and scientific conceptions of the universe almost uniformly based on Aristotle. Newton's explanation of the universe was convincing to the scientific community until the breakthroughs of Albert Einstein and Werner Heisenberg in the first half of the 20th century. These stunning achievements were not enough for Newton, who also made important discoveries in optics that led to new theories concerning the properties of light and colors, which culminated in the invention of the reflecting telescope. Despite the efforts of gifted writers such as John Locke and Voltaire, who published popular and popularized explanations of Newton's ideas in 1704 and 1733 respectively, it took decades for Newton's ideas to percolate through the educated strata of western society. Such fundamental conceptual reordering of people's understanding of the universe demonstrated the possibilities of human endeavor and took the prestige of English science and technology to new heights, justifying the broad and deep transformation envisioned by the *philosophes*.

The Enlightenment emphasized the diffusion of ideas. Frenchmen Denis Diderot (1713–1784) and Jean le Rond d'Alembert (1717–1783) led a great collaborative enterprise to rationalize and categorize existing knowledge. They published a 24-volume compendium of existing knowledge, the *Encyclopédie*, between 1751 and 1772. Diderot and d'Alembert had to overcome the opposition of powerful individuals in the Church hierarchy and state administration. Other 18th-century projects of diffusion and rationalization included the creation of the periodic table of elements and Swede Carl von Linné's (or Linnaeus, 1707–1778) development of a means of classifying plants and animals into categories. The organization and publication of current scientific knowledge set the stage for later accomplishments.

Although science made few direct contributions to manufacturing technology during the first few decades of the Industrial Revolution, it did accomplish something vital. The Scientific Revolution bequeathed a new inductive method of testing ideas that focused on experimentation. The wave of scientific discoveries, clever experiments, and geographical explorations that followed helped to convince the average person that an improvement of the human condition was not only possible but underway. As a result of the Enlightenment, the prospect of "progress," both in understanding and materially, gradually overcame the pessimistic views of people like Thomas Malthus that had dominated European society for a millennium. In the 19th century, this faith in progress became firmly entrenched as technological change and industrialization first transformed the day-to-day life of western Europeans, and ultimately, much of the world.

The Enlightenment also shaped agricultural improvement. Arthur Young (1741–1820), a leading English agricultural writer, emphasized the importance of education, the development of new knowledge, and the utility of helping agricultural entrepreneurs to escape the binding restrictions of customary practice through innovation, all hallmarks of the Enlightenment. Young's fervor for agricultural improvement was shared by an impressive number of other people in Great Britain and throughout western Europe, bringing the benefits of the new ways of thinking to ever wider audiences.

See also: Agricultural Revolution; Education; "Industrious Revolution"; Productivity; Role of the State; Wedgwood, Josiah; Document: "The Enlightenment's Focus on Education and the Usefulness of Knowledge"

Further Reading

Day, C. R. *Education for the Industrial World: The École d'Arts et Métiers and the Rise of French Industrial Engineering.* Cambridge: Cambridge University Press, 1987.

Jacob, Margaret C. *The First Knowledge Economy: Human Capital and the European Economy, 1750–1850.* Cambridge: Cambridge University Press, 2014.

Jones, Peter M. *Industrial Enlightenment: Science, Technology and Culture in Birmingham and the West Midlands 1760–1820.* Manchester: Manchester University Press, 2008.

Mokyr, Joel. *The Gifts of Athena.* Available online at http://www.nes.ru/NES10/cd/materials/Mokyr-2chapters.pdf.

FACTORY ACTS From 1802, the British Parliament passed a series of "factory acts" to regulate the industrial employment of child labor. These legislative acts attempted to mitigate the very worst excesses of child exploitation, though with minimal success until improved mechanisms for enforcement began to be developed in the 1830s and 1840s. Although the effect of children's labor on morals was the initial motivation of the factory acts, their scope expanded to cover female labor and the length of the work day. The factory acts were paralleled by legislation in other countries, but Britain's efforts went the furthest and the fastest in curbing the abuse of factory labor for later generations of workers that endured the Industrial Revolution. The factory acts gave birth to modern industrial regulation of the labor force.

The 1802 Health and Morals of Apprentices Act was introduced by rich mill owner Sir Robert Peel. It applied only to those young people (under 18) sent to work in textile mills by their parish in exchange for financial or material support for their impoverished families. Widely used as cheap labor and with no recourse because they could not leave and had no protectors, these apprentices were exploited horribly. This act limited the work day to 12 hours, six days a week, and outlawed night work. Employers were required to provide a place to sleep, decent clothing, and some sort of education. In textile factories with more than 20 employees, ventilation was mandated and the mill had to be whitewashed at least twice a year. The act was to be enforced by local magistrates known as justices of the peace who were supposed to appoint visitors to investigate whether the requirements of the law were met. Because many justices of the peace were more closely allied to the mill owners and because taking care of apprentices cost money that had to be raised by local taxes, which the justices usually wanted to keep as low as possible, the law was generally ignored. Mill owners increasingly turned to unregulated "free" labor instead of relying on parish apprentices.

In the aftermath of the Napoleonic Wars, the British Parliament again took up factory regulation on the instigation of Robert Owen. Peel agreed to sponsor the project, but it took three years of parliamentary investigations and numerous concessions that gutted the bill before the passage of the Cotton Mills and Factories Act in 1819. This measure forbade the employment of children under the age of 9 and restricted children aged 9–16 to 12 hours' work per day between the hours of 5 a.m. and 9 p.m. (six days a week), but only in cotton factories. Again, justices of the peace were supposed to enforce the act, but no funds for inspection were allocated, rendering this bill, like its predecessor, almost completely without practical effect.

The tide of reform that followed widespread popular unrest in 1830–1831 included important limitations on child factory labor. A narrow Labour in Cotton Mills Act passed in 1831 excluded night work for anyone under the age of 21 working in a factory, but was clearly understood as a stopgap measure. The creation of a parliamentary commission spearheaded by Anthony Ashley-Cooper, later Earl of Shaftesbury, and Michael Sadler led to a scathing report that prompted the establishment of more extensive restrictions on child labor and created more effective means of enforcement, though large loopholes continued to exist.

The Factory Act of 1833 forbade children under the age of nine from working in textiles (except silk mills). Children between 9 and 13 could not work more than eight hours without getting an hour-long lunch break. They were also to receive two hours of education per day (in addition to going to work) and could be employed no more than 48 hours a week. For children aged 14 to 18, the length of the day's labor that required a formal meal break was 12 hours. Nobody under 18 years old could work between 8:30 p.m. and 5:30 a.m. Factories were to be regularly inspected and a dedicated professional corps of inspectors was established that was independent of local authorities and did not require ministerial authorization to act.

The humanitarian impulses that led to the enfranchisement of Catholics in 1831, the parliamentary Reform Act of 1832, and the abolition of slavery in the United Kingdom and its colonies in 1833 did not stop mill owners from objecting strenuously to the passage of the Factory Act. They complained to the House of Commons that such limitations were "prejudicial to the Cotton Trade" and "impracticable" because "Free labourers cannot be obtained to perform the night work, but upon very disadvantageous terms to the manufacturers." The continued success of Britain's textile industry empowered the next generation of reformers to push for new restrictions on the work day in all factories without exception and to apply the same constraints established in 1833 to young people and to women.

An 1844 Factory Act affected all textile mills (except lace and silk) and banned women and youths between 13 and 17 from working more than 12 hours a day. Children under the age of 13 could work no more than 6.5 hours a day and children under the age of 8 could not be employed. Three years later, a Ten Hour Act was applied to women and youths with total hours reduced to 63 and then 58 hours by May 1848. In 1850, the workday was set to either 6 a.m. to 6 p.m. or 7 a.m. to 7 p.m. and women and youths could work a maximum of 10.5 hours a day (with 1.5 hours of breaks). Six more Factory Acts were passed between 1853 and 1878 that extended the rules on children, youths, and females established for textiles to all other factories.

The factory acts were a series of small steps in the direction of reform. It took more than 30 years to pass effective limitations on child labor in the cotton industry and another 45 years for those restrictions to be applied to all factory work. There was widespread pressure to improve the conditions of labor from elites, the middle classes, and workers themselves. The continued vigor of British industry and the tremendous wealth gained from the Industrial Revolution allowed these halting reforms from above to be implemented before the eruption of major violence. The factory acts showed that an industrial economy can allow the working classes to gain a share of the benefits without destroying profitability. This model was widely copied and even surpassed by Britain's industrial rivals in the second half of the 19th century.

See also: Discipline; Education; Factory System; Owen, Robert; Pollution, Health, and Environment; Role of the State; Second Industrial Revolution; Standard of Living; Workforce; Document: "Conditions in the Mines"; Document: "Living and Working in Manchester"; Document: "Robert Owen on Education and the Evils of Child Labor"

Further Reading

Burnette, Joyce. "Women Workers in the British Industrial Revolution." Available online at https://eh.net/encyclopedia/women-workers-in-the-british-industrial-revolution-2/.

"1833 Factory Act." Available online at http://www.nationalarchives.gov.uk/education/resources/1833-factory-act/.

Harris, Ron. "Government and the Economy, 1688–1850." In *The Cambridge Economic History of Modern Britain*, vol. 1, *Industrialisation, 1700–1860*, ed. Roderick Floud and Paul Johnson. Cambridge: Cambridge University Press, 2004.

Quinault, Roland. "The Industrial Revolution and Parliamentary Reform." In *The Industrial Revolution and British Society*, edited by Patrick O'Brien and Roland Quinault. Cambridge: Cambridge University Press, 1993.

Tuttle, Carolyn. "Child Labor during the British Industrial Revolution." Available online
    at https://eh.net/encyclopedia/child-labor-during-the-british-industrial-revolution/.

FACTORY SYSTEM   The seemingly inexhaustible demand for cotton textiles led entrepreneurs to develop the factory system as a more efficient way of
organizing manufacturing to maximize production. The essential characteristics of the factory were the concentration of workers at one site rather than in
the home, and the mechanization of production with concurrent increased
division of labor and hierarchical management. The use of machinery imposed geographical constraints—mechanization required a nearby power
source, either water or coal. Thus, industrialization was regional more than
national, clustering around rivers and coal deposits. This new sort of production lowered costs, permitting greater profit while allowing prices to be reduced, bringing goods within the purchasing reach of more people, increasing
potential demand. The creation and spread of the modern factory system
within the confines of the British textile industry during the late 18th century
was the most tangible sign of the coming transformation of western civiliza-
tion: the Industrial Revolution.

The first modern factory was a cotton mill at Cromford in Derbyshire,
England, established by the inventor Richard Arkwright. When it opened in
1771, it had space for a complete set of machines and was purpose-built to be
lit by candle for night work. The machines were run by large waterwheels. In
1769, Arkwright had founded a horse-powered workshop not far from James
Hargreaves's jenny-mill in Nottingham to utilize his inventions in partnership with a bar-owner and a banker, but the partners simply did not have
enough capital to outfit the manufactory the way he wanted. So, he formed
an association with two rich hosiers: Jedediah Strutt and Samuel Need who
funded Cromford. At first, Strutt and Need purchased the mill's entire output
for their stocking knitting businesses, but, in 1773, the three partners established a weaving workshop to make England's first all-cotton calicoes in imitation of goods imported from India.

Cromford became the model for a huge number of other establishments.
It swiftly grew to house several thousand spindles and 300 workers. Only
15 years later, there were 140 Arkwright-type water-powered mills spinning
cotton. By 1800, England was home to 900 cotton-spinning factories of
which 300 were large mills (with more than 50 workers) patterned on Arkwright's. Almost all of these establishments utilized water power. Initially, few,
even unskilled workers sought employment at Cromford because the rural
site was picked for maximizing water power capacity, not for convenience or
ease of access. (Unskilled workers were preferred because they did not have to
unlearn other techniques, they did not mind the closer supervision demanded

by factory labor, and they were willing to be trained to work the machines.) In the short run, Arkwright solved the labor problem by accepting a huge number of youthful apprentices from poor houses all over Britain. The child and teenage apprentices lived at the mill and were bound (i.e., they could not leave) to work for Arkwright either until they reached the age of 18 or for seven years, whichever was longer!

Arkwright's long-term answer to his labor problem was to return to the region of his birth. He set up his factories in the relatively poor region of Lancashire where domestic industry was well established. Lancashire also had a large number of small streams and shallow rivers that were perfect for turning waterwheels. The region enjoyed excellent access to the sea through the port of Liverpool. Other entrepreneurs followed him both in moving to the province to benefit from the same cost advantages and by taking thoroughgoing advantage of child, female, convict, and apprentice labor.

The British pioneered the factory system, and it spread most rapidly there. As a result, the manufactured goods produced in the British Isles tended to be cheaper and in many cases better (thanks to the mechanization of many operations) than those made in other countries, allowing ever-increasing economies of scale. British industrial dominance in the first half of the 19th century was founded on relatively inexpensive goods made with machinery and a high level of division of labor by workers with unique craft skills in economic sectors with highly elastic demand. Yet these advantages did not survive changes in the production process, the development of other countries' industrial sectors, and in consumer demand that ultimately sounded the death knell for British dominance, but not until after 1870.

Factories pre-dated the Industrial Revolution in the sense that large buildings that housed many workers collaborating in the manufacture of some product had existed for centuries. Silks, tapestries, porcelain, weapons, and some ships were made at sites that qualified as factories. But in the 18th century, in order to satisfy the burgeoning market for cotton textiles, a hierarchical management emerged that was interested in implementing mechanization, substituting water or coal for human energy, and instituting a greater division of labor. Such means of maximizing production necessitated a much more thorough control over labor and the work process. These characteristics were the difference between a factory derived from the term "manufacture" and a factory system. This shift, along with reliance on water and coal power, transformed the means of production by lowering costs. Because of competition both from India and from other European countries, such saving went into reducing prices to increase demand rather than increasing profits. Lower profit per unit was acceptable when volume was skyrocketing. The creation and spread of the modern factory system within the confines of the British textile sector during the late 18th century represented the true beginnings of the Industrial Revolution.

See also: Arkwright, Richard; Cartwright, Edmund; Coal; Consumer Revolution; Cotton; Discipline; Division of Labor; Domestic Industry; Factory Acts; Hargreaves, James; "Industrious Revolution"; Jacquard, Joseph-Marie; Lancashire; Owen, Robert; Productivity; Slater, Samuel; Tariffs and Excise Taxes; Waltham System; Wedgwood, Josiah; Document: "The State of the Poor"; Document: "Lowell Mill Girls"; Document: "Robert Owen on Education and the Evils of Child Labor"

Further Reading

Hackett, Lewis. "Industrial Revolution." Available online at http://history-world .org/Industrial%20Intro.htm.

Hounshell, David A. *From the American System to Mass Production, 1800–1932: The Development of Manufacturing Technology in the United States.* Baltimore: Johns Hopkins University Press, 1984.

Hudson, Pat. "Industrial Organization and Structure." In *The Cambridge Economic History of Modern Britain*, vol. 1, *Industrialisation, 1700–1860*, ed. Roderick Floud and Paul Johnson. Cambridge: Cambridge University Press, 2004.

Mantoux, Paul. *The Industrial Revolution in the Eighteenth Century: An Outline of the Beginnings of the Modern Factory System in England*, rev. ed. New York: Harper & Row, 1961.

Mokyr, Joel. "The Rise and Fall of the Factory System: Technology, Firms, and Households since the Industrial Revolution." Available online at http://faculty .wcas.northwestern.edu/~jmokyr/pittsburgh.PDF.

FITCH, JOHN   After a successful trial of his steamboat on the Delaware River in 1787 in front of delegates from the Constitutional Convention, American John Fitch received the first patents for this new form of transportation, in the United States and in France, both in 1791. Fitch also ran the first commercial steamboat service across the Delaware River between Philadelphia and Burlington, New Jersey, though it ran only for a single summer before it failed due to lack of customers. Despite his patents, Fitch could not find backers, in part because those patents only provided limited protection. Although a good designer and builder, he was a poor entrepreneur. His contributions have generally been overlooked in favor of Robert Fulton's.

Fitch was born in 1743 in the British colony of Connecticut and died in 1798 in Bardstown, Kentucky, by his own hand. A jack of all trades, Fitch worked on farms, as a silver- and gunsmith, as a surveyor and would-be land speculator, and as a clockmaker. During the Revolutionary War, he fought for the Continental Army. He then traveled west to survey and lay claim to new territories in the Ohio River valley, where he was captured by Native Americans. He survived captivity and settled north of Philadelphia where he began to experiment with steamboats in 1785 at the same time as several competitors, most notably engineer James Rumsey.

Racing to stay ahead of his rivals and to find financial sponsors, Fitch staged a spectacle in front of delegates to the Constitutional Convention in August 1787. This steamboat featured two horizontal racks of oars on either side of the vessel rather than a paddle wheel. It ran successfully in the Delaware and Schuylkill Rivers. Several delegates even took a ride on the new invention. Fitch's hopes for federal financial support were disappointed, but he took on Henry Voigt as a partner and built an improved 60-foot steamboat with stern-mounted oars. In the summer of 1790, this steamboat, able to carry up to 30 passengers, made many round-trips between Philadelphia and Burlington. The business failed: customers were few and far between.

Despite the bankruptcy of his business, Fitch received the first U.S. patent for steamboats in August 1791; his French patent was awarded later the same year. However, the newly established Patent Commission only awarded Fitch a monopoly on his most recent design rather than the monopoly on steamboats that he sought. Other inventors received related patents on the same day, which undermined Fitch's efforts to find financial supporters or partners. Fitch went to France hoping to capitalize on his French patent, but failed to find backers amid the turmoil of the French Revolution.

Fitch returned to the United States in 1793 and attempted to claim land around Bardstown, Kentucky, that he had surveyed in the 1780s, but squatters had already taken up residence. A lengthy court battle followed—as he continued to experiment with steam engines—during which Fitch despaired and committed suicide in 1798. Fitch's career shows how difficult it was for inventors, even those with patent protection, to profit from their inventions without powerful patrons or partners. His experiences also show that inventors can take various routes to solving the same technical difficulties and demonstrates that the design that becomes popular is not always selected due to superior technology.

See also: Patent(s); Role of the State; Steam Engine; Transportation by Water

Further Reading

"John Fitch: First Steamboat." Available online at http://www.pbs.org/wgbh/they madeamerica/whomade/fitch_hi.html.

"The John Fitch Steamboat Museum." Available online at http://www.craven-hall .org/fitch-steamboat-museum/.

Prager, Frank, ed. *The Autobiography of John Fitch*. Philadelphia: Memoirs of the American Philosophical Society, 1976.

Sutcliffe, Andrea. *Steam: The Untold Story of America's First Great Invention*. New York: St. Martin's Press, 2004.

HARGREAVES, JAMES   Englishman James Hargreaves developed the spinning jenny in 1764 and patented it in 1770. A spinning jenny could do the work of numerous spinners and make higher quality, more even, and finer thread. This pioneering invention contributed greatly to resolving a technical bottleneck in cotton textile production, enabling a spectacular increase in output that drove the Industrial Revolution.

Hargreaves (1720–1778) was born in Lancashire and spent his first 20 years working as a carpenter and a weaver near Blackburn. As a result, he had both mechanical skills and an intimate knowledge of the process of weaving, though little formal education. He was asked by a neighbor, a calico printer named Robert Peel who founded a manufacturing dynasty, to build a carding machine. Not long afterward, legend has it, he saw an overturned spinning wheel that continued to revolve: this image supposedly gave him the idea for his jenny. His relatively simple machine consisted of a rectangular frame mounted on four legs with a row of vertical spindles at one end. Two parallel wooden rails were mounted on a carriage that slid back and forth. Cotton that had been carded and roved could then be passed between the two rails and wound on the spindles. A spinner could move the carriage with one hand and turn the handle for the spindles with the other, thereby drawing the thread and simultaneously twisting it. Hargreaves's first model had eight spindles, but this number was rapidly increased. A decade later, a spinning jenny could accommodate up to 80 spindles.

Although he successfully solved a vexing technical problem, Hargreaves suffered numerous setbacks while trying to profit from his invention. These difficulties were typical of those faced by innovators in this era. Hargreaves began to construct machines for sale in 1767, but he did not seek a patent for three more years, a decision that had major financial consequences. Once it became clear that the spinning jenny saved considerable labor, local cotton spinners who feared for their jobs during a sharp economic downturn broke down his door and smashed his machines. Two years later, the same thing happened again. Hargreaves did not seem to fear further violence from rebellious workers despite moving out of the frying pan and into the fire. He relocated to Nottingham, a major locus of machine-breaking throughout the 18th and 19th centuries. Instead, Hargreaves experienced far greater difficulties with unscrupulous entrepreneurs and unsympathetic judges. With a partner, he set up a spinning mill that ran successfully, but his hope to become wealthy was based on selling his machines. They were cheap to make; they required only a skilled craftsman to make precision parts that moved seamlessly. His problem was that other manufacturers copied his design with ease and then refused to pay the patent fees. He sued, but the court found that since his machines had been used before he patented them, his patent was meaningless. Hargreaves did not die penniless, as another legend has it; he left an estate worth £4,000, but this was a pittance compared to the economic value of his invention. A decade after his death, at least 20,000 spinning jennies were at work in Great Britain with thousands more to be found on the continent. The device was also swiftly adapted to wool and later linen and silk. Each machine did the work of at least eight people. The spinning jenny completely altered the production of cotton textiles and played a major role in sparking the Industrial Revolution.

See also: Arkwright, Richard; Cotton; Discipline; Division of Labor; Education; Lancashire; Luddites; Patent(s); Productivity; Slater, Samuel; Waltham System; Document: "Resisting Mechanization: The Luddites"

Further Reading

"James Hargreaves." Available online at http://www.famousinventors.org/james -hargreaves.

MacLeod, Christine. *Inventing the Industrial Revolution: The English Patent System, 1660–1800.* Cambridge: Cambridge University Press, 2002.

Mantoux, Paul. *The Industrial Revolution in the Eighteenth Century: An Outline of the Beginnings of the Modern Factory System in England*, rev. ed. New York: Harper & Row, 1961.

Timmins, Geoffrey. *Four Centuries of Lancashire Cotton.* Preston: Lancashire County Books, 1996.

"INDUSTRIOUS REVOLUTION"   The "Industrious Revolution" refers to an explanation of the origins of the Industrial Revolution. The term is closely linked to the notion of a Consumer Revolution and was developed by Akira Hayami, a Japanese demographer, but in the historical literature on the Industrial Revolution, the idea is associated with Jan de Vries, a Dutch-born, U.S.-trained historian of Europe, especially the Dutch Republic. Over the course of the era between 1600 and 1800, increased demand for various consumer goods led households to decide that consumption of these products were worth providing more labor, especially the labor of women and children, to be able to earn enough money to afford them. This "Industrious Revolution" explains how the working classes participated in the Consumer Revolution—experienced mostly by the middle-classes—and why some people worked longer hours to counterweigh the generally falling wages of the period up to 1830. The term is currently at the center of a major academic debate on the Industrial Revolution: accepting the idea has important implications for explanations of economic behavior.

According to its proponents, the "Industrious Revolution" responded to both demand- and supply-side factors and places the Industrial Revolution in a broader context. By getting families to decide to work longer hours, "industriousness" increased production by expanding the supply of labor. At the same time, the elasticity of household labor supply meant that demand for consumer goods could be satisfied, thereby allowing demand to grow even more rapidly. Such a conception of the origins of the British Industrial Revolution understands this transformation as essentially a supply-side phenomenon.

Households became more industrious in two main ways. First, labor was reallocated through the reduction of leisure time. Men, women, and children performed not just more labor, but, more importantly, worked increasingly for wages. Instead of making what the household needed, families that worked for wages progressively purchased not only what they needed, but what they wanted. This shift in the nature of production and consumption permitted greater specialization and helped to increase the productivity of labor. This process preceded and was independent of the organizational and technological developments associated with the first Industrial Revolution.

The "Industrious Revolution" is a complex notion that may explain certain aspects of popular behavior in the 17th and 18th centuries, but it is less clear whether this concept explains the onset of modern economic growth through industrial transformation, as its adherents claim. Was demand for consumer goods the cause or the effect of the pressure of declining wages on the family economy? Within those increasingly industrious families, was the "Industrious Revolution" a means by which male heads of household appropriated the benefits of the wage labor of women and children? Was there a compelling linkage between industriousness and industrial transformation? The answers to these questions and others like them are hotly debated. Beyond the simple yet important fact that in the 17th and 18th centuries consumption of consumer goods increased and went further down the social scale than ever before, proponents of the idea have struggled to marshal convincing evidence to tie it to broader economic trends and transformations. In its contemporary usage, focus on the "Industrious Revolution" privileges a supply-side explanation of the origins of the Industrial Revolution by ignoring or at least undervaluing issues of class, the standard of living, and changes in the nature of production. The existence and role of an "Industrious Revolution" and its relationship to the Consumer Revolution will continue to motivate research into the origins of the Industrial Revolution for the foreseeable future.

See also: Colonialism; Consumer Revolution; Cotton; Discipline; Division of Labor; Domestic Industry; Lancashire; Pollution, Health, and Environment; Productivity; Standard of Living; Tariffs and Excise Taxes; Wedgwood, Josiah; Workforce; Document: "The State of the Poor"; Document: "Conditions in the Mines"; Document: "Living and Working in Manchester"

Further Reading

Allen, Robert C., and Jacob Louis Weisdorf. "Was There an 'Industrious Revolution' before the Industrial Revolution? An Empirical Exercise for England, c. 1300–1830." Available online at http://www.economics.ku.dk/research/publications/wp/dp_2010/1014.pdf/.

Burnette, Joyce. "Women Workers in the British Industrial Revolution." Available online at https://eh.net/encyclopedia/women-workers-in-the-british-industrial-revolution/.

De Vries, Jan. *The Industrious Revolution: Consumer Behavior and the Household Economy, 1650 to the Present*. Cambridge: Cambridge University Press, 2008.

Ogilvie, Sheilagh. "Consumption, Social Capital, and the 'Industrious Revolution' in Early Modern Germany." *Journal of Economic History* 70, no. 2 (2010): 287–325. Available online at http://www.econ.cam.ac.uk/Ogilvie_ESRC/publications/Ogilvie-2010-JEH.pdf.

INTERCHANGEABLE PARTS Interchangeable parts are practically identical. Pieces are made to similar enough specifications that they can be taken from one model of a machine and put into another. Developed in France for military purposes during the 18th century, interchangeable parts required substantial state investment to overcome the resistance of workers and pay the higher prices that such flexibility cost. Although skilled metalworkers could produce interchangeable parts for many devices, the invention or adaptation of a variety of machine tools allowed greater precision. In the 19th century, interchangeable parts began to be developed in many industrializing economies, but this approach became particularly important in North America where it was incorporated into both armory practice and the American System of Manufactures.

The practice of interchangeable parts had been developed by the state-run Arsenal of Venice in the early-modern era. In shipbuilding, certain wooden parts were cut to rigorous specifications to allow quick and easy assembly, but this applied to only a few parts that could be readily standardized. French artillery officers of the 18th century were the chief proponents of the idea of interchangeable parts in machines with metal components. Inspector general of artillery Jean-Baptiste Gribeauval, ordered the standardization of components in large artillery pieces in the 1750s, which was applied experimentally to muskets in the late 1770s. Although the trials were promising, the opposition of skilled gunsmiths who did not want to be told how to do their jobs was considered too implacable to ramp up to full-scale production.

Honoré Blanc (1736–1801), an experienced mechanic and gunsmith, revived the idea. He set up a workshop to make gunlocks, the critical piece. In 1785, Blanc staged a public experiment in which he had another gunsmith assemble a gunlock, choosing randomly from a bin with the parts to make 50 muskets. The demonstration succeeded brilliantly, but workers' opposition again postponed setting up production. When France went to war in 1792, however, Blanc broke down the process of manufacturing muskets into as many simple tasks as possible with the goal of using this division of labor to undermine opposition to interchangeable parts. The government supported Blanc's efforts, but artisanal resistance slowed down the process. Production at Blanc's workshop at Roanne using a number of purpose-built gauges, tools, and machines began in 1797. After his death, this enterprise produced about 10,000 fully interchangeable gunlocks annually in the first years of the 19th century, constituting about 5 percent of the needs of Napoleonic France at a price 20 percent higher than those made using traditional methods. But when state subsidies ended, so did production.

American mechanic Eli Whitney attempted to replicate Blanc's process. He won a contract with the U.S. War Department to make 10,000 muskets by September 1800. Whitney built or invented a set of purpose-built machines capable of manufacturing many of the key parts with precision. It took Whitney until January 1809 to fulfill his contract; he used the goal of interchangeable parts as an excuse to justify the delays. Although Whitney never developed a set of machines capable of manufacturing interchangeable parts, he did propagate the idea, setting the stage for John Hancock Hall (1781–1841) to achieve interchangeability in 1824 at the Harpers Ferry armory. Based on that tardy beginning, the manufacturing techniques spread to other armories and workshops and from there to other industries. After 1850, interchangeable parts became an integral part of U.S. manufacturing.

See also: American System of Manufactures; Armory Practice; Division of Labor; Iron and Steel; Productivity; Role of the State; Tariffs and Excise Taxes; Whitney, Eli; Workforce

Further Reading

Alder, Kenneth. *Engineering the Revolution: Arms and Enlightenment in France, 1763–1815.* Princeton, NJ: Princeton University Press, 1997.
Lienhard, John H. "Interchangeable Parts." Available online at http://www.uh.edu/engines/epi1252.htm.

Meyer, David R. "The Roots of American Industrialization, 1790–1860." Available online at https://eh.net/encyclopedia/the-roots-of-american-industrialization-1790–1860/.

Roser, Christoph. "230 Years of Interchangeable Parts—A Brief History." Available online at http://www.allaboutlean.com/230-years-interchangeability/.

Smith, Merritt Roe. *Harpers Ferry Armory and the New Technology: The Challenge of Change.* Ithaca, NY: Cornell University Press, 1977.

IRON AND STEEL   Iron was essential to building the machines and infrastructure that made the Industrial Revolution. Although steel, an alloy of iron and carbon, had been made beginning many centuries before the Common Era, it was not cost effective for widespread employment except for certain specialized uses such as swords. Experimentation across the 18th century improved iron production, which facilitated mechanization in a wide variety of industries, making an industrial revolution possible.

Across the early modern era, the British iron industry was the largest, most innovative and internationally competitive in the world. Britain had large deposits of iron ore, but when greater strength or higher quality was needed, it imported ore from countries on the Baltic Sea, particularly Sweden and Russia. Wrought (malleable) iron was generally smelted by combining pig iron (crude cast into ingots known as "pigs") with charcoal, a vegetable fuel that did not transmit impurities to the finished product. In 18th-century England, however, charcoal was in short supply because of a general shortage of wood, which led Abraham Darby to experiment with coke beginning in 1709. As a result of ongoing scarcity, roughly one-third of British iron production relocated to the 13 North American colonies, especially to Pennsylvania, where wood was plentiful as well as easy and cheap to move on the many rivers of the region. The definitive loss of these colonies in 1783 provided a significant cost incentive to the British to further their use of coal as a replacement fuel. Thus, the development of the iron and coal industries was inextricably linked in the 18th and 19th centuries.

As in textiles, experimentation by those Britons directly involved in the production process was the key to improving technique. Iron-masters discovered how to apply heat indirectly. A reverberatory furnace stirred molten pig over a bed of coal until it became wrought iron, preventing direct contact between the coal and the iron. This process, known as "puddling," was developed by Englishman Henry Cort (1740–1800) in 1783–1784 and perfected in the 1790s. Further improvements made iron produced with coal as fuel of equal or higher quality to traditional production using charcoal while maintaining puddling's huge cost advantage. Cort's methods also permitted 15 tons of iron to be processed in 12 hours. A forge-hammer could usually but not always produce a single ton in the same time. These innovations enabled a rapid expansion of iron production in the late 1790s, and even faster growth in the first decades of the 19th century as machines made from metal became ever-more crucial to economic development. From 23,000 tons produced annually around 1720, Britain's annual output attained 3.5 million tons by the end of the 1850s.

Although iron was the indispensable component of machines and infrastructure in the age of the Industrial Revolution, steel too played a role. Steel is an iron alloy that contains 1–2 percent carbon: it is stronger than low-carbon (less than 1 percent) wrought iron, and more malleable than high-carbon (cast or) pig iron. The major improvement that took place during the 18th century was the development of the technique to make crucible or cast steel by English instrument maker Benjamin Huntsman around 1742. His breakthrough was to mix bars of steel with an alkali in a clay crucible and then heat them with coke. Cast steel had many uses, but it was still quite expensive and rather brittle. Only precision instruments, certain tools like files, and some bladed weapons were worth the expense. Although most of the machines that "made" the Industrial Revolution would have benefitted from higher-quality steel construction, iron or even wooden construction was much more economical and easier to make. Many 18th- and early 19th-century manufacturing processes were not optimal, but they worked well enough to begin a revolutionary transformation. Improved iron production made the Industrial Revolution while the emergence of economical means of producing steel in the 1860s was the basis of the Second Industrial Revolution and the eventual eclipse of Britain in metalworking.

See also: American System of Manufactures; Armory Practice; Coal; Factory System; Interchangeable Parts; Productivity; Railroads; Role of the State; Second Industrial Revolution; Steam Engine; Tariffs and Excise Taxes; Watt, James

Further Reading

Carr, James C., and Walter Taplin. *A History of the British Steel Industry.* Cambridge, MA: Basil Blackwell, 1962.

Casson, Herbert Newton. "The Romance of Steel: A History of the United States Steel Industry." Available online at http://www.rodneyohebsion.com/steel.htm.

Landes, David. *The Unbound Prometheus: Technological Change and Industrial Development in Western Europe from 1750 to the Present.* Cambridge: Cambridge University Press, 1969.

Misa, Thomas J. *A Nation of Steel: The Making of Modern America, 1865–1925.* Baltimore: Johns Hopkins University Press, 1995.

Spoerl, Joseph S. "A Brief History of Iron and Steel Production." Available online at http://www.anselm.edu/homepage/dbanach/h-carnegie-steel.htm.

JACQUARD, JOSEPH-MARIE Joseph-Marie Charles, whose family nickname was "Jacquard," developed an attachment for the programmable loom that made the machine practical, transforming the textile industry. Jacquard's attachment could be fixed on many different types of looms and enabled automatic weaving of intricate patterns by raising or lowering the threads. This machine helped France compete with Britain in many high-value categories of textiles and facilitated the emergence of the factory system on the continent of Europe. The basic principles remain in operation today and Jacquard's approach to programming his loom, through punched paste-board cards joined together on a continuous chain in which each card corresponded to a row of the design, formed the basis for other programmable machines, including the earliest computers.

Jacquard was born in 1752 in Lyon, France, where his father was a master silk weaver. (He died outside the same city in 1834.) Self-educated, Jacquard squandered his inheritance along with his wife's dowry, which forced him to earn a living as a manual laborer. He fought in France's armies during the Revolution. After discharge, Jacquard returned to Lyon, where he sought to automate silk weaving to eliminate a major bottleneck in production. In 1800, he patented an improved draw loom that received a bronze medal at the 1801 Paris industrial exposition, then developed a loom to weave fishing nets two years later before making his major breakthrough in 1804. What inspired Jacquard's attachment was looking at earlier inventors' failed approaches to automating looms on display in a Paris museum. Jacquard's invention was a significant improvement on and combination of these earlier models that had never been used profitably in full-scale production.

Jacquard's first loom excited the fears of Lyon's large population of weavers who were afraid that his invention would eliminate their jobs. They attacked Jacquard and destroyed his loom. The weavers' opposition made entrepreneurs afraid to try the Jacquard loom. Emperor Napoleon Bonaparte, however, was so impressed by the possibilities of the new loom that he purchased the patent and gave it the city of Lyon, thereby granting them a monopoly. In exchange, Jacquard received an annual pension of 3,000 francs and a royalty of 50 francs for each loom he made that went into operation over the next six years. By the end of that period, there were 11,000 Jacquard looms in operation in France with further improvements coming in 1815 that increased the speed and reliability of Jacquard's attachment.

In addition to transforming the manufacture of high-end textiles and helping France to compete with its cross-channel rival in some product categories, Jacquard's invention was adapted to other uses. During the 1820s and 1830s, Englishman Charles Babbage modified the punched-card system to run his calculators and other programmable machines. Most historians of science and technology believe that Babbage's devices were the forerunner of contemporary methods of computer programming. Today, Jacquard-style weaving is still widespread, but now a computer scans the design and operates the loom.

See also: Chaptal, Jean-Antoine; Discipline; Patent(s); Productivity; Role of the State; Workforce

Further Reading

Essinger, James. *Jacquard's Web: How a Hand-Loom Led to the Birth of the Information Age*. Oxford: Oxford University Press, 2004.
"The Jacquard Loom." Available online at http://www.gadagne.musees.lyon.fr /index.php/history_en/content/download/2939/27413/file/zoom_jacquard _eng.pdf.
Jenkins, D. T. *The Cambridge History of Western Textiles*, vol. 1. Cambridge: Cambridge University Press, 1994.
"Joseph-Marie Jacquard." Available online at http://history-computer.com/Dream ers/Jacquard.html.

LANCASHIRE   The county of Lancashire, located in northwestern England, was the hub of the British Industrial Revolution. Starting as a relatively poor area, industrialization made Lancashire into one of the richest areas in Europe. The county's rapid transformation stemmed from a combination of natural resources, geographical advantages, and entrepreneurial action that, taken together, turned Lancashire into the laboratory of industrial change. Lancashire's experience reminds us that the first Industrial Revolution did not occur on a national scale, but rather must be understood regionally or even locally.

Bounded by Wales to the southwest, Yorkshire's West Riding to the east, Cheshire to the south, Westmoreland and Cumberland to the north, Lancashire had certain geographic advantages. Liverpool, Britain's chief western port for the Atlantic trade, provided access to raw materials and markets. Myriad fast-running streams were potential power sources for factories and mills. Large deposits of coal and iron allowed the development of ancillary industries. As population growth and the creation of large farms put pressure on penniless small farmers and agricultural laborers, they increasingly turned to domestic industry to supplement their incomes. A large, impoverished yet skilled labor force trained in the manufacture of woolens helped draw entrepreneurs to set up shop in Lancashire.

With cotton imported through Liverpool, entrepreneurs established water-powered spinning mills beginning in the 1760s. Technical bottlenecks encouraged innovators like James Hargreaves and Richard Arkwright to tinker with new machines and ways of organizing production. The combination of factors that led to rapid industrial growth attracted more entrepreneurs to a 30-mile-wide circle around Manchester. New-built canals like the Duke of Bridgewater's delivered coal, and foundries provided the iron used to make machines and factories and later steam engines and railroad tracks. Seemingly infinite demand for cotton textiles and the county's growing ability to supply good-quality textiles at rock bottom prices drove the British Industrial Revolution and carried the rest of Lancashire and indeed all of England along with it.

The county's population doubled to more than 700,000 between 1761 and 1801, making it the fastest growing area in England during an era of rapid overall population growth. By the latter date, nearly a quarter million men, women, and children labored in Lancashire's cotton industry. In 1851, the county's population surpassed 2 million with nearly 375,000 people working in the cotton trades. At its height around 1861, almost 450,000 men and women made cotton goods in Lancashire. During the Industrial Revolution, Lancashire produced between 55 percent and 70 percent of Britain's total output of cottons, which grew to become the largest industry in the country. In 1831, the two counties of Lancashire and its neighbor, the West Riding, housed approximately 55 percent of the manufacturing jobs in the entire United Kingdom. The radical transformation of economy and society associated with the first Industrial Revolution occurred first and most thoroughly in Lancashire. For most of the period, industrialization was a regional, not a national, phenomenon: it was centered on the county of Lancashire.

See also: Agricultural Revolution; Arkwright, Richard; Bridgewater, Duke of; Cartwright, Edmund; Coal; Consumer Revolution; Cotton; Discipline; Division of Labor; Domestic Industry; Factory System; Hargreaves, James; "Industrious Revolution"; Iron and Steel; Luddites; Owen, Robert; Patent(s); Productivity; Role of the State; Standard of Living; Steam Engine; Tariffs and Excise Taxes; Transportation by Water; Workforce; Document: "Defending the Factory System"; Document: "Living and Working in Manchester"; Document: "Robert Owen on Education and the Evils of Child Labor"

Further Reading

Mantoux, Paul. *The Industrial Revolution in the Eighteenth Century: An Outline of the Beginnings of the Modern Factory System in England*, rev. ed. New York: Harper & Row, 1961.

Marshall, Dorothy. *Industrial England 1776–1851*. New York: Routledge, 1973.

Timmins, Geoffrey. *Made in Lancashire: A History of Regional Industrialisation*. Manchester: Manchester University Press, 1998.

Trueman, C. N. "Lancashire and the Industrial Revolution." Available online at http://www.historylearningsite.co.uk/britain-1700-to-1900/industrial-revolu tion/lancashire-and-the-industrial-revolution/.

Walton, John K. "Factory Work in Victorian Lancashire." Available online at http://www.bbc.co.uk/legacies/work/england/lancashire/article_1.shtml.

LIEBIG, JUSTUS VON   Justus von Liebig inaugurated modern laboratory-based scientific teaching at the University of Giessen (which has since been renamed after him) around 1825. He made major contributions to agricultural and biological chemistry and is usually considered the founder of organic chemistry. Liebig was also an entrepreneur who believed that science should have practical application. He created a company that trademarked the Oxo brand beef bouillon cube that is still sold today. Through his teaching methods, Liebig revolutionized the interaction of science, industry, and the state while demonstrating the profound productive impact of research-oriented universities.

Justus Liebig (1803–1873) was from Darmstadt, the capital of Hesse in what became western Germany. His family ran an apothecary and made art supplies, where he learned the basics of laboratory work. After university, he moved to Paris in 1822 to work with Joseph-Louis Gay-Lussac, perhaps the foremost chemist of the era. Only 18 months later, he was named a professor at Giessen at the tender age of 21. In 1825, Liebig set up a laboratory focused on teaching graduate students and founded what became the premier academic journal in the fields of chemistry and pharmacology to disseminate the findings of his team's experiments. The steady stream of scientific advances and profitable applications coming out of Liebig's program at Giessen attracted the best students from around the world and inspired other universities to imitate his teaching methods. In 1852, seven years after being named a baron and gaining the right to add the "von" to his name, Liebig moved to the University of Munich in Bavaria where he spent the rest of his career.

Liebig's own contributions to science included developing devices to perform organic analysis and demonstrating certain principles of chemical structure that gave rise to modern biochemistry. Outside the classroom, Liebig's most important breakthroughs came in the application of science to agriculture. He identified what nutrients plants needed to grow fastest and invented the first nitrogen-based fertilizer. In addition, he formulated the Law of the Minimum, which describes the effect of specific nutrients on plants. These findings laid the foundations of modern industrial-style agriculture. He disseminated them in his textbook *Organic Chemistry and Its Application to Agriculture and Physiology* published in 1840.

With breakthroughs coming so rapidly, Liebig and his students made it impossible to ignore the potential economic benefits of state support for university-based research and scientific and technical education more generally. Through scientific advances, states could develop innovative ways to compete with more established industrial powers or to develop totally new industries that expanded the scope of industrialization. Following up on Liebig's successes, many German universities emerged as effective centers of scientific and technological research, tackling industrial problems with academic discipline. They also provided a strong grounding in scientific and technological issues to nearly all university students. With this knowledge, German officials, professionals, and entrepreneurs adapted to changing technologies and were more likely to take advantage of opportunities stemming from scientific advances. With his unmatched achievements and deep coterie of students, Justus von Liebig became perhaps the key figure in fostering the emphasis on scientific and technical education in German-speaking Europe.

See also: Chaptal, Jean-Antoine; Education; Productivity; Role of the State

Further Reading

Brock, William H. *Justus von Liebig: The Chemical Gatekeeper*. Cambridge: Cambridge University Press, 1997.

"Justus von Liebig and Friedrich Wöhler." Available online at http://www.chemherit age.org/discover/online-resources/chemistry-in-history/themes/molecular -synthesis-structure-and-bonding/liebig-and-wohler.aspx.

Rossiter, Margaret W. *The Emergence of Agricultural Science: Justus Liebig and the Americans, 1840–1880*. New Haven, CT: Yale University Press, 1975.

Wilson, Kelpie. "Justus von Liebig and the Birth of Modern Biochar." Available online at http://www.ithaka-journal.net/english-justus-von-liebig-and-the-birth-of -modern-biochar?lang=en.

LUDDITES   The Luddites were English workers who unsuccessfully resisted mechanization in 1811–1817. Named after a supposed Leicester stocking maker's apprentice named Ned Ludham who in 1779 responded to his master's reprimand by taking a hammer to a stocking frame, the followers of "Ned Ludd," "Captain Ludd," or sometimes "General Ludd" targeted this machine for destruction during a deep economic downturn. Centered in the Midlands, before moving to Yorkshire and Lancashire, the Luddites destroyed only those machines that directly threatened their jobs. Although the Luddites are remembered as opposing all technology and standing in the way of "progress," in fact, the Luddites' use of violence and hostility to technological change were limited to those machines that directly jeopardized their livelihood. Government repression of worker resistance greatly exceeded the original acts of violence. The failure of the Luddites and their demonization in popular culture demonstrates the domination of British elites and the relative weakness of worker resistance to industrialization in England.

Early in February 1811, the Luddites began operation in the Midlands triangle formed by Nottingham, Leicester, and Derby in the lace and hosiery trades. Over the next year, Luddite bands conducted at least 100 separate attacks that destroyed about 1,000 frames (out of England's total of 25,000) valued at £6,000–10,000. These Luddites did not attack all machines or act indiscriminately; they only attacked special frames making cheap knockoffs that undermined the jobs of skilled workers. The woolens workers of Yorkshire imitated their compatriots beginning in January 1812, but these Luddites were more generally opposed to mechanization. The cotton weavers of Lancashire rose up in April as armed crowds attacked large factories. Thousands participated in these activities, including many whose employment was not threatened. Taken together, these initial episodes of Luddism caused perhaps £100,000 of damage. Further waves of machine-breaking in the Midlands where a few hundred additional stocking frames were destroyed took place in the winter of 1812–1813, in the summer and fall of 1814, and in the summer and fall of 1816 that sputtered into early 1817. Other than hurting some employers, the Luddites only managed to slow down mechanization in the woolens, lace, and hosiery trades. They had slight impact on the vital cotton industry. In short, the Luddites had little impact on the course of British industrialization.

The government's response was disproportionate, even excessive. To begin the conflict against Napoleon in Spain in 1808, the British sent less than 10,000 troops, but the British state deployed 12,000 troops against the Luddites in 1812. Parliament made frame-breaking a capital crime (carrying the death penalty) that same year. Leading up to the Luddite movement, Parliament passed the Two Acts restricting individual liberties in 1795, suspended the writ of habeas corpus that forced the government to charge those in detention with specific crimes, outlawed any and all worker associations in 1799–1800, and eliminated the ability of magistrates to set minimum wages in 1809 for woolens and minimum wages more generally in 1814. Thousands of spies were engaged and sent to identify the Luddites, especially the leaders. The army was not only sent in to stop the Luddites, it was permanently redeployed as 155 military barracks were built in industrial districts to ensure that property owners and magistrates had easy access to overwhelming force when challenged by militant workers. There were only two fatal victims of Luddite violence against property, though there were dozens of casualties during the attacks themselves. For instance, in repulsing the Luddite attack on Daniel Burton's factory at Middleton in Lancashire on April 18, 1812, five were killed and 18 wounded. With frame-breaking a crime, British courts hanged more than 30 Luddites in 1812–1813, dozens were transported to Australia, and hundreds more were imprisoned, some for long stretches. Clearly, the state supported the mill owners by discouraging working-class militancy with every weapon at its disposal.

The Luddites built on a long tradition of working-class violence against innovative machines or industrial techniques that threatened employment. In a wide variety of industries, 18th-century British workers turned to machine-breaking when more peaceful protests had no effect. James Hargreaves's first spinning jenny was dismantled and burned in 1767, Richard Arkwright's cotton mill at Chorley was destroyed in 1776, and the first factory containing Edmund Cartwright's power-looms was burned in 1792. Major waves of violence against machines took place in 1776–1780, 1785, 1792, 1799–1802, and 1810–1813. Nor did machine-breaking disappear with the followers of Ned Ludd. Machine-breaking accompanied extensive rural rioting in East Anglia in 1816 and again in 1822. In 1826, Lancashire endured a wave of machine-breaking more extensive than in 1811–1812: 21 factories were assaulted and 1,000 looms valued at £30,000 smashed. Three years later, power-looms were targeted by Manchester's working classes. During the Captain Swing riots, which ran from 1829 to 1832 with a high point in late August 1830, agricultural laborers relied on arson, but machine-breaking was an important means of expressing popular anger. As a result of more than 1,500 separate incidents, an impressive proportion of England's threshers were destroyed along with quite a bit of industrial machinery. The Plug Plots led by Staffordshire miners in 1842 concluded the era of machine-breaking in Britain.

The Luddites failed to stop or even slow down mechanization for more a few months. In the aftermath of their attack on machines, the British state took even more overt action to control the working classes on behalf of innovating entrepreneurs. The domination of the labor force developed by British industrialists and enforced by the government was essential to the emergence of industrial society. The lingering memory of Luddite opposition to their own technological obsolescence and the weakness of their response demonstrated concretely the nature of power relations between the workers and elites during the first Industrial Revolution.

See also: Arkwright, Richard; Cartwright, Edmund; Cotton; Discipline; Hargreaves, James; Lancashire; Role of the State; Socialism; Workforce; Document: "Defending the Factory System"; Document: "Living and Working in Manchester"; Document: "Resisting Mechanization: The Luddites"

Further Reading

Binfield, Kevin, ed. *Writings of the Luddites*. Baltimore: Johns Hopkins University Press, 2004.

Horn, Jeff. *The Path Not Taken: French Industrialization in the Age of Revolution, 1750–1830*. Cambridge, MA: MIT Press, 2006.

"The Luddite Link." Available online at http://ludditelink.org.uk/.

"The Luddites at 200." Available online at http://www.luddites200.org.uk/the Luddites.html.

Randall, Adrian. *Before the Luddites: Custom, Community and Machinery in the English Woollen Industry, 1776–1809*. Cambridge: Cambridge University Press, 1990.

MERCANTILISM   All early-modern governments attempted to improve the economy of the territory under their control. This goal has been associated with the state policy of mercantilism, which attempted, in part, to increase exports in order to create a favorable balance of trade while maximizing the supply of precious metals. This approach conflated stocks of hard money in hand and the total amount of national wealth. European mercantilist policies focused on managing foreign trade, but also supported a variety of institutions such as the guilds. This approach to economic development favored both low cost and luxury producers who could capture and keep markets abroad. States sought to garner exclusive trading privileges through treaties and all colonies were exploited to benefit the mother country. Consumers thus suffered in favor of producers. Mercantilism was practiced by all early-modern European states to a greater or lesser degree, but nowhere was mercantilism more intertwined with political culture than in Great Britain.

Conserving domestic markets and resources motivated the promulgation of a series of English Navigation Acts beginning in 1651. Intended to protect the domestic merchant marine from Dutch competition, these acts mandated that goods from Asia, Africa, and the Americas could only be imported into Britain or its colonies in British ships. Goods from Europe either had to be carried by British ships or by ships of the origin of the goods in question. Certain colonial commodities like sugar, tea, and tobacco were required to be shipped directly to a British port even if their ultimate destination was somewhere else (this was why the proportion of re-exports of colonial goods was so high.) Although the British were, by far, the most successful at enforcing their Navigation Acts because of their growing naval supremacy, nearly all European nations had similar legislation on the books in the 17th and 18th centuries.

Mercantilism led all European states to license associations of investors to explore, colonize, and trade with certain areas. These associations were chartered by the state, which provided some support but usually left the vast majority of the activities of these associations unregulated. Chartered companies could institute laws, fight wars, make treaties (subject to state approval), and enjoyed a monopoly of trade and/or colonization in their area of operation. The English established chartered companies to trade with Muscovy (1555), the Levant (1581), East Indies (1600), and Hudson's Bay (1670). Other charters entrusted colonization to the Virginia Company (1606) and the Massachusetts Bay Company (1629). The Netherlands established East India (1602) and West India (1621) companies, while the French established a number of such companies to trade with the Caribbean, West Africa, the Levant, and the Indian Ocean. Many other states including Denmark, Sweden, Austria, and several German lands also created chartered companies. Several of these companies, most notably the Dutch East India, the English East India, and Hudson's Bay became virtual states within states ruling vast territories with minimal government supervision (or expense!), earning enormous profits for investors. These state-sponsored companies extended the European presence to new areas, tied the global economy together, and vastly expanded world trade.

The British state also regulated the import and export of food. From 1689 to 1846, the notorious English Corn Laws forbade the export of grain unless prices were extremely cheap, thanks to a bumper crop. The intent was to encourage domestic grain production by guaranteeing that a relative scarcity would keep prices high. Until 1772, additional legislation mandated state oversight of internal trade in grain, meal, flour, bread, and meat. Although the government sometimes enforced lower prices in times of dearth, in general, these regulations kept food prices above the norm for northwestern Europe and limited food consumption for the average Briton. Mercantilism, especially in Britain, benefited economic and political elites at the expense of the standard of living of the vast majority of the population.

The fundamental dependence of 18th-century economic growth on mercantilism by the European powers especially Great Britain in the 17th and 18th centuries has been obscured by the gigantic shadow cast by the immensely influential work of Adam Smith. For far too many economists, economic historians, and politicians, Smith's well-known attack on mercantilism and state action more generally in favor of a more individualistic focus on industry and free trade has assumed the status of dogma. That Smith was criticizing rather than describing contemporary practice appears to have been either forgotten or deliberately overlooked. No matter how Smith has been read by his successors, it must not be forgotten that the economic preconditions for industrialization were fostered in a thoroughly exploitative, mercantilist economic system.

See also: Agricultural Revolution; Colonialism; Consumer Revolution; Cotton; Domestic Industry; Enlightenment; "Industrious Revolution"; Productivity; Role of the State; Standard of Living; Transportation by Water; Document: "Child on Interest, Trade, and Money"; Document: "Adam Smith on the Division of Labor"

Further Reading

Hont, Istvan. *Jealousy of Trade: International Competition and the Nation-State in Historical Perspective*. Cambridge, MA: Belknap Press, 2005.

Horn, Jeff. *Economic Development in Early Modern France: The Privilege of Liberty, 1650–1820*. Cambridge: Cambridge University Press, 2015.

LaHaye, Laura. "Mercantilism." Available online at http://www.econlib.org/library/Enc/Mercantilism.html.

"Mercantilism." Available online at http://www.landofthebrave.info/mercantilism.htm.

Stern, Philip J., and Carl Wennerlind, eds. *Mercantilism Reimagined: Political Economy in Early Modern Britain and Its Empire*. Oxford: Oxford University Press, 2013.

OWEN, ROBERT Robert Owen (1771–1858) was a Welsh factory manager who demonstrated that overweening exploitation of the working classes was not required to earn huge profits. He pushed for reform of the factory system in the name of the negative effects of industrialization on the British national character. In later life, Owen's critique of industrial society led him to embrace socialism as a means of preserving the egalitarian and communal lifestyles of the rural population.

Owen worked as a draper in London and Manchester, and after 1792 managed a mill in the latter city. He became a member of Manchester's Literary and Philosophical Society where he was profoundly influenced by the Enlightenment. Owen also worked for the city's Board of Health where he saw the effects of the Industrial Revolution on the first generations of workers. He married Caroline Dale, the daughter of the co-owner of a water-powered cotton mill (with Richard Arkwright) located in New Lanark, Scotland, and took over its management in 1800. Owen got a stake in the enterprise, which expanded to encompass four large mills. Based on his experiences in Manchester, Owen was dissatisfied with the condition of the workers. He put his ideas on social reform into action by founding schools for children employed in his mills and by reducing the length of the workday from 13–14 hours to 10.5 and then, in 1810 to 10 hours. His goal was an eight-hour day. He also instituted infant childcare at the mills, a first in the United Kingdom, and eliminated the exploitative practice of paying workers in a type of token that could only be redeemed at a "trunk" store controlled by the mill owner that generally sold low-quality goods at exceptionally high prices. The workers rewarded Owen's dedication to their welfare with far greater effort. Their productivity made New Lanark highly profitable. During the 29 years he directed the mills, he more than doubled the capital of the investors, but his expensive measures led him to bring in new partners in 1813 (including Jeremy Bentham) who were willing to let him try out his social experiments.

The success of New Lanark underpinned Owen's efforts to improve the welfare of workers. He published an essay entitled "Observations on the Effect of the Manufacturing System" in 1815 that was intended to persuade Parliament to limit the exploitation of child labor in British factories: some of his reform proposals were enacted in the Factory Act of 1819. Owen publicly embraced socialism in 1817 while commenting on the English Poor Law, and increasingly saw a rural lifestyle as preferable to any other. Building on the model of a new kind of community being formed nearby in Orbiston, Scotland, in 1825, Owen invested the bulk of his money in a utopian community established at New Harmony, Indiana. This social experiment failed after less than two years. Owen moved to London and increasingly focused on lobbying for labor reform and spreading socialist propaganda. His long career provided a concrete reminder of both the potential and the drawbacks of Enlightened responses to industrialization as well as proof positive that profits and the well-being of the workers were not mutually exclusive.

See also: Agricultural Revolution; Arkwright, Richard; Cotton; Discipline; Education; Enlightenment; Factory Acts; Factory System; "Industrious Revolution"; Lancashire; Productivity; Role of the State; Socialism; Standard of Living; Workforce; Document: "Robert Owen on Education and the Evils of Child Labor"

Further Reading

Claeys, Gregory. *Machinery, Money and the Millennium: From Moral Economy to Socialism 1815–1860*. Princeton, NJ: Princeton University Press, 1987.

Donnachie, Ian. "Education in Robert Owen's New Society: The New Lanark Institute and Schools." Available online at http://infed.org/mobi/education-in-robert-owens-new-society-the-new-lanark-institute-and-schools/.

"Robert Owen." Available online at http://www.newlanark.org/world-heritage-site/robertowen.shtml.

"Robert Owen (1771–1858)." Available online at http://robert-owen-museum.org.uk/Robert_Owen_1771_1858.

Royle, Edward. *Robert Owen and the Commencement of the Millennium*. Manchester: Manchester University Press, 1998.

PATENT(S) Patents protect intellectual property. Based on an English law dating from 1624 and amended many times since, Britain and all other states grant patents or a monopoly of use for a specified amount of time to individuals or groups of individuals and then restrict the ability of others to make use of an idea without the consent of the patent holder. Governments can only assure patent rights within their own borders though they often make arrangements with other states to respect each other's patents. Patents improved production by making it easier for the developer to benefit economically from new machines or technical advances. During the Industrial Revolution, patents nurtured innovation, especially though not exclusively in Great Britain.

During the industrial age, patents involved three fundamental interests that were often in conflict. Governments wanted to preserve their national advantages in machinery, worker expertise, or scientific knowledge. Individuals or groups who developed new techniques or more efficient machines sought to maintain their exclusivity, while also capitalizing on their discoveries. Lastly, because the scientific community was international in scope, the steady advance of scientific knowledge meant that researchers sometimes reached similar conclusions almost simultaneously. These disparate interests, combined with inherent advantages and disadvantages of national scientific cultures, and differences in resources and infrastructures, meant that some scientific advances or technological innovations spread immediately, while others stagnated for decades. States tried to hold onto their advantages by extending the life of certain patents while systematically allowing the imitation of other patents. The leads and lags associated with the spread of technological and scientific developments increasingly concerned governments, as the protection or acquisition of such knowledge impacted not only the economy, but also a state's military preparedness.

Throughout the industrialized world, patents for inventors were instituted to encourage technological innovation. The number of patents issued grew steadily during the 18th and accelerated in the early 19th century. Other countries established similar laws in the same period. Britain legally prohibited the export of many important machines until 1843, but this ban only slowed the flow of workers, machines, and ideas across national borders. Technology transfer was often personal, arriving in the form of an individual or small group bearing the scientific knowledge necessary to make or operate a certain machine or the craft skills needed to construct the machinery. During the Industrial Revolution, patents shaped the flow of technology transfer.

See also: Arkwright, Richard; Cartwright, Edmund; Chaptal, Jean-Antoine; Cockerill, William; Cotton; Crystal Palace; Fitch, John; Hargreaves, James;

Jacquard, Joseph-Marie; Role of the State; Second Industrial Revolution; Steam Engine; Watt, James; Whitney, Eli

Further Reading
Griffin, Emma. *A Short History of the British Industrial Revolution*. Houndsmills, UK: Palgrave, 2010.

Henderson, David R. "Patents." Available online at http://www.econlib.org/library /Enc1/Patents.html.

Khan, B. Zorina. "An Economic History of Patent Institutions." Available online at https://eh.net/encyclopedia/an-economic-history-of-patent-institutions/.

MacLeod, Christine. *Inventing the Industrial Revolution: The English Patent System, 1660–1800*. Cambridge: Cambridge University Press, 2002.

Pursell, Carroll W., ed. *Technology in America: A History of Individuals and Ideas*, 2nd ed. Cambridge, MA: MIT Press, 2010.

POLLUTION, HEALTH, AND ENVIRONMENT   Population growth, urbanization, and industrialization vastly increased the health problems of Europe during the age of the Industrial Revolution and beyond. Rapid population growth especially in overcrowded cities with insufficient sanitation facilities compounded the threat of disease in general while harsh working conditions in factories and mines amplified the incidence of diseases like coal workers' pneumoconiosis and tuberculosis. Only after 1850 did the state and the scientific/medical community take effective action to improve the health of the working classes and of urban areas more broadly, with most of the benefits coming near the end of the 19th century. Limiting pollution and the degradation of the environment stemming from industrialization only became important considerations in the 20th century.

During the Industrial Revolution, dirt from coal smoke darkened the buildings and the landscape, already splattered by mud in the unpaved streets. Breath came short amid the coal fumes, but other smells often masked it because of crowding in cities and industrial districts. Garbage and human waste littered the streets, particularly in poorer areas. Supplemented by animal wastes, such refuse got into the drinking water, already in short supply in most cities, causing disease. Disease preyed on malnourished and overworked urban populations throughout the period, leading to spectacular declines in life expectancy with peaks during catastrophic natural disasters like the cholera epidemic of 1831 or the Europe-wide potato blight of the late 1840s. Children and pregnant women suffered disproportionately. In 1840, workers in Manchester, England, could anticipate an average life-span of only 17 years because of very high rates of infant mortality, whereas the average for all of England was a still horrific 40 years. Nor was Manchester unique. Dr. G. Calvert

Holland oversaw a demographic investigation of the city of Leeds in 1842. The average age of death for the gentry, manufacturers, and their families was 44. For shopkeepers, it was 27, and for laborers, it was a terrifying 19! The aggregate average was 21, which demonstrated the preponderance of laborers in the population. Dr. Holland reported, "We have no hesitation in asserting, that the sufferings of the working classes, and consequently the rate of mortality are greater now than in former times. Indeed, in most manufacturing districts the rate of mortality in these classes is appalling to contemplate. . . ."

At the same time that industrial wages were being reduced to—or even below—the poverty line, workers were angry that because of neglect the work environment was increasingly unhealthy. The effects of water-logged mine shafts, closed rooms full of wool particles, breathing coal dust, performing difficult repetitive motions, badly constructed machines, dangerous raw materials (toxic materials like mercury, lead, arsenic, and chlorine were commonly used in many industries), and extremes of heat and cold were all magnified by exhaustion, sleep deprivation, and poor diet. These environmental conditions led directly to pneumonia, arthritis, rheumatism, bursitis, carpal tunnel syndrome, eye strain, and tuberculosis. Machines sheared off fingers and explosions led to the loss of legs. Mine collapses and falls left battered and broken bodies behind them. Chemical poisoning rendered people paranoid and palsied. Clearly, workers' health was not a priority for either entrepreneurs or the state during the first several generations of industrialization.

The scientific community in partnership with governments and some entrepreneurs did make some advances in public health such as vaccination. Many natural substances effective against disease had been known for centuries or millennia; the practice of inoculation, the injection of a disease to prevent a more drastic appearance, had been practiced since the Renaissance. In 1798, the English physician Edward Jenner (1749–1823) took the first step in controlling smallpox by injecting a milder form of the disease into a healthy individual as a means of building up resistance to it, and preventing the illness from reappearing in a more virulent form. Hotly debated by contemporaries because nearly all believed that people contract disease when they breathe odors of decay or putrefying excrement (the miasmatic theory of disease), vaccination slowly became standard practice throughout western Europe. In Britain, Parliament signaled its acceptance of its efficacy with the Vaccination Act of 1853. Smallpox vaccination was the culmination of centuries of trial and error, rather than scientific understanding of why this method worked. Only in the later 19th century did directed scientific inquiry reveal the causes and vectors of disease: what mattered was that it seemed to work.

Pushed by outbreaks of cholera in 1831–1832 and 1848–1849, along with the omnipresence of many other diseases in urban industrial Europe, states and concerned individuals devoted increased attention to problems of public health. Poor Law Commissioner Edwin Chadwick took the lead in publicizing urban decay and its attendant health risks. In response, Britain began to clean up its cities by passing the first public health law in 1848, which set up a national health board with broad authority to create more modern sanitary systems. Chadwick and others interested in public health emphasized the need for clean drinking water. In the 1840s and 1850s, close observation by public health officials, many of them doctors, revealed the limitations of the miasmatic theory of disease. They suggested that the vector of contagion for a disease was passed through excrement or decaying matter rather than by miasmas. This observation set the stage for the bacterial revolution, which, after 1870, transformed the health of Europe and ultimately the world. The lack of interest by elites and governments in stopping pollution, improving health, and protecting the environment until the twilight of the Industrial Revolution is closely intertwined with the late onset of benefits to the working classes' standard of living.

See also: Coal; Factory Acts; Factory System; Iron and Steel; Lancashire; Owen, Robert; Productivity; Railroads; Role of the State; Second Industrial Revolution; Socialism; Standard of Living; Document: "The State of the Poor"; Document: "Conditions in the Mines"; Document: "Living and Working in Manchester"

Further Reading

"Effects of the Industrial Revolution." Available online at http://webs.bcp.org/sites/vcleary/ModernWorldHistoryTextbook/IndustrialRevolution/IREffects.html#publichealth.

"The Environmental Impact of the Industrial Revolution." Available online at https://taapworld.wikispaces.com/The+Environmental+Impact+of+the+Industrial+Revolution.

Mathias, Peter. *The First Industrial Nation: An Economic History of Britain, 1700–1914*, 3rd ed. London: Routledge, 2001.

McLamb, Eric. "The Ecological Impact of the Industrial Revolution." Available online at http://www.ecology.com/2011/09/18/ecological-impact-industrial-revolution/.

Porter, Roy. *The Greatest Benefit to Mankind: A Medical History of Humanity from Antiquity to the Present.* New York: W. W. Norton, 1999.

PRODUCTIVITY Productivity was a vital component of the broadly based changes that transformed first British and then western society as a whole during the Industrial Revolution. In economics, the term refers to the effectiveness of effort and is measured by the rate of output per unit of input.

Almost any factor involved in manufacturing, especially capital, land, transportation, energy, and labor, can become more or less productive based on the quality of inputs. These broad measures can be broken down by economic sector, industry, or to account for specific features like technological change. Economists often focus on "Total Factor Productivity," which is defined as that portion of output not explained by the amount of inputs. In other words, Total Factor Productivity measures how efficiently and intensely inputs are used. In one form or another, the issue of productivity has been at the heart of investigations of the processes of change during the British Industrial Revolution. The reason for this emphasis is that it has been demonstrated that improvements in labor productivity and the increase in manufacturing output were far slower and came far later than would seem to make sense given the overall rate of industrial growth. Investigations of productivity have driven discussion of the standard of living, the role of the state, the "Industrious Revolution," and many other dynamic questions relating to the Industrial Revolution.

Current scholarly estimates of the rates of productivity growth in various industries and sectors suggest that technology contributed much less than had been thought to industrial transformation before 1800. For the period as a whole, newly industrialized sectors accounted for nearly two-thirds of productivity growth in the British economy between 1780 and 1860. While cotton textiles and machine building enjoyed high productivity growth rates, almost all other industries grew slowly if at all. Even in these exemplary industries, productivity growth did not greatly exceed what had been achieved in preceding decades. During the key "take-off" period of 1770 to 1800, Total Factor Productivity was stagnant. By some accounts, greater supplies of increasingly efficient energy contributed more than 90 percent to productivity growth between 1800 and 1850.

Generally speaking, even in the first half of the 19th century, productivity growth stemmed from improvements in transportation and massive increases in the quantity and efficiency of energy use as coal and water replaced human and animal power. The effects of technologies linked to the steam engine on productivity were gradual and less important than had been assumed. These findings suggest that the Industrial Revolution was the result less of increases in the productivity of labor based on technological change than of an enhanced transportation system and enlarged supplies of capital and energy. Such an understanding of the process of industrialization suggests that far greater attention must be paid to coal, water power, and transportation in explaining Britain's advantages.

Technological change linked to the productivity of labor has been at the heart of most explanations of the British Industrial Revolution. This focus has crowded out other factors in understanding shifts in labor productivity. The heights of English inventive creativity were also the years that the state removed traditional protections of worker rights in order to enforce the labor discipline sought by entrepreneurs, with force if necessary. With food prices kept artificially high by the mercantilist Corn Laws, wages stagnant or in decline, and the looming example of popular insurrection on the other flank of the Channel, British workers only entered factories and mills because they had little other choice. Aversion for labor discipline helps to explain why parish apprentices, immigrants, women, and children played such disproportionate roles in early industrialization. It seems quite possible that whatever improvements came from technological change were cancelled out by these factors, in which case technological change assumes a much more ambivalent position in understandings of the role of productivity in the Industrial Revolution.

Scholarly research has also found that labor productivity had been steadily improving since the 16th century. In fact, the growth rates, especially in agriculture but also in industry, were higher before 1750 than during the Industrial Revolution. That this growth stalled in the second half of the 18th century deserves greater attention, as does agriculture's continuing to outperform industry in labor productivity. These considerations point toward a longer term framework for understanding why an industrial revolution took place at all, much less in Britain during this era.

See also: Agricultural Revolution; American System of Manufactures; Armory Practice; Colonialism; Consumer Revolution; Cotton; Discipline; Division of Labor; Domestic Industry; Education; Factory System; "Industrious Revolution"; Patent(s); Role of the State; Standard of Living; Steam Engine; Tariffs and Excise Taxes; Wedgwood, Josiah; Workforce; Document: "Adam Smith on the Division of Labor"; Document: "The State of the Poor"

Further Reading

Field, Alexander J. "Productivity." Available online at http://www.econlib.org/library/Enc/Productivity.html.

Griffin, Emma. *A Short History of the British Industrial Revolution*. Houndsmills, UK, Palgrave, 2010.

O'Brien, Patrick, and Roland Quinault, eds. *The Industrial Revolution and British Society*. Cambridge: Cambridge University Press, 1993.

Shackleton, Robert. "Total Factor Productivity Growth in Historical Perspective." Available online at https://www.cbo.gov/sites/default/files/113th-congress-2013-2014/workingpaper/44002_TFP_Growth_03–18–2013_1.pdf.

Wrigley, E. A. *Energy and the English Industrial Revolution*. Cambridge: Cambridge University Press, 2010.

RAILROADS   Railroads were tangible signs of the Industrial Revolution. The first commercial railroad ran between Liverpool and Manchester, England, and began operation in 1830. Steam-powered locomotives dramatically lowered land transport costs for goods and passengers opening up vast swaths of the globe to development, bringing western economic needs and priorities to areas that previously had been protected by their remote location. The railroad also had major economic and social effects that marked the last generation of the first Industrial Revolution and paved the way for the second wave of industrial transformation after 1870.

Based on Richard Trevithick's high-pressure steam engine, and constantly improved by talented British engineers, the railroad emerged as a viable technology in 1814. Initially steam trains ran back and forth to the pit-heads of coal and iron mines, and then in 1830 the *Rocket*, a locomotive built and developed by George Stephenson, first traveled from Liverpool to Manchester at the impressive speed of 16 miles per hour. In its first year, the line carried more than 400,000 passengers, making transporting humans more profitable than carrying freight, a situation that continued until the 1850s. The financial success of this line, in the heart of the rapidly industrializing region of Lancashire, spurred many imitators.

Within 20 years, a web of railroad tracks traversed the British Isles; other networks spread rapidly across western Europe and North America. By 1870, extensive railroad systems crisscrossed most of the European continent. In addition, the United States and the British colonies of Canada, Australia, and especially India boasted their own vast railroad systems. On the eve of the First World War, railroads covered the continents of Asia, North America, and Africa and tied the disparate parts of the world together as never before. Along with the steamboat and the telegraph, the railroad accelerated the speed of life and the speed of change just as the maximum speed of the railroad increased from 16 mph in 1830, to 50 mph in 1850, to nearly 100 mph by 1914.

Railroads had powerful economic and social effects. They lowered the cost of transporting heavy goods, allowing more remote areas to become part of the global economy. Manufactured goods and raw materials now flowed across the planet much more easily and, most importantly, much more cheaply than ever before. With markets widening and costs falling, larger and larger factories could be built, allowing greater and greater potential profits. The ease and relative affordability of transportation meant that industrial production now could occur far from sources of raw materials. As a result, cities boomed and the urban working classes replaced farmers as the largest single occupational group in most industrialized societies.

In the United States and other "second wave" industrial nations, railroads as well as the other internal improvements had particularly powerful economic and social effects. By lowering the cost of transporting heavy goods, railroads provided remote areas with cheap access to distant markets. Before the railroad, the paper industry of western Massachusetts paid 8–24 cents per ton-mile to get their goods to market. By 1865, their freight charges had dropped to 4.5 cents per ton-mile.

Railroads also required strong government support. Completed in 1833, the Camden and Amboy railroad linked New York and Philadelphia to become the first working line in North America. Given a monopoly by the state of New Jersey, this railroad company became one of the largest corporations in the United States. The cost of building the United States' lines was significantly cheaper than in England or in Europe. By 1865, thanks to the support of various states and the federal government as well as the initiative of private citizens, the United States had 35,000 miles of railroad track, 3.5 times that of the United Kingdom. Yet the 10,000 miles of British track constituted a dense web; this was not the case in the United States. For Americans, because of the regional concentration of industry and the reliance on water power, the railroad was often the first tangible sign of the Industrial Revolution. Railroads, together with steamboats, perpetuated the factory system and brought the necessities of industrialization to new areas, thereby playing a major role in creating a truly global economy.

See also: Brunel, Isambard Kingdom; Coal; Colonialism; Crystal Palace; Division of Labor; Iron and Steel; Lancashire; Pollution, Health, and Environment; Productivity; Role of the State; Second Industrial Revolution; Steam Engine; Transportation by Water

Further Reading

Jensen, Richard. "Railroad History." Available online at http://www.americanhistory projects.com/downloads/railroad.htm.

Miner, Craig H. *A Most Magnificent Machine: America Adopts the Railroad, 1825–1862*. Lawrence: University of Kansas Press, 2010.

O'Brien, Patrick. *The New Economic History of the Railways*. London: Routledge, 2014.

"Railroad History, An Overview of the Past." Available online at http://www.american -rails.com/railroad-history.html.

Savage, Christopher, and T. C. Barker. *Economic History of Transport in Britain*. London: Routledge, 2012.

ROLE OF THE STATE   State action was essential to industrialization in Great Britain and to those nations that began the process two to three generations later, including France, Belgium, Prussia, and the United States. Government action took a number of forms, both indirect and direct, that can appear insignificant to modern eyes but were necessary to industrialization. To consider the Industrial Revolution without recognizing that state action made it possible is to misrepresent the process of economic development in the 18th and 19th centuries.

In early modern Europe, state intervention in the economy is generally known as mercantilism. Mercantilism involved control of trade and shipping. The Navigation Acts as established in 1651 required goods imported from Africa, the Americas, and Asia into Britain or its colonies to arrive in British hulls while European cargoes had to be brought either by ships from Britain or from the country of origin. Almost all European nations enacted similar laws. Chartered companies were also established by European governments to explore, colonize, and trade with certain areas. Governments left these companies largely unregulated. The most powerful ones became virtual states within a state ruling huge territories and generating enormous profits that helped pay for industrialization. The British state also controlled the price of grain through the Corn Laws in force between 1689 and 1846 while other laws regulated internal trade in grain, meal, flour, bread, and meat until 1772. These elements of mercantilism were essential elements of the early modern state's approach to economic oversight. Mercantilism helped to create the wealth and economic conditions needed to industrialize while protecting the power of elites from successful challenge until the eve of the Second Industrial Revolution.

War was the crucible of government intervention in the economy. Great Britain and France fought eight wars between 1688 and 1815 occupying 65 of the intervening 127 years. Britain spent an enormous proportion of its military budget on its navy. The navy defended the island nation from invasion and protected British trade and the empire while menacing enemy coastlines and colonies. England's small regular army was backed up by local militia. The militia were of limited value in repelling an invasion, but had significant capability to repress domestic threats by workers or rebellion in Scotland and Ireland.

The sheer number and scope of these wars forced the British state to tax and spend on a scale beyond that of any contemporary government. In the 17th century, the British state collected 2–4 percent of national income and 6 percent in wartime. For the era 1689–1815, that figure jumped to 12 percent. Between 1670 and 1815, total revenue from taxes increased by a factor of 17 while national income tripled. Great Britain was the most highly taxed society of the time, but other competing states like France, Spain, Prussia, and the Dutch Republic took many steps down this same path.

Despite this huge increase in tax revenue, the English state could only afford to fight this series of increasingly expensive, world-spanning conflicts by borrowing huge sums through the London capital market. The Bank of England was created in 1694 to help the government manage and consolidate its debt and to lower the rate of interest paid by the state. After the defeat of Napoleon, interest payments on government debt amounted to 56 percent of the state's income. A further 31 percent was spent on defense. There can be no doubt that, like its chief European competitors, Great Britain was a military regime. The state's development of efficient and effective means of borrowing money and limiting interest charges helped Britain win wars, slow the economic gains of its rivals, gain colonies, and allow investments in industrialization and transportation to be made.

The British state was also increasingly willing to deploy first law and then force to support the interests of entrepreneurs. Local justices of the peace controlled wages and prices: they generally rejected salary demands not linked to rising prices. The enclosure of fields was mandated by Act of Parliament, and resistance to the division of common land was overcome by force. The same process accompanied the creation of the turnpike trusts when they infringed on or replaced local interests. Labor was also controlled more thoroughly than in the past. The system of lengthy apprenticeships was maintained and strengthened and the traditional rights of skilled workers to resist the demands of their employers were steadily eroded until they were finally eliminated in 1809–1814. Combinations of workers were outlawed while combinations of entrepreneurs were encouraged. Strikes by miners and industrial workers were broken up by force whenever property was threatened. The English legal system also enforced social control in dealing with vagrancy and unemployment. Since many jobs were seasonal, a very high proportion of workers were unemployed at some point in an annual cycle. Those who did not have a current means of support could be sent back to the parish of their birth where they were put into a workhouse, imprisoned in a house of correction, or even transported to Georgia or later Australia. This Poor Law, like most of the actions of the British state in the 18th century, maintained or even increased the servility and dependence of the lower socioeconomic ranks of English society. This dependence probably made labor more productive, thereby contributing to economic growth, but it did little to achieve social peace.

Government resources were also used to improve transportation. Britain invested directly to develop ships, docks, harbors, and weapons. Turnpikes and canals were created or upgraded thanks to government-granted monopolies. The state also spent heavily to attract skilled workers and inventors from abroad with monetary incentives and tax breaks. For technologies or craft practices that could not be so acquired, the state resorted to commissioning and/or rewarding industrial spies. From the 17th century, a patent law protected the

inventions or improvements of innovators. In imitation of continental academies, King Charles II supported the establishment of the Royal Society to explore the world of science in 1660. Although much of this sort of activity was
"behind the scenes," the mercantilist British state was an effective supporter of
economic development throughout the period.

The fundamental dependence of 18th-century economic growth on state
action has been obscured by the gigantic shadow cast by the immensely influential work of Adam Smith. For far too many economists, economic historians, and politicians, Smith's well-known attack on mercantilism and state
involvement in the economy in favor of a more individualistic focus on industry and free trade has assumed the status of dogma. That Smith was criticizing
rather than describing contemporary practice appears to have been either forgotten or deliberately overlooked. No matter how Smith has been read by his
successors, it must not be forgotten that the British state fostered the economic preconditions for industrialization in a thoroughly exploitative, mercantilist economic system that it dominated.

See also: Agricultural Revolution; American System of Manufactures; Ar-
mory Practice; Brunel, Isambard Kingdom; Chaptal, Jean-Antoine; Coal;
Cockerill, William; Colonialism; Consumer Revolution; Cotton; Credit;
Crystal Palace; Discipline; Education; Enlightenment; Factory Acts; Factory
System; Fitch, John; Hargreaves, James; "Industrious Revolution"; Inter-
changeable Parts; Iron and Steel; Jacquard, Joseph-Marie; Liebig, Justus von;
Luddites; Mercantilism; Patent(s); Pollution, Health, and Environment;
Railroads; Royal Society of Arts; Second Industrial Revolution; Tariffs and
Excise Taxes; Transportation by Water; Wedgwood, Josiah; Whitney, Eli;
Document: "Conditions in the Mines"; Document: "Adam Smith on the
Division of Labor"

Further Reading

Harris, Ron. "Government and the Economy, 1688–1850." In *The Cambridge
    Economic History of Modern Britain*, vol. 1, *Industrialisation, 1700–1860*, ed.
    Roderick Floud and Paul Johnson. Cambridge: Cambridge University Press,
    2004.
"The Industrial Revolution-Role of the State." Available online at http://www
    .intriguing-history.com/industrial-revolution-role-of-state/.
Magnusson, Lars. *Nation, State and the Industrial Revolution*. New York: Routledge,
    2009.
Mathias, Peter. *The First Industrial Nation: An Economic History of Britain, 1700–
    1914*, 3rd ed. London: Routledge, 2001.

ROYAL SOCIETY OF ARTS The Society for the Encouragement of Arts, Manufacture, and Commerce was founded in 1754 by William Shipley. The society first met at Rawthmell's Coffee House, Covent Garden, London. The group was based on Irish and French models of organizations devoted to philosophical exploration, the arts, and the development and spread of knowledge regarding useful machines and agricultural techniques. Among its 11 founding members were two high-ranking nobles, Lord Romney and Viscount Folkestone; two medical doctors; three gentlemen deeply interested in science; and a watchmaker, with Shipley who earned his living as a dancing master. The organization ran on dues collected from the members and stayed largely independent of the government until the society was granted a royal charter in 1847 and received the right to use the term "royal" in 1908. Today is it known as the Royal Society of Arts or RSA and has over 27,000 members in the English-speaking world and in Belgium.

Dedicated to the fulfillment of Enlightenment ideals of social justice through practical innovation, the society brought together scientists, tinkerers, industrialists, government officials, and other like-minded people from a broad spectrum of social groups. The society also awarded a variety of prizes, which allowed the group to encourage certain types of invention while recognizing excellence. During the age of the Industrial Revolution, prizes were offered in six categories: Agriculture; Manufacture; Chemistry; Mechanics; Polite Arts; and Colonies and Trade. From 1783, the group also published a newsletter *Transactions*, which disseminated its goals and accomplishments widely. The society took the lead in many projects for the greater good of commerce, industry, and the populace as a whole such as organizing the Crystal Palace Exhibition of 1851.

This group was only the most well-known and influential of such learned groups, which included the Royal Society that focused on science, and a host of provincial groups. Taken together, learned societies encouraged the interaction of those interested in science, technology, and their applications with government officials while spreading both theoretical and practical knowledge. This interaction played a hotly debated role in boosting British technological creativity and in British industrial leadership. The issues in dispute concern whether Britain enjoyed unique institutions that encouraged the communication and collaboration between those interested in the practical application of science and those devoted to the development of knowledge for its own sake.

See also: Brunel, Isambard Kingdom; Chaptal, Jean-Antoine; Crystal Palace; Education; Enlightenment; Patent(s); Role of the State

Further Reading

Baird, Ileana, ed. *Social Networks in the Long Eighteenth Century: Clubs, Literary Salons, Textual Coteries.* Cambridge: Cambridge University Press, 2014.

"History." Available online at https://www.thersa.org/about-us/archive-and-history/.

Jacob, Margaret C. *Scientific Culture and the Making of the Industrial West.* Oxford: Oxford University Press, 1997.

Mokyr, Joel. *The Gifts of Athena: Historical Origins of the Knowledge Economy.* Princeton, NJ: Princeton University Press, 2004.

SECOND INDUSTRIAL REVOLUTION   The Second Industrial Revolution began around 1850 and continued until the outbreak of World War I in 1914. In a major shift from the first Industrial Revolution, "pure" science played a major role in developing new industries—in large part because of growing interaction among scientists, entrepreneurs, and state officials. Steel, chemicals, and electricity were the characteristic industries of the Second Industrial Revolution as textiles, iron, and coal had been for the first industrial transformation. The Second Industrial Revolution was spearheaded by Germans and Americans, taking over leadership from the British and French. If the original Industrial Revolution inaugurated modern economic life, the second placed western industrial society at the apex of a globe-spanning economic system.

The Second Industrial Revolution built on the foundations of the first. States and universities sponsored institutions to systematize scientific knowledge, particularly in electricity and chemistry. These institutions focused on the practical application of science to industry. As technical education spread widely and deeply, manufacturing was transformed as the production process was broken down through the division of labor and machines were developed to replace or improve on human labor as in the American System of Production. The Second Industrial Revolution substituted capital for labor as human physical skills were replaced by improvements in management and design. This trend culminated in the emergence of the factory assembly line early in the 20th century.

The Second Industrial Revolution capitalized on the improvements in transportation made by railroads, steamships, canals, and turnpikes. The world shrank as the telegraph and telephone permitted communication across vast distances, even across the oceans. During the period between 1870 and 1914, raw materials from the hinterlands of the European and North American continents became readily available while western political power—in large measure based on burgeoning military might generated by industrialization—stretched across Africa and much of Asia, bringing new areas into the global economy. People moved within and between countries as never before. A world-spanning division of labor subordinated the economies of colonies and western dependencies to the industrial centers of Europe, North America, and later Japan.

Population growth, urbanization, and migration fueled demand as consumerism spread throughout global society. Manufacturing techniques improved sufficiently to put many goods within financial reach of huge segments of the population. Britain and to a lesser degree France provided the capital for industrialization in most of the follower nations as governments sought to contain the worst excesses of domestic exploitation through legislation to avoid political unrest that might threaten the control of elites. States also invested heavily in economic development, both directly by funding railroads and indirectly by supporting technical education. Producers formed cartels to guarantee profits and maintain market share while minimizing the risks of the trade cycle.

The Second Industrial Revolution emerged during an era of increasingly free trade. In the aftermath of the Anglo-French Commercial Treaty in 1860, international commercial barriers fell drastically or disappeared. However, following the onset of a global depression in 1873 based on the overproduction of many commodities resulting in deflation, tariffs began to reappear toward the end of the decade. Only after the return of economic good times near the end of the century did trade barriers again begin to fall. Control over resources and access to markets were thus important issues in most countries and were used to justify the nearly complete control over other parts of the planet exercised by western and westernized economies.

Because industrialization came relatively late to the United States, many Americans confuse the results of the Second Industrial Revolution with those of the first. It is important, however, to recognize that these are distinct phenomena based on very different factors. Just as Britain had its era of industrial glory based on unique, unrepeatable circumstances, so too did the United States. The transition to a Second Industrial Revolution demonstrates the evolution of the global economy and the dangers of assuming that industrial predominance will last.

See also: American System of Manufactures; Armory Practice; Brunel, Isambard Kingdom; Credit; Education; Factory Acts; Liebig, Justus von; Patent(s); Pollution, Health, and Environment; Railroads; Role of the State; Standard of Living; Transportation by Water

Further Reading
Basalla, George. *The Evolution of Technology*. Cambridge: Cambridge University Press, 1988.

Hounshell, David A. *From the American System to Mass Production, 1800–1932: The Development of Manufacturing Technology in the United States.* Baltimore: Johns Hopkins University Press, 1984.

Mokyr, Joel. "The Second Industrial Revolution." Available online at http://faculty .wcas.northwestern.edu/~jmokyr/castronovo.pdf.

Pollard, Sidney. *Peaceful Conquest: The Industrialization of Europe 1760–1970.* Oxford: Oxford University Press, 1982.

"Second Industrial Revolution." Available online at http://ushistoryscene.com/article /second-industrial-revolution/.

SLATER, SAMUEL   Samuel Slater was an English emigrant who became known as the "father of the American Industrial Revolution." Slater was a self-nominated industrial spy who took advantage of the rewards offered by various U.S. states to provide the latest model cotton textile machines from England. Between 1790 and 1835, Slater and his partners set up mills that were the first of their kind in North America, though they had existed for generations in Europe. They could not compete internationally; they survived only because of a high degree of government financial support and tariff protection. Slater and his partners also benefited greatly from the conflict between the United States and the United Kingdom that ultimately led to war in 1812–1815.

Born in England to a wealthy family, Samuel Slater (1768–1835) was apprenticed to Jedediah Strutt, one of Richard Arkwright's first and most important partners. From Strutt, one of the largest textile manufacturers in Britain, Slater learned both management and the technical side of manufacturing. In 1789, he finished his apprenticeship, which included a stint as a mill supervisor, and decided to emigrate to the United States. He was drawn by the hefty bounties offered by several American states to anyone who could bring or build the latest model cotton textile machines. Slater arrived in New York, but he was disgusted by the machines and organization of the group that offered the bounty. Instead, he moved to Pawtucket, Rhode Island, to work with Quaker merchant Moses Brown who had employed a number of skilled workmen and constructed several prototype machines.

Slater rejected Brown's existing designs. Instead, from memory, he drew up plans for the Arkwright carding machine and spinning frame and then had the craftsmen assembled by Brown build the machines. The mill began operation in 1790 with workers walking on treadmills to power the machines; the following year, this plant became the first U.S. factory to produce cotton yarn with water-powered machinery. It operated on the British pattern: 12 hours a day, 6 days a week with a heavy complement of child laborers aged 7 to 12 who worked for very low wages. Slater became a partner, but soon formed another firm that built a separate mill in Pawtucket. Both mills made yarn that was sold to independent weavers. These enterprises were kept going by the embargo on British goods imposed in 1807. The ban enabled Americans to replace temporarily the British in many domestic markets. Later, Slater founded a number of other mills for both cotton and wool scattered around New England, including one at the modestly named Slatersville (now part of North Smithfield), Rhode Island. These water-powered mills contained both spinning and weaving operations within the same factory building and became quite widespread after 1815.

Slater elaborated a deeply paternalistic approach to finding and disciplining labor. He recruited young, unmarried women and recent immigrants. At Slatersville, families lived and worked in the community surrounding the mill. Tenement houses, a store, and even a Sunday school (the first one in a factory in the United States) were provided for the workforce by the company. In the aftermath of the 1829 downturn, however, Slater lost control of several of his mills. To restore his business prospects, Slater increasingly focused on finding (often short-term) competitive advantages and then maximizing profit before moving on. To achieve greater efficiency on the model of Robert Owen, Slater and his sons loosened their paternalist control over the labor force.

Slater took advantage of government incentives and tariff protection, the financial resources of Quaker merchants, and the machine-making skills of Yankee artisans along with the strong work habits of their laborers to become one of the most successful men in New England. When the business environment became rockier, his managerial practice evolved to become more efficient. Slater, like his models Arkwright and Strutt, was not a technical innovator; rather, he was an economic opportunist whose most important expertise was in management where he became the prototype for a new, more capitalistic businessman.

See also: American System of Manufactures; Arkwright, Richard; Armory Practice; Cartwright, Edmund; Cotton; Discipline; Division of Labor; Education; Factory System; "Industrious Revolution"; Productivity; Role of the State; Tariffs and Excise Taxes; Waltham System; Wedgwood, Josiah; Workforce

Further Reading

Hindle, Brooke, and Steven Lubar. *Engines of Change: The American Industrial Revolution 1790–1860*. Washington, DC: Smithsonian Press, 1986.

Prude, Jonathan. *The Coming of Industrial Order: Town and Factory Life in Rural Massachusetts, 1810–1860*. Amherst: University of Massachusetts Press, 1983.

"Samuel Slater: American Factory System." Available online at http://www.pbs.org /wgbh/theymadeamerica/whomade/slater_hi.html.

"Samuel Slater: Father of the American Industrial Revolution." Available online at http://www.woonsocket.org/slaterhist.htm.

Tucker, Barbara M. *Samuel Slater and the Origins of the American Textile Industry, 1790–1860.* Ithaca, NY: Cornell University Press, 1984.

SOCIALISM   Socialism emerged in the first half of the 19th century as a response to the inequalities inherent in the political system that facilitated the Industrial Revolution. Early socialists were usually intellectuals rather than workers; they sought a restructuring of society to replace the competition integral to individualism and exploitation with egalitarianism and cooperation. As socialists developed their ideas, the common element was a social and economic system distinguished by social or collective ownership—often through the medium of control of the state—of the means of production along with cooperative management of the economy. Socialism also refers to the political theories and movements that sought to establish such a system. During the age of the Industrial Revolution, the many varieties of socialism were marginal movements with little impact and few followers, but these groups became a far greater threat to the status quo after 1850.

The term "socialism" first appeared in print in 1803 in Italian: it only entered public discussion in the 1820s and 1830s. The first generation of socialist thinkers included Englishman Robert Owen (1771–1858) and two Frenchmen: Charles Fourier (1772–1837) and Claude-Henri de Rouvray, count of Saint-Simon (1760–1825), among a host of others concerned with the socioeconomic transformation then well underway. Although a large number of "socialist" groups emerged, the most influential adopted and adapted the ideas of Owen, Fourier, and Saint-Simon. These thinkers and their followers were frustrated by the growing inequality of the industrial system in which factory owners grew rich while working-class families had to deploy the labor of women and children to complement the wages of the "breadwinner" not just to keep body and soul together, but to afford a few of the goods associated with the Consumer Revolution. In good Enlightenment fashion, the early socialists hoped to convince economic elites to forego voluntarily maximizing their profits in order to allow workers to lead better lives. Such optimism about human nature proved to be one of the major limiting factors in the early socialist movement, leading German socialist theorist Karl Marx (1818–1883) to dismiss these dedicated reformers and their followers as ineffectual "utopians" with no grasp on reality whose ideas had no practical application.

Saint-Simon, an aristocrat who renounced his title to support the French Revolution, advocated public control of the means of production in order to minimize inequality. Marx built on Saint-Simon's ideas that the form of economic relations differentiated the various forms of societies and that history demonstrated an enduring cyclical pattern of construction and deconstruction. Fourier was born into the French middle class: he rejected industrialization as harmful both to individuals and to communities. He preferred agricultural societies in which most goods were made in the home for domestic use because they were more likely to enable humans to master their passions and attain what he referred to as a natural state of harmony. Owen had several advantages over his French colleagues. He was a self-made man who amassed a considerable fortune as a textile entrepreneur, most notably at New Lanark, Scotland, where he treated workers with respect. Owen put a number of his ideas into practice before nearly driving himself into bankruptcy with the establishment of what was intended to be a self-sustaining, cooperative community at New Harmony, Indiana. In the aftermath of this community's failure in 1827, Owen devoted the rest of his life to spreading socialist ideas and lobbying for government-sponsored reforms on behalf of the working classes.

Few factory workers endorsed the ideas of these early socialists. Artisans whose livelihoods were under assault by mechanization were, by far, the most likely supporters of socialist ideas until the 1870s. Perhaps factory workers found the ideas too optimistic, too abstract, expressed in ways that their limited educations made difficult to grasp, or the plans were too far removed from their own realities, but for whatever reason(s), early socialism attracted few workers. This remained the case even after Marx and his collaborator, Prussian-born English industrialist Friedrich Engels (1820–1895) introduced an explicitly political element into the movement with *The Communist Manifesto* (1848), calling for an immediate social revolution that would turn society upside down. Despite this clarion call, throughout the 19th century, many and probably most socialists limited themselves to advocating for industrial reform to curb the excesses of the capitalist system. Only after European governments inaugurated their own reforms at the height of British dominance, limited as they were, did significant numbers of factory workers espouse socialism.

Socialism emerged as a bogeyman for elites and the middle classes who sought ways to prevent calls for change in defense of the status quo. Although Owen and Fourier explicitly disavowed political action on behalf of their ideas, and the Saint-Simonians did not go beyond lobbying, the fundamental challenge of socialism—its focus on equality, collective ownership, and cooperation—threatened the position of economic elites dependent on the exploitation of workers and their inherited positions in society that provided them ownership of the means of production. By thoroughly scapegoating socialist ideas and practices, elites and their agents sought to avoid change and protect their positions. In the aftermath of the revolutions of 1848, workers increasingly recognized that the middle classes would not act consistently in their interest, which eventually led many to adopt more radical, even revolutionary, means of achieving change. However, the adoption of Marxist ideas on the need for a revolution to remake society belongs to the era of the Second Industrial Revolution, not the first. The emergence of socialism in the early 19th century was a harbinger that the working classes would not accept the growing inequality of industrial society forever.

See also: Colonialism; Consumer Revolution; Discipline; Division of Labor; Enlightenment; Factory Acts; Factory System; Luddites; Owen, Robert; Pollution, Health, and Environment; Role of the State; Second Industrial Revolution; Standard of Living; Workforce; Document: "Conditions in the Mines"; Document: "Defending the Factory System"; Document: "Living and Working in Manchester"; Document: "Robert Owen on Education and the Evils of Child Labor"

Further Reading

"History of Socialism." Available online at http://www.philosophybasics.com/branch_socialism.html.

Laidler, Harry W. *History of Socialism: An Historical Comparative Study of Socialism*. New York: Routledge, 1969.

Lindemann, Albert S. *A History of European Socialism*. New Haven, CT: Yale University Press, 1984.

"Marxists Internet Archive." Available online at https://www.marxists.org/.

"Responses to the Industrial Revolution." Available online at http://webs.bcp.org/sites/vcleary/ModernWorldHistoryTextbook/IndustrialRevolution/responsestoIR.html.

STANDARD OF LIVING   The standard of living refers to the bulk of the population's well-being. In the context of the 18th and 19th centuries, the term is contentious because a significant proportion of commentators both then and now assert that the British working classes' standard of living improved dramatically because of the Industrial Revolution. Recent research has corrected this view by demonstrating that almost all the gains in workers' standard of living came after 1830, more than 50 years after the onset of industrialization.

Britain's output grew impressively during this era, partly in response to a burgeoning population. Because few industries grew as fast as cotton textiles, metallurgy, or even woolens, Britain as a whole actually experienced relatively slow growth, punctuated by periodic crises during the critical era from 1780 to 1850. As a result, average living standards rose gradually and tentatively in the heyday of industrialization. For the entire period, the standard of living increased, at most, by 30 percent. Since this improvement followed a period of falling wages in the first decades of industrialization (1760–1780), industrialization did not improve British living standards—especially for the burgeoning working classes—as much or as rapidly as many would like to believe. The Industrial Revolution imposed harsh sacrifices on the typical household economy.

Real wages increased about 16 percent from 1760 to 1820, an increase that is distorted by the decline of average real family incomes by approximately 14 percent from 1791–1795 to 1816–1820. From that point, real wages improved a dramatic 41 percent from 1820 to 1850. These improved real wages were partially the result of a vastly extended work week. Without formal vacations, in 1760, an average employed British adult labored nearly 50 hours a week. By 1850, when nearly half of British workers labored in mines, mills, workshops, and factories, that figure had climbed to more than 61 hours a week. Women and children had to work outside the home to survive because an adult male often did not earn enough to support a family. Pushed by declining hourly wages and increasing hours of labor for men, perhaps two-thirds of married women earned wages or had an occupation in the late 18th century. In 1851, census data indicates that 36 percent of children aged 10–14 worked for wages after half a century of legislative efforts to curb that practice.

The fall in real wages was masked by the increased labor of the entire family. This intensification of labor was also sufficient to support a large increase in consumption of about 75 percent in 1750–1850. Workers' growing participation in the Consumer Revolution gave the impression of an improving standard of living. This was the "Industrious Revolution" in operation.

Other measures tell a more ambivalent story. The height of British army recruits—a unique source that provides insight into nutrition and health conditions—declined by 1.3 percent. In 1850, the average British male was probably shorter than he had been a century before. Continental Europe did not experience a similar drop. Such data might be explained in part by greatly increased consumption of sugar, tobacco, and alcohol. British life expectancy at birth had stood at 42.7 years in 1581, but fell rapidly until it reached a mere 25.3 years in 1726. By 1826, it was back to 41.3 years before declining to 39.5 years in 1850. Of course, some groups enjoyed consistently longer lives, but as a whole, mid-Victorian British life expectancy was less than it had been under Queen Elizabeth. This data suggests that there were serious shortcomings to the British standard of living during the Industrial Revolution.

The standard of living must also take into account the speedy expansion of the British population from approximately 6.3 million in 1761 to 14.9 million in 1841. This expansion was most rapid from 1791 to 1831. Such growth was particularly impressive given the heavy emigration from Britain to the colonies and to the United States as well as the long years of war that punctuated this era. Declining mortality played an important role, especially for infants and young children, but increasing fertility was a greater factor in the impressive increase in British population. People had more children for several reasons. The mean age of marriage fell from 28 for males and 26 for females in the decade 1680–1689 to 25 for men and 23 for women in 1830–1837. Women increasingly expected to marry. Married women were also slightly more likely to have children and to minimize the spacing between births. These shifts in nuptiality were an essential component of the increased fertility of the period. Greater willingness to have children and the likelihood of those children surviving are a vital measure of the positive evolution of the standard of living during the age of the Industrial Revolution.

Not only was the population growing, but people also moved to urban areas. The proportion of urban dwellers more than doubled from 21 percent in 1750 to 45 percent a century later. Cities offered jobs, access to educational opportunities, and entertainment among many other familiar benefits, but at the same time they were centers of disease, lawlessness, and poverty where life expectancy was quite low and falling during most of the first Industrial Revolution. Only after 1850 did governments begin to deal with these difficult problems with manifest advantages for the standard of living of the British people.

In short, the British Industrial Revolution relied on exploiting the working classes, lowering real wages, forcing men to work far longer hours, and requiring women and children to work outside the home to support the family. Although fertility improved, child mortality declined, and consumption increased, the falling height of army recruits and sinking overall mortality suggests that the effects of industrialization had a generally negative effect on the British people's, much less the working classes', standard of living. Only once Britain had enjoyed at least two generations as the "workshop of the world" and defeated rival France in the Revolutionary and Napoleonic wars did the benefits of the Industrial Revolution "trickle down" to the population at large. It is the period *after* the first Industrial Revolution when most of the gains in the standard of living stemming from the Industrial Revolution were enjoyed, by the great-grandchildren (or even great-great grandchildren) of those workers who toiled in the first factories that touched off this revolutionary transformation.

See also: Arkwright, Richard; Coal; Colonialism; Consumer Revolution; Cotton; Discipline; Division of Labor; Domestic Industry; Factory Acts; Factory System; "Industrious Revolution"; Lancashire; Luddites; Owen, Robert;

Pollution, Health, and Environment; Role of the State; Second Industrial Revolution; Socialism; Workforce; Document: "Living and Working in Manchester"; Document: "Conditions in the Mines"; Document: "Adam Smith on the Division of Labor"; Document: "The State of the Poor"

Further Reading

Daunton, Martin J. *Progress and Poverty: An Economic and Social History of Britain 1700–1850*. Oxford: Oxford University Press, 1995.

Griffin, Emma. *A Short History of the British Industrial Revolution*. Houndsmills, UK: Palgrave, 2010.

King, Steven, and Geoffrey Timmins. *Making Sense of the Industrial Revolution: English Economy and Society, 1700–1850*. Manchester: Manchester University Press, 2001.

Nye, John V. C. "Standards of Living and Modern Economic Growth." Available online at http://www.econlib.org/library/Enc/StandardsofLivingandModern EconomicGrowth.html.

Steckel, Richard H. "A History of the Standard of Living in the United States." Available online at https://eh.net/encyclopedia/a-history-of-the-standard-of-living-in -the-united-states/.

STEAM ENGINE This external combustion machine uses heat in the form of expanding or rapidly condensing steam to generate mechanical work. Although the potential of boiling water to produce power had been known since the first century CE, only in the 17th century were practical, though highly inefficient, means invented to put this knowledge into practice. James Watt's various improvements turned a machine used primarily as a pump to remove water from mines into the workhorse of the Industrial Revolution. Steam engines were the critical invention in creating the factory system and enabling the development of steam-driven transportation that characterized the 19th century.

In 1606, a Spanish inventor Jerónimo de Ayanz y Beaumont invented a rudimentary steam engine to pump water. Thomas Savery patented a pump with hand-operated valves that sucked water from mines using condensed steam to create a vacuum in 1698. Thomas Newcomen added a piston that separated condensing steam from the water in 1712. It was used in a coal mine, where fuel was essentially free. A few other such "atmospheric engines" were built where similar conditions applied, but it was clear that major improvements were necessary for steam engines to become widely used.

Some of Britain's best engineers worked to improve the steam engine. The most successful ones had experience designing and building precision tools. In the 1760s, John Smeaton (1724–1792), an instrument maker from Leeds, upgraded existing designs, doubling their efficiency. James Watt (1736–1819), an instrument maker from Glasgow, spent two decades tinkering with the engine, solving several technical problems. His improvements saved a huge amount of coal and permitted the machine to be moved, which made the steamboat and the railroad possible. British entrepreneurs and craftsmen rapidly applied an upgraded engine he built in 1778 to run all sorts of industrial machines. Constantly improved, the steam engine was essential to successful mechanization and to the emergence of the factory system. However, Watt's engines were too large and did not produce enough pressure to run a steam-powered vehicle. Only after another Englishman, Richard Trevithick, developed such an engine in 1800 did it become possible to build steamboats and railroads, the era's most vital advances in transportation.

The development of the modern factory is often linked to the steam engine. This is not accurate as many early factories instead relied on water power. It was not until 1783 that steam power was first used in a factory, albeit indirectly. Richard Arkwright's Manchester mill used a Newcomen engine to pump water to drive the machines in the dry season when the water pressure was insufficient to turn the waterwheel. The first fully steam-driven factory was at Papplewick, Nottinghamshire, which began operation in 1785. Watt wrote to his partner, Matthew Boulton, "If you come home by way of Manchester, please do not seek orders for cotton-mill engines, because I hear that there are so many mills erecting on powerful streams in the North of England, that the trade must soon be overdone, and consequently our labour may be lost." Other sources of power did not disappear or even fade away even after the efficiency of steam engines improved.

For decades, steam did not represent a huge improvement over other sources of power. All but a few of the 496 Boulton and Watt steam engines sold by that firm produced only 15–16 horsepower per hour. They were limited by the current state of metalwork, which could not fabricate parts capable of withstanding greater steam pressure. Thus, for more than 30 years, a steam engine did not provide appreciably more power than wind or water could generate. Until the dawn of the 19th century, the steam engine's great advantage was its mobility and its independence of the weather. However, the enormous investment in steam engines and the mechanization it permitted did encourage a round-the-clock use of machinery. Constant employment of expensive machines by two shifts of workers had dramatic effects on total output and heightened the need to discipline the labor force to get them to accept permanent night work. The true age of steam in manufacturing did not begin until after 1800 when Watt's patent expired. By 1835, three-quarters of the machines in the cotton industry were run by steam.

In addition to its traditional spheres of agriculture and mining and its vital places in textile mills and iron foundries, steam power was applied to run a host of other machines. Matthew Boulton set up six presses to make coins for Britain's Mint. Brewers and canal masters used steam engines primarily as pumps. Others were interested in transportation. William Murdock, a Boulton and Watt employee, devised a steam-driven wheeled carriage. In 1801, Henry Bell began to experiment with a steamboat [based on successful French experiments undertaken in 1783], and a decade later, he established steamer service on Scotland's Clyde River. Steamships required ever-improving pressure to supply the motive power. These lessons were applied later to the steam locomotive, which was the key to building a network of railroads and commenced a revolution in land transport.

The constant improvement to the steam engine that took place in the 18th and 19th centuries relied on the experience of artisans and iron makers with using coal as fuel and their willingness to experiment with new machines. The result of this technological creativity was the coal-driven steam engine, which ultimately placed almost unlimited and reliable power at humanity's disposal, replacing the dependence on human or animal power. The steam engine was the characteristic machine of the Industrial Revolution.

See also: Arkwright, Richard; Brunel, Isambard Kingdom; Coal; Cotton; Crystal Palace; Factory System; Iron and Steel; Patent(s); Productivity; Railroads; Role of the State; Second Industrial Revolution; Transportation by Water; Document: "Defending the Factory System"; Document: "Living and Working in Manchester"

Further Reading

"A Brief History of Steam Power." Available online at http://johno.myiglou.com /SteamHistory.htm.

Hunter, Louis C. *A History of Industrial Power in the United States, 1730–1930*, vol. 2, *Steam Power*. Charlottesville: University of Virginia Press, 1985.

"Industrial History: The History of the Steam Engine." Available online at http:// www.thomasnet.com/articles/custom-manufacturing-fabricating/steam-engine -history.

Jacob, Margaret C. *Scientific Culture and the Making of the Industrial West*. Oxford: Oxford University Press, 1997.

Musson, A. E., and Eric Robinson. *Science and Technology in the Industrial Revolution*. Manchester: Manchester University Press, 1969.

TARIFFS AND EXCISE TAXES   Tariffs are taxes—either set at a general rate or on specific goods—on imports and exports that are generally collected at the border. An excise tax applies to particular commodities or products made and sold within a country's borders. They are usually assessed either at the point of production or at the point of sale. Taken together, tariffs and excise taxes were major sources of revenue for all European states. As part of the approach to economic policymaking usually referred to as mercantilism, governments used these fiscal instruments to favor some industries and protect certain producers. The prevalence of these levies demonstrates the limitations in practice of the economic principles articulated by Adam Smith that free trade accelerated industrial growth and economic realities. Tax policy was one of the most important ways that the state influenced economy and society during the age of the Industrial Revolution.

In the 17th century, high tariffs encouraged European states to develop their colonial empires and trading relations outside Europe to guarantee access to raw materials, luxury goods, and markets. Tariffs also enabled manufacturers to make goods to substitute for imports like Indian calico cotton cloth. European equivalents did not have to be internationally competitive; they just had to be able to compete behind the government's tariff walls. In some places like Great Britain, imported grain was also highly taxed to protect the incomes of landowners who benefited from higher food prices. These Corn Laws were first instituted in 1670 and amended frequently in the 18th century, then reinstated fully in 1815, and remained in force until 1846. At the same time, mercantilist governments realized that excise taxes stifled initiative and encouraged smuggling. They therefore moved to reduce or eliminate these duties whenever possible. During the 18th century, state officials lowered both tariff and excise rates to encourage trade and industry. The chief exception was Britain where the excise emerged as the government's chief means of paying off its enormous wartime debts.

The ebb and flow of customs and excise rates can best be explained through the lens of political economy. Governments maintained, increased, or reduced rates for fundamentally political reasons rather than strictly economic motives. For most of the 18th century, the British excise on goods like beer, malt, hops, soap, salt, candles, and leather brought in at least 40 percent of the state's total revenue and, in some years, as much as 55 percent. Although tariff rates were generally on the wane, improved collection and the broadly based expansion of trade volumes meant that receipts doubled over the course of the century to about one-third of revenue. British tariff rates on most goods were exceptionally low before the series of wars with France forced the government to raise vast sums to support its military adventures. In 1689, tariff rates were 5 percent on most goods, rising to 15 percent in 1704 and 25 percent in 1759. Further increases stalled in 1786–1792 before continuing their ascent. By 1820, tariff rates reached 60 percent before falling gradually to about 20 percent in 1850. Given the dependence of the British manufacturing economy on imported raw materials and the island nation's reliance on exports, elevated customs rates—much higher than Britain's closest economic rivals such as France and the Netherlands—during the era of industrial take-off suggests that Britain might have grown faster and with far less hardship for the laboring classes if it had practiced what Adam Smith preached. The loss of 13 North American colonies largely due to trade policy is also surely relevant. Lobbying and the operation of patronage networks played dominant roles in determining the specifics of trade policy throughout the era. Free trade was a goal (for some) but certainly never a reality during the first Industrial Revolution.

European states and the United States all relied on the tariff and the excise for the bulk of government revenue. In the 1780s, as industrialization got under way, tariff rates continued to drop, most concretely with the Anglo-French Commercial Treaty of 1786 that lowered taxes on many items, in large measure because many governments led by France saw closer trade ties as a way of avoiding the animosities that led so frequently to war. On the continent, excise levies also fell, especially in the 1790s as France eliminated guilds and economic privileges that fragmented the national market. The success of French arms led to the eradication of those same institutions throughout western and central Europe. Despite their reputation as free-traders, Britain went in a different, more regressive direction, distorting the market by heightening excise rates on certain goods and maintaining high tariff walls to protect infant industries and elite incomes.

British reliance on regressive taxation while their competitors were removing barriers to competition challenges many assumptions about the process of industrialization. This situation also flies in the face of what most economists consider best practice. British political economy provides the best explanation for why it bucked the trend and why their strategy worked. The ability of British elites—seconded by the state—to dominate their workers helps to explain why food prices could remain so high without causing riots and rebellions. The tremendous benefits of Britain's colonial empire and global commercial ties, along with the negative effects of Revolutionary politics and military defeat that stifled continental industrialization for at least a generation, also played major roles in this situation. Achieving the highest possible rates of economic growth was never the goal of British political economy during the Industrial Revolution. Preserving the power of entrenched elites and special interests was, as the role of tariffs and excise taxes demonstrates concretely.

In the second wave of industrializing nations like the United States and the German lands, excise taxes declined rapidly as both sources of revenue and as tools of state economic policy. Tariffs, however, remained high especially in the United States to shelter infant industries and encourage import substitution. After 1815, the German lands of Prussia, Bavaria, Württemberg, and Hesse-Darmstadt suffered from the breakup of the French low-tax trading zone developed by Emperor Napoleon I. They recognized that lowered barriers could encourage commerce and industry. From a hesitant beginning in 1818, Prussia sponsored a customs union, the Zollverein, that by 1834 encompassed German-speaking Europe (other than Austria). The Zollverein's moderate tariff rates, about half of the United Kingdom's, recognized that retaliation for high rates was a major threat for economies dependent on both exports and imports that were not in the dominant financial and military position enjoyed by the British in the first half of the 19th century.

It is highly significant that concrete movement toward genuine free trade on the part of the first industrial nation occurred only at the very end of the era. The abolition of the Corn Laws in 1846 and a general lowering of tariff rates led eventually to a free trade treaty between the United Kingdom and France in 1860, which encouraged the elimination of trade barriers around the world. The effects of free trade on industrialization, however, are part of the story of the Second Industrial Revolution, not the first, which was strongly affected by the persistence of excise taxes and high tariffs resulting from the political economy of the various states undergoing industrialization.

See also: Chaptal, Jean-Antoine; Colonialism; Education; Enlightenment; Mercantilism; Productivity; Railroads; Role of the State; Second Industrial Revolution; Wedgwood, Josiah; Document: "Child on Interest, Trade, and Money"; Document: "Adam Smith on the Division of Labor"

Further Reading

Asakura, Hironori. *World History of the Customs and Tariffs.* Brussels: World Customs Association, 2003.

Ashworth, William. *Customs and Excise: Trade, Production, and Consumption in England, 1640–1845.* Oxford: Oxford University Press, 2003.

Brewer, John. *The Sinews of Power: War, Money and the English State, 1688–1783.* Cambridge, MA: Harvard University Press, 1989.

Nye, John V. "The Myth of Free-Trade Britain." Available online at http://www.econlib.org/library/Columns/y2003/Nyefreetrade.html.

"The Second American Party System and the Tariff." Available online at http://www.taxhistory.org/www/website.nsf/Web/THM1816?OpenDocument.

TRANSPORTATION BY WATER   Until the development of railroad networks after 1850, water transport was significantly cheaper than moving either goods or people by land. Although states poured resources into improving roads, building turnpikes and bridges, as well as other means of speeding and easing transport by land, water transportation remained far easier and less expensive. Thus, access to navigable rivers or the seacoast was a major geographical advantage to trade and industry. The development of steamboats as well as a network of canals along with improvements to ports and docks lowered costs further and gave new areas access to the global economy. Improved water transport enabled and supported the Industrial Revolution.

At the dawn of the 18th century, British road transport costs averaged about 1 shilling per ton-mile, while shipping via inland waterways cost about 2.5 pence per ton-mile and coastal shipping even less. This difference of at least 480 percent in shipping costs demonstrates the extreme expense of transporting heavy or bulky goods by land and the benefits of extending and improving transportation by water.

The island nature of the British state was a tremendous material resource. It was also a key to building an effective transportation network. Even without man-made improvements, nowhere in Britain is more than 70 miles from the sea, and very few places are more than 30 miles from navigable water. The Severn and the Trent river systems provide water carriage to the industrial Midlands, and the Thames and the Wash Rivers allow easy transport to major agricultural regions. In the 17th, 18th, and 19th centuries, the British state seconded by numerous entrepreneurs expended considerable capital on improving waterways, building canals, and ensuring access to the rivers and streams as sources of industrial power. These efforts were not unique; in fact, Britain was following in the wake of various continental countries in water transport. But because of the compactness of the island, the reach of the navigable rivers, and the plentiful ports, the improvements made to the British water system were more effective in creating a national transportation network and thus a national market than was possible on continental Europe.

The differential in shipping costs encouraged greater investment and innovation in canal building. Cheap coal was so critical to the British economy that canals were constructed solely to transport it to market. Beginning around 1750, canals were constructed along the Severn, Trent, and Mersey Rivers and their tributaries. Later canals linked the river systems or facilitated access to inland areas like southern Wales that had vital resources but no outlet to the sea. With a few notable exceptions like the canal constructed by the Duke of Bridgewater to link his estates to Manchester and Liverpool, the construction of most canals was financed through joint-stock companies to mobilize the enormous sums needed. By 1830, England and Wales had 3,876 miles of inland canals, up from 1,399 in 1760. From 1780 to 1830, Britain's canals contributed a 0.8 percent annual increase in transport productivity.

In the United States, canals tied the interior of the continent to the Atlantic Ocean and thus to the global economy. The most notable of the large number of canals built during this era was the Erie Canal financed by the state of New York. Stretching 363 miles, the canal was completed in 1825. By joining the Hudson River and Lake Erie, the so-called Eighth Wonder of the World crossed the Appalachian Mountains to link the port of New York with markets hundreds of miles in the interior and vice versa. Because of the expense of building and maintaining canals, the vast distances to be traversed, the limited tax revenues of local and state governments in the United States, and the emergence of the railroad as a transportation rival, less than 3,400 miles of canals were built during the Industrial Revolution. Canals linked several key hubs like the Great Lakes and the river systems of the Midwest, but the exorbitant cost of building—an average of $37,580 per mile—ensured the dominance of the railroad after 1830.

Harbors and rivers were dredged and deepened to permit additional or further access. Even before the use of steam revolutionized ocean transport, sailing ships were modified through different rigging and hull design to increase carrying capacity while lessening the number of men needed to sail the vessel. On ships entering London from Spain and Portugal, the tonnage grew rapidly: the number of tons per man swelled from 7.9 in 1686 to 9.1 in 1726 and 12.6 in 1766. Shipping contributed a 1.4 percent annual increase in transport productivity between 1780 and 1860. Gradual improvements took England's transportation network to a level beyond their European competitors and set the stage for further advances once steam power was added to the mix.

Steamboats were a major innovation in water transportation because they could travel more easily upstream on rivers and were not dependent on the weather or the tide. The possibility of using a steam engine to turn a wheel outfitted with paddles to propel a boat or ship was tried in a number of places in the 1780s concurrent with James Watt's improvements to the machine. Marquis Claude de Jouffroy first achieved the feat in 1783 on the Saône River in France, building on an abortive attempt in 1776 by his mentor. Four years later, American John Fitch made a more successful trial in the Delaware River in a small boat using a rack of oars instead of a paddle wheel. In 1790, Fitch and a partner Henry Voigt began service across the Delaware in an improved craft. Although the business soon failed, Fitch got both U.S. and French patents for steamboats in 1791.

Robert Fulton is often credited with developing the steamboat, which is clearly incorrect. Rather Fulton's accomplishment was to make the steamboat a commercial success. He received a monopoly from the state of New York thanks to the support of powerful investor, banker, and diplomat Robert

Livingston (Fulton married Livingston's niece.) His paddle-wheeled steam-boat the *Clermont*'s five-day roundtrip voyage from New York City to Albany in 1807, traveling five knots against the current, was a sensation. In conjunction with the Erie Canal, the steamboat made access to the American interior significantly faster and cheaper. The first steamboat reached New Orleans by way of the Ohio and Mississippi Rivers in 1811. Soon steamboats traveled regular routes on the Hudson, Delaware, James, Susquehanna, Ohio, Missouri, and Mississippi Rivers (among many others) as well as their tributaries and the Great Lakes. Thirteen years after Fulton's feat, the number of steamboats plying the Ohio and Mississippi river systems reached 69; it rose to 187 in 1830 and 536 in 1850. Not only could steamboats go upriver far more easily, but by the mid-1820s, they could also travel up to 100 miles a day, whereas other boats could achieve 20 miles only under good conditions. The emergence of steamboats also helped to spread knowledge of engines and precision metallurgy, especially along the Ohio River and its tributaries. In Pittsburgh, Wheeling, Cincinnati, and Louisville, industrial development followed in the wake of this knowledge.

In Britain, the first commercial steamboat began operation in 1812, and the continent followed soon afterward. Steamboats took over much of the ferrying business across the Irish Sea and the Channel and along the coasts. The first iron steamboat was launched in Britain in 1821, setting the stage for greater military use of the steamboat. Beginning with Isambard Kingdom Brunel's *Great Western*, which steamed between Bristol and New York from 1838, steamships began to take over transoceanic routes. This evolution was speeded greatly by the replacement of paddles with far more efficient screw propellers in the 1840s. Between 1840 and 1860 the number of British steamships increased fivefold and represented almost 10 percent of the nation's total shipping tonnage.

Improvements in water transportation had myriad effects. Important technical innovations were developed in shipbuilding, hull design, dredging and river management, and the building of locks and sluices, among other things. Engineers of all types and the construction industries in general benefitted directly from the development of the transportation net. British financial practice evolved to raise the sums needed to improve waterways, ports, and shipping. Various organizations within British society learned to work together to link up the disparate parts of the network. Developing the technical expertise of Britain's human capital, mobilizing finance capital and evolving forms of organization promoted the emergence of industrial society in the late 18th century.

The economic implications of the improvements in British transportation were dramatic. Despite the piecemeal character of canal building, with no national planning either attempted or implemented, an island-spanning network was created, linking the major urban centers together and reaching out into most rural areas. Food prices fell, not by reducing the incomes of those who worked the land, but by lowering market prices by reducing transport costs. Most commodity prices also dropped, especially that of coal. The economic benefits of an improved transportation network were so clear that entrepreneurs relocated production to take advantage of natural resources, especially if coal was available nearby. All in all, roads, canals, and shipping permitted first the development and then the integration of British markets by substantially lowering transaction costs. Polities with larger landmasses like France, the United States, and Russia also benefited from enhanced water transport, but their economic spurts came later, with the railroad. The establishment of a cheap and reliable system of transportation by water was among the major contributors to the emergence of an industrial revolution in Britain.

See also: Bridgewater, Duke of; Brunel, Isambard Kingdom; Coal; Credit; Fitch, John; Iron and Steel; Mercantilism; Productivity; Railroads; Role of the State; Steam Engine; Document: "The State of the Poor"

Further Reading

Daunton, Martin J. *Progress and Poverty: An Economic and Social History of Britain 1700–1850*. Oxford: Oxford University Press, 1995.

Rodrigue, Jean-Paul. "The Industrial Revolution and Transportation (1800–1870)." Available online at https://people.hofstra.edu/geotrans/eng/ch2en/conc2en/ch2c1en.html.

Szostak, Rick. *The Role of Transportation in the Industrial Revolution: A Comparison of England and France*. Montreal: McGill University Press, 1991.

Ville, Simon. "Transport." In *The Cambridge Economic History of Modern Britain*, vol. 1, *1700–1860*, ed. Roderick Floud and Paul Johnson. Cambridge: Cambridge University Press, 2004.

"Waterways of England and Wales: Their History in Maps." Available online at http://www.canalmuseum.org.uk/history/maps.htm.

WALTHAM SYSTEM   The Waltham system was created beginning in 1813 by the Boston Manufacturing Company in a purpose-built water-powered cotton textile factory along the Charles River in Waltham, Massachusetts. It was the brainchild of Boston merchant Francis Cabot Lowell (1775–1817). The "system" was based on the use of a workforce that consisted overwhelmingly of girls and young women who lived in company-owned boardinghouses in exchange for dramatically lower wages. The Waltham factory's financial success inspired many imitators and led the company to create its very own mill town in 1822: they named it Lowell. The Waltham system as expressed in

Lowell was productive until the Civil War and beyond. It set the stage for what became known as the American System of Manufactures at the dawn of the Second Industrial Revolution.

Lowell began the process of creating the Waltham system with a bit of industrial espionage. During a two-year trip to England, he, like Samuel Slater before him, attempted to memorize the design of an important textile machine in the factories he visited, in this case, the power-loom. When he returned to the United States, he and mechanic Paul Moody reconstructed the machines, adapting them to the materials available. With a new textile machine ready to put to use, Lowell and a group of partners founded the Boston Manufacturing Company in 1813 to supply the demand that had accumulated because of the British blockade during the War of 1812. As with many European enterprises, they raised capital by selling shares mostly to their friends, relations, and business acquaintances; the firm was ultimately capitalized at an impressive $600,000. The model of a joint-stock or share-holder corporation rapidly became widespread in American business.

Along the Charles River in Waltham, Massachusetts, Lowell constructed a brand-new brick building. Water power was used to mechanize the conversion of raw cotton into cloth. Although frequently given credit in the United States for being the first to integrate the entire production process in a single structure, the British, French, Belgians, and Prussians had established such mills a generation before. As an integrated factory, Waltham was significant, however, because it abandoned New England's long-standing reliance on domestic manufacture. Its corporate structure and management practices became the model for other American factories, especially when the coarse cotton cloth it produced sold well.

Nearly the mill's entire labor force of 300 was composed of girls fresh from the farm. The girls, some as young as 15, received much lower wages than men, but they could live in company boardinghouses that were clean and respectable—they even had official chaperones. For these girls, the factory was an escape from the farm and a means of engaging in religious and educational activities, all while earning cash wages. The boardinghouses enabled these girls to abandon part-time agricultural work: they were now industrial workers. Enough Waltham-type mills were constructed that finding sufficient girls to staff the factories became difficult. The original Waltham mill, however, had no problem attracting and keeping a loyal workforce.

Although Lowell himself died young, the system he created yielded extremely high profits. When the Boston Manufacturing Company expanded and created its own mill town in 1822 along the Merrimack River, the directors named it after him. The company chose a site with a 30-foot waterfall that could accommodate the largest waterwheels in North America; they were capable of running in any season and in any weather. Ultimately, the industrial city of Lowell housed 20 mills and 6,000 workers (5,100 of whom were women aged 15–29). By the end of the 1820s, 10 of the largest corporations in the United States made use of the hydraulic system established in Lowell. In 1850, Lowell produced 20 percent of all U.S.-made cotton cloth.

When not at work (13 hours a day), the young women of Lowell, like their Waltham progenitors, lived in dormitories, separated from their families, where they were subject to disciplinary "moral instruction," including the requirement to "attend public worship . . . and to conform strictly to the rules of the Sabbath." They were also to keep clean, while avoiding both "ardent spirits" and "frivolous and useless conversation." This heavy-handed managerial paternalism was a way of combating social opposition to women working outside the home and of attracting laborers, but the positive aspects and relatively high pay lasted only as long as the good times. When a sharp downturn hit in the mid-1830s, Lowell's vaunted mills also experienced labor problems when management tried to cut wages by a quarter. Despite the ambivalent elements of managerial practice of Lowell and the mills in Lowell, the Waltham system's innovations in management and factory organization became the seed of what became known as the American system of production and the foundation of U.S. industrial competiveness.

See also: American System of Manufactures; Cartwright, Edmund; Consumer Revolution; Cotton; Crystal Palace; Domestic Industry; Factory System; "Industrious Revolution"; Productivity; Second Industrial Revolution; Standard of Living; Tariffs and Excise Taxes; Workforce

Further Reading

Dublin, Thomas. "Women and the Early Industrial Revolution in the United States." Available online at https://www.gilderlehrman.org/history-by-era/jackson-lincoln/essays/women-and-early-industrial-revolution-united-states.

Malone, Patrick M. *Waterpower in Lowell: Engineering and Industry in Nineteenth-Century America*. Baltimore: Johns Hopkins University Press, 2009.

Temin, Peter, ed. *Engines of Enterprise: An Economic History of New England*. Cambridge, MA: Harvard University Press, 2002.

"The Waltham-Lowell System." Available online at http://www.nps.gov/lowe/learn/photosmultimedia/waltham_lowell.htm.

WATT, JAMES   Scots-born James Watt was an instrument maker at the University of Glasgow who dramatically improved the efficiency of the Newcomen steam engine, making it far more versatile, which permitted its application to a wide variety of industrial uses. His 1769 patent was extended in

1775 by Act of Parliament to run until 1800. In partnership with Matthew Boulton, Watt began manufacturing steam engines at the former's Soho Engineering Works located in Birmingham, England. Their well-built and well-maintained, relatively reliable engines helped to build support for the new machine and contributed greatly to Britain's industrial prowess in the initial phases of the Industrial Revolution.

James Watt was born in Greenlock, Scotland, in 1736. Largely self-educated, he went to London to learn the trade of mathematical instrument maker in 1755. Two years later he returned home to become instrument maker for the University of Glasgow. Watt was called upon to repair the university's model of a Newcomen engine. During the 1760s, with the financial support of English inventor John Roebuck, Watt experimented with improving the efficiency of the Newcomen engine, particularly the relationship of the density of steam to factors such as temperature and pressure. With his first patent issued in 1769, Watt overcame the wasteful use of steam by designing a separate condensing chamber that both improved steam pressure on the piston and removed the need to cool the cylinder, thereby preventing heat loss and maximizing fuel use.

In 1775, Matthew Boulton (1728–1809) purchased Roebuck's interest in Watt's engine and began to manufacture engines at the Soho Engineering Works in Birmingham. Over the next several years, Watt developed other innovations that he also patented. These included introducing pistons that moved up and down (a reciprocal motion), which could drive machines such as the power-loom through the addition of a rod and crank, which turned in a circle (rotary motion). In addition, Watt implemented a double-acting system in which steam was admitted alternately to both ends of the cylinder. Finally, Watt developed a "steam governor" that automatically regulated the speed of an engine by linking output to input, a concept fundamental to automation.

Boulton and Watt's first engine, installed in 1776, pumped water from a coal mine. Engine manufacture made use of the Soho Works' highly trained metal craftsmen to fabricate the necessary precision parts. Thus, it took a combination of sufficient capital, trained workers, many different types of complex machines, and more than one inventive genius to dramatically improve the steam engine.

Boulton and Watt benefitted from powerful state protection through the patent system that gave them a monopoly, which they guarded fiercely. Both Boulton and Watt also conceived of themselves as scientists, joining and participating faithfully in several different learned societies such as the Society of Arts and indulging their interest in many different subjects. This activity enhanced their national and international reputations and assisted in the sale of their engines both at home and abroad, while also ensuring their value to the state that enforced their patent rights.

In 1800, Boulton and Watt's patent rights expired and Watt retired from business, ostensibly to devote himself solely to science. At this point, Britain had more than 500 operational Boulton and Watt engines. Several dozen more had been sold on the continent and a significant number of copies of their design had been made in places where English patent rights could not be enforced. As a sign of his importance to the study of efficiency and power, an electrical unit of measurement, the watt, was named after him, which also recognized that it had been Watt who coined the term "horsepower" to describe the energy output of an engine.

Watt's designs and willingness to oversee the quality of the machines he and Boulton built made his reputation as a scientist and inventor, which helped him become known to subsequent generations as the inventor of the steam engine, even though such engines had been in existence for generations before Watt took out his first patent. Watt did, however, vastly increase the efficiency of the steam engine, paving the way for further improvements and facilitating the mechanization so fundamental to the Industrial Revolution.

See also: Coal; Credit; Division of Labor; Iron and Steel; Patent(s); Productivity; Role of the State; Royal Society of Arts; Transportation by Water; Workforce

Further Reading

"James Watt." Available online at http://www.famousscientists.org/james-watt/.

Lira, Cara. "Biography of James Watt." Available online at http://www.egr.msu.edu/~lira/supp/steam/wattbio.html.

Musson, A. E., and Eric Robinson. *Science and Technology in the Industrial Revolution.* Manchester: Manchester University Press, 1969.

Tann, Jennifer, ed. *The Selected Papers of Boulton and Watt.* Cambridge, MA: MIT Press, 1981.

Tann, Jennifer, and M. J. Breckin. "The International Diffusion of the Watt Engine, 1775–1825." *Economic History Review* 31 (1978): 541–64.

WEDGWOOD, JOSIAH   English industrialist Josiah Wedgwood pioneered techniques in making pottery, in marketing his wares, and in using his political connections to gain state support for his enterprise and for his industry. Wedgwood was a new model entrepreneur who combined technological expertise, managerial proficiency, and political acumen. During the Industrial Revolution, successful entrepreneurship, especially in fields just starting to undergo transformation, required this kind of varied skill set.

Wedgwood (1730–1795) was from a family of potters in Staffordshire. At the age of nine, he went to work for his brother in the family business and later served as his apprentice. When his brother refused to make him a partner, Wedgwood left to work for others. By 1759, he opened his own pottery works where he not only made the models and prepared the clay mixes but also ran the business. Wedgwood opened a new factory named Etruria in 1769 near Stoke-on-Trent with partner Thomas Bentley.

At first, Wedgwood specialized in simple, durable, everyday earthenware. His hearty cream-colored line was dubbed Queen's ware after Queen Charlotte, who named him "Queen's potter." Wedgwood searched constantly for product innovation to combat competition from the quality porcelain of Asia and the royal Sèvres works in France. Declining sales of creamware led him to experiment with barium sulphate from which he produced distinctive green jasperware in 1773. This porcelain featured separately molded reliefs, usually in white. The use of other color schemes like black on red to imitate Greek vases required numerous trials and reliable kilns. As part of the experiments, Wedgwood invented a pyrometer to correctly measure kiln temperature. These experiments helped bring Wedgwood's scientific accomplishments to others: he joined several scientific groups including the Society of Arts to publicize his work. Other decorative themes taken from ancient Roman and Egyptian art made Wedgwood's goods into pieces of art: his pottery went far beyond being just useful objects. But he also produced table china with whatever fad of the day seemed likely to sell.

Wedgwood was also an innovator in factory organization, marketing, and politics. He built a village for his workforce to live in. The village provided decent housing, but ownership of their housing gave Wedgwood enormous control over his workers' lives and those of their families. Machines were introduced to replace the potter's wheel, but it was by increasing the division of labor and in imposing a thoroughgoing industrial discipline that Wedgwood developed cost and quality advantages. In exchange for relatively high wages, he sought to "make such machines of the Men as cannot err," a strategy that helped to transform Staffordshire from a poor region of artisanal enterprises into a rich manufacturing district.

To gain prestige and win customers, Wedgwood wooed royalty all over Europe. He sent expensive masterpieces both to them and to British ambassadors in their capitals, all prominently featuring his trademark. Beyond his hopes for patronage, he figured that elites set the fashion for luxury goods and influenced taste. Then he sold imitations to the masses in Europe and North America at double the prices charged by his competitors. Another means of catching the public's eye was by establishing a luxurious showroom first in London, then in other cities where the wealthy congregated. Traveling salesmen, another innovation for a manufacturer of luxury goods, blanketed England, the Continent, the British Empire, and the United States. His motto was "Fashion is infinitely superior to merit."

Finally, Wedgwood gathered together like-minded manufacturers to lobby the government for effective protection from foreign competition. A General Chamber of Manufacturers (1785–1787), of which Wedgwood was the most influential member, shaped a trade agreement in 1785 that subordinated Irish industry to England's and then successfully pressured the government to reopen negotiations for even more favorable terms for British manufactures in a commercial treaty signed with France the following year. At his death, Wedgwood left a prodigious fortune of £500,000. His sons and nephew took over the business, and Wedgwood products are still sold all over the globe. Wedgwood was one of the first industrial pioneers to create an enduring brand through relentless control over labor, constant innovation, and persistent political influence.

See also: Colonialism; Consumer Revolution; Discipline; Division of Labor; Education; Factory System; Patent(s); Productivity; Role of the State; Royal Society of Arts; Tariffs and Excise Taxes

Further Reading

Dolan, Brian. *Wedgwood: The First Tycoon*. New York: Viking, 2004.
"Josiah Wedgwood." Available online at http://www.thepotteries.org/potters/wedg wood.htm.
"Josiah Wedgwood (1730–1795): The Industrialist." Available online at http://aboli tion.e2bn.org/people_33.html.
"Lives of the Wedgwoods: Josiah Wedgwood I." Available online at http://www .wedgwoodmuseum.org.uk/learning/discovery_packs/pack/lives-of-the-wedg woods/chapter/josiah-wedgwood-i-1730–95.
McKendrick, Neil, John Brewer, and J. H. Plumb. *The Birth of a Consumer Society: The Commercialization of Eighteenth-Century England*. Bloomington: Indiana University Press, 1982.

WHITNEY, ELI   Eli Whitney was an American inventor and manufacturer whose contributions transformed the U.S. economy, both in the short and the long run. Whitney invented the cotton gin, which enabled short-staple, green-seed cotton produced with slave labor to spread throughout the Southern states. In the United States, he is usually given credit (incorrectly) for elaborating how mass production of metal goods could be based on interchangeable parts. Whitney's long career also demonstrated the vital role of the state in entrepreneurial success or failure.

Eli Whitney was born in Westboro, Massachusetts, in 1765 and died in 1825. His father was a well-to-do farmer who did not support his son's decision to go to Yale College to become a teacher. After graduation in 1792, he went to Georgia where he recognized the need for a machine to get rid of seeds and clean dirt from raw green-seed cotton. His simple machine or "gin" invented in 1793 yielded cotton ready to start the manufacturing process. Whitney patented his machine the following year and went into business with another Yale graduate named Phineas Miller to make his gins.

The new partnership was frustrated because Southern planters preferred to pirate the machine rather than pay the fees owed to Whitney and Miller. The partners brought numerous lawsuits (always in Southern states) against planters for patent infringement, always unsuccessfully. The business went bankrupt in 1797 and might have deterred Whitney from further entrepreneurship.

The decision of several states, led by South Carolina in 1801 but including North Carolina and Tennessee, to pay Whitney something for his invention, saved him. The partners were paid considerable sums, almost all of which went to settle their legal expenses and debts. Only two years later, the states repudiated their arrangements and sued for the recovery of their money. Whitney had to apply—successfully—to Congress for protection in 1804.

A major reason for congressional support is that Whitney had moved on to a new project. In 1798, he contracted with the War Department to manufacture 10,000 muskets at $13.40 each for the U.S. Army to be delivered by September 1800. The War Department needed Whitney because the two national armories could not furnish the military's needs in timely fashion. Whitney was no better: it took him until January 1809 to fulfill his contract.

The means by which Whitney undertook to manufacture the weapons proved to be critical. This choice enabled him to keep his government contracts and patronage. Instead of having a skilled worker make and assemble each part or each weapon, Whitney strove to manufacture a set of uniform or interchangeable parts that would fit any musket. Based on French examples, Whitney invented a series of purpose-built machines, most notably a milling machine that enabled unskilled laborers to make many key parts with a high level of precision by following a template. In combination with armory practice, Whitney's approach marked the beginning of what came to be known as the American System of Production. Although Whitney's muskets cost far more than the weapons made by the national armories and he never achieved complete interchangeability, he received a second order for 15,000 muskets in 1811 and fulfilled the contract in two years.

Whitney's career demonstrates that the federal government was unable to fulfill its legal obligations to patent holders, but was willing to invest in technological advances. His experience also highlights the vital role of defense spending in supporting key infant industries. In the first few decades of the

19th century, other gunsmiths achieved Whitney's goal and the principle of uniformity with interchangeability as a target was implemented in the manufacture of clocks, locks, furniture, and hardware. This advance helped to transform the economy of the Northeast as much as the cotton gin changed the South.

See also: American System of Manufactures; Armory Practice; Consumer Revolution; Cotton; Division of Labor; Factory System; Interchangeable Parts; Patent(s); Productivity; Role of the State; Tariffs and Excise Taxes; Workforce

Further Reading

"Eli Whitney: The Inventor." Available online at http://www.eliwhitney.org/7 /museum/about-eli-whitney/inventor.

Hounshell, David A. *From the American System to Mass Production, 1800–1932: The Development of Manufacturing Technology in the United States.* Baltimore: Johns Hopkins University Press, 1984.

Phillips, William H. "Cotton Gin." Available online at https://eh.net/encyclopedia /cotton-gin/.

Thomson, Ross. *Structures of Change in the Mechanical Age: Technological Innovation in the United States, 1790–1865.* Baltimore: Johns Hopkins University Press, 2009.

WORKFORCE   The men, women, and children who "made" the Industrial Revolution, particularly during the first decades of industrialization, rarely had much choice in the matter. Factory and mine labor was backbreaking, exhausting, unhealthy, and required a type of work discipline that did not come easy to those accustomed to agricultural labor. Owners, managers, and foremen deployed a variety of methods to "break" the workforce. Getting people to work as long, as hard, when, and where they wished were the keys to efficiency. Labor productivity—achieved in part through mechanization and the substitution of water and steam for human and animal power, but also by imposing discipline on the workforce—was the key to earning the profits that drove entrepreneurs to initiate an industrial revolution. As their standard of living demonstrated concretely, the workforce enjoyed few if any benefits during the first several generations of industrialization.

A vital part of the process of industrialization was the substitution of women and children for more expensive (and more truculent) male labor. Women and children were always paid less to perform the same tasks. The use of machines was generally reserved for a small cadre of skilled male laborers because it was claimed that the devices required greater physical strength to use—this assertion was only partly true—while the bulk of other tasks benefitted from the more dexterous fingers of women and children. In economic terms, this exchange deskilled the labor force and permitted a thoroughgoing substitution of capital for labor.

Women and children were the bulk of the labor force in the cotton textile sector during the first century of industrialization. A British survey undertaken in 1818 found that adult women comprised a little over half the workers in cotton textiles with children representing another third. In Scotland, the reliance on women and girls was even greater. Female labor, overwhelmingly women under 30, especially teenagers, made up over 60 percent of the cotton workers in Glasgow and approached 70 percent in work sites situated outside urban areas. The labor of women made the cotton textile industry productive and profitable.

Children labored at least as much as women. In 1851, a British commission found that one-third of children over 10 and under the age of 15 worked outside the home. This figure drastically underrepresented the number of children in the work force because it did not count those employed in domestic industry or agriculture. At least half and usually a far higher percentage of nominally school-age children worked full time during the age of the Industrial Revolution.

Nor was the labor of children voluntary. Parents could legally commit their children to work. This was not just the standard use of juveniles to perform domestic chores or to help their parents. Destitute English parents sent their children up to the age of 21 out to work for the parish in exchange for financial support. A parent could also apprentice their child for seven years to a master or entrepreneur. In neither case could the child leave or do anything about their working conditions. From the age of four or five, children worked the same 12–14 hour shifts as adults; they suffered disproportionately from frequently unhealthy and dangerous working conditions.

The conditions for many children indentured to the parish who were involved in industry and mining strongly resembled the indentured adult laborers sent out to the colonies to labor for a fixed number of years in exchange for their passage. Children could be dispatched more than 200 miles away from their families, isolating them completely. Only in 1816 did Parliament impose a 40-mile limit. Other attempts were made to improve the lives of children, but the first measure to have any real effect was the Factory Act of 1833 (passed, not coincidently, the same year that Britain prohibited slavery). This measure outlawed work for children under the age of 9 and limited it for children aged 9–13 to 8 hours per day. Night work was forbidden. The measure also restricted children aged 14–18 to working a mere 12 hours a day. Thus, until the closing decades of the Industrial Revolution, children could be and were exploited in huge numbers.

The deliberate and systematic substitution of the labor of women and children represented a considerable savings. In the mid-19th century, in the capital of the British cotton industry—the city of Manchester—the highest paid female factory worker made a quarter of what the highest paid male laborer earned. The lowest paid male worker made 13–15 shillings a week while the highest paid female workers earned 7–11 shillings. These wages were perhaps 20 percent higher than nonfactory wages; they had to be significantly higher to convince skilled or free labor to accept the harsh discipline and unpleasant working conditions of the factories.

Children earned far less. Apprentices and parish appointees worked mostly for room, board, and a mostly hypothetical training in the techniques appropriate to the industry. At best, they made one-sixth to one-eighth the wages of an adult worker and suffered not just "the slings and arrows of outrageous fortune," but from the straps, whips, and fists of their overseers.

Managers sought to make their workers as reliable as the machines they tended. The reaction of workers to industrial discipline varied widely. A large number of laborers accepted their new situations and made the best of it. Workers tried to innovate or get ahead in some way and to use the system to their advantage. Others went along grudgingly, often because they had no other alternative, but they tolerated their situation. A significant proportion, however, felt they were being taken advantage of and resisted the labor demands of the Industrial Revolution, at least to some degree. For many British workers, resistance took the form of emigration, often to the United States or the empire. For others, the traditional labor tactics of coalition and combination, slowdown, and strike were used to oppose workplace innovation or to preserve customary practices. In some trades, in some times, and in some places, these tactics had considerable success, at least in the short term. Other laborers turned to more "modern" forms of resistance and complaint such as politics and/or unions.

Workers justifiably resented many aspects of the process of industrialization. Entrepreneurs and labor forces always have certain areas of conflict, but the emergence of a hierarchical and centralized system of management responsible for the production, distribution, and sale of manufactured goods was especially frustrating for the workforce. The increasing complexity of the economic system, the growing division of labor, and the spread of the tentacles of the new economy around the world all combined to alienate the people who actually made the goods from economic decision making. The working classes lost any true control over or even influence within the production process.

Management's habit of firing recalcitrant workers and the enormous numbers of jobs made redundant by mechanization also angered the laboring classes. The argument that the total number of industrial jobs was increasing was accurate, but as the shifting sex and age breakdown of factory workers demonstrates, those who got the new jobs were not the same people who were being laid off. Technological and managerial obsolescence combined to render whole segments of the working class without a means of earning a living and enabled elites to lower wages with relative impunity.

The imposition of industrial discipline was also a major bone of contention between masters and men. The elimination of holidays, the increasing length of the work day and work week, and following the dictates of the clock were innovations that impinged on the free time, independence, and habits of a huge proportion of the population. In some sectors, the institution of payment by output but with regularly increased quotas, rather than payment by the hour, was also detested. Workers believed that this form of remuneration destroyed their control over workplace rhythms and ignored the differences in energy and outlook that stem from the passage of the seasons. Nor did workers like the recourse to corporal punishment, especially against women and children. The fact that employers also attempted to destroy or prevent any attempt at labor organization to redress grievances also irked workers, who believed rightly that their customary rights and traditional protections were being trampled on.

In England, traditional safeguards against lowering wages too far had existed for hundreds of years before the onset of industrialization. At the bidding of manufacturers, Parliament steadily abrogated such protections over the course of the 18th century. There was considerable discussion about whether to institute a minimum wage to guarantee the well-being of the workforce. But establishing a legal minimum wage or fixing some relationship between wage levels and the price of food were both rejected out of hand by the government as being too binding on manufacturers and potentially injurious to the national economy: the struggle against Revolutionary and then Napoleonic France was used to justify continued sacrifices by the working classes.

The workforce suffered dramatic declines in certain aspects of their standard of living during the Industrial Revolution that they attempted to make up for in other ways. As British workers adapted to the time-clock, new production methods, and the needs of the machine, entrepreneurs forged a greatly enhanced productivity to achieve an industrial revolution. The exploitation of the workforce generated tremendous profits, but had drastic long-term consequences. Karl Marx and Friedrich Engels based their analysis of the flaws of capitalism, in particular their argument that the profits of the current economic system came at the expense of enormous human suffering by the working classes, on first-hand observation of British conditions. All European societies in the 18th and 19th centuries faced the same social, political, and religious pressures for reform, but British entrepreneurs could rely on the state to support their efforts to convince and/or force the working classes to contribute their labor. The workforce did not benefit from the Industrial Revolution at all before 1830, and the bulk of improvements to their lives and lifestyles did not begin until 1850.

See also: American System of Manufactures; Coal; Colonialism; Cotton; Discipline; Division of Labor; Domestic Industry; Education; Enlightenment; Factory Acts; Factory System; "Industrious Revolution"; Lancashire; Luddites; Owen, Robert; Pollution, Health, and Environment; Productivity; Role of the State; Socialism; Standard of Living; Waltham System; Wedgwood, Josiah; Document: "Resisting Mechanization: The Luddites"; Document: "Living and Working in Manchester"; Document: "Robert Owen on Education and the Evils of Child Labor"; Document: "Conditions in the Mines"; Document: "Lowell Mill Girls"; Document: "The State of the Poor"; Document: "Defending the Factory System"

Further Reading

Burnette, Joyce. "Women Workers in the British Industrial Revolution." Available online at https://eh.net/encyclopedia/women-workers-in-the-british-industrial -revolution-2/.

Griffin, Emma. *A Short History of the British Industrial Revolution.* Houndsmills, UK: Palgrave, 2010.

Rule, John. *The Labouring Classes in Early Industrial England, 1750–1850.* London: Routledge, 1986.

Thompson, E. P. *The Making of the English Working Class.* London: Vintage, 1966 1963).

Tuttle, Carolyn. "Child Labor during the British Industrial Revolution." Available online at https://eh.net/encyclopedia/child-labor-during-the-british-industrial -revolution/.

Primary Documents

CHILD ON INTEREST, TRADE, AND MONEY

Josiah Child (1630–1699) was an English merchant, economic writer, and government official whose ideas, particularly those in Brief Observations Concerning Trade and Interest of Money *(1668) powerfully influenced British mercantilism, monetary policy, and colonial policy. After making a fortune as a military supplier, Child became involved in the East India Company, becoming its elected governor. He received a baronetcy for his efforts.*

. . . The Profit That People [the Dutch] have received, and any other may receive, by reducing the Interest of Money to a very Low Rate.

This in my poor opinion, is the CAUSA CAUSANS of all the other causes of the Riches of that people; and that if Interest of Money were with us reduced to the same rate it is with them, it would in a short time render us as Rich and Considerable in Trade as they are now, and consequently be of greater dammage to them, and advantage to us, then can happen by the Issue of this present War, though the success of it should be as good as we can wish, except it end in their Total Ruine and Extripation.

To illustrate this, let us impartially search our Books, and enquire what the State and condition of this Kingdom was, as to Trade and Riches, before any Law concerning Interest of Money was made. The first whereof that I can find, was Ann 1545, and we shall be Informed that the Trade of England then was Inconsiderable, and the Merchants very mean and few: And that afterwards, viz, Anno. 1635 with ten Years after Interest was brought down to eight per cent there was more Merchants to be found upon the Exchange worth each One thousand Pounds and upwards, then were in the former dayes, viz. before the year 1600 to be found worth One hundred Pounds each.

And since Interest hath been for about twenty Years at six per cent notwithstanding our long civil Wars, and the great complaints of the deadness of Trade, there are more men to be found upon the Exchange now worth Ten thousand pounds Estates, then were then of One thousand pounds. . . .

If we look into the Countrey, we shall find Lands as much Improved since the abatement of Interest, as Trade, etc. in Cities; that now yeelding twenty Years purchase, which then would not have sold for above eight or ten at most. . . .

More might be said, but the Premises being considered, I judge will sufficiently demonstrate how greatly this Kingdom of England hath been advanc't in all respects for these last fifty years: And that the abatement of Interest hath been the cause thereof, to me seems most probable; because as it appears it hath been in England, so I find it is at this day in all Europe, and other parts of the World: Insomuch that to know whether any Country be rich or poor, or in what proportion it is so, no other question needs to be resolved, but this, viz. What Interest do they pay for Money? Neer home we see it evidently, in Scotland and Ireland, where ten and twelve per cent is paid for Interest, the people are poor and despicable, their Persons ill cloathed, their Houses worse provided, and Money intollerably scarce, notwithstanding they have great plenty of all provisions, nor will their Land yield above eight or ten years purchase at most.

In France where Money is at seven per cent, their Lands will yield about eighteen years purchase; and the Gentry who may possess Lands, live in good condition, though the Peazants are little better then Slaves, because they can possess nothing but at the will of others.

In Italy Money will not yield above three per cent to be let out upon real security; there the people are rich, full of Trade, well attired, and their Lands will sell at thirty five to fourty years purchase, and that it is so, or better, with them in Holland, is too manifest. . . .

Now if upon what hath been said, it be granted that de facto, this Kingdom be richer at least four-fold (I might say eight fold) then it was before any Law for Interest was made, and that all Countries are at this day richer or poorer in an exact proportion to what they pay, and have usually paid for the Interest of Money; it remains that we enquire carefully, whither the abatement of Interest be in truth the Cause of the Riches of any Country, or only the Concomitant or Effect of the Riches of a Country; in which seems to lie the Intricacy of this Question.

To satisfie myself wherein, I have taken all opportunities to discourse this point, with the most Ingenious men I had the Honour to be known to, and have search't for, and read all the Books that I could ever hear were printed against the Abatement of Interest, and seriously considered all the Arguments and Objections used by them against it: All which offer to the consideration of wiser Heads, viz. THAT THE ABATEMENT OF INTEREST IS THE CAUSE OF THE PROSPERITY AND RICHES OF ANY NATION, and that the bringing down of Interest in this Kingdome, from six to four, or three per cent will necessarily, in less than twenty Years time, double the Capital Stock of the Nation. . . .

Source: Josiah Child, *Brief Observations Concerning Trade and Interest of Money*. London: Elizabeth Calvert, 1668. Modeled on http://avalon.law.yale.edu/17th_century/trade.asp.

THE STATE OF THE POOR

Frederick Morton Eden (1766–1809) was a British nobleman who became an important figure in the insurance industry. However, his chief claim to fame was a compilation of information about the life of the poor during the Age of Revolution. He did some fieldwork, but he obtained most of the data from correspondence with clergymen and by sending out investigators with specially designed questionnaires. The results demonstrate some of the realities of the working-class experience and some of the fallacies of elite perceptions concerning the lives of laborers.

I most sincerely agree with those who regret that the labourer does not get more for his shilling than is usually the case; the misfortune, however, does not arise from (what is so often most unjustly reprobated) his being obliged to purchase the few articles he has occasion for, from petty retail shops, but because either through ignorance, custom or prejudice, he adheres to ancient improvident systems in dress, diet, and in other branches of private expenditure. . . . Instead of the ill-grounded complaints, which have so often been reiterated by writers on the Poor, that the wages of industry are in general too inadequate to provide the labourers with those comforts and conveniences which are befitting his station in the community, they would better serve the cause of the industrious peasant and manufacturer by pointing out the best means of reducing their expenses, without diminishing their comforts.

There seems to be just reason to conclude that the miseries of the labouring Poor arose, less from the scantiness of their income (however much the philanthropist might wish it to be increased) than from their own improvidence and unthriftiness; since it is the fact, and I trust will be demonstrated in a subsequent part of this work, that in many parts of the kingdom, where the earnings of industry are moderate, the condition of the labourers is more comfortable than in other districts where wages are exorbitant. . . .

It must be confessed that the difficulty of introducing any species of food which requires much culinary preparation into the South of England arises in a great measure from the scarcity and high price of fuel. It is owing to this cause that even the labourer's dinner, of hot meat on a Sunday, is generally dressed at the baker's, and that his meals during the rest of the week consist almost wholly of bread purchased from the same quarter.

In the Midland and Southern counties, the labourer in general purchases a very considerable portion, if not the whole of his clothes from the shop-keeper. In the vicinity of the metropolis, working people seldom buy new clothes; they content themselves with a cast-off coat, which may be usually purchased for about 5s., and second-hand waistcoats and breeches. Their wives seldom make up any article of dress, except making and mending clothes for the children. In the North, on the contrary, almost every article of dress worn by farmers, mechanics and labourers, is manufactured at home, shoes and hats excepted—that is, the linen thread is spun from the lint, and the yarn from the wool, and sent to the weavers and dyers, so that almost every family has its web of linen cloth annually, and often of woolens also, which is either dyed for coats or made into flannel etc. Sometimes black and white wool are mixed, and the cloth which is made from them receives no dye; it is provincially called *kelt*. There are, however, many labourers so poor that they cannot even afford to purchase the raw material necessary to spin thread or yarn at home, as it is some time before a home manufacture can be rendered fit for use. It is generally acknowledged that articles of clothing can be purchased in the shops at a much lower price than those who made them at home can afford to sell them for, but that in the wearing those manufactured by private families are very superior both in warmth and durability.

Source: Frederick Morton Eden, *The State of the Poor: or A History of the Labouring Classes in England, from the Conquest to the Present Period*, 3 vols. London: J. Davis, 1797, II: 491–92, 495, 547, 554–55.

LOWELL MILL GIRLS

Harriet J. Hanson Robinson (1825–1911) worked in the textile mills of Lowell, Massachusetts, for 14 years from the age of 10. In her autobiography, Loom and Spindle *(1898), she described her life and involvement in the strike of 1836. Robinson became deeply involved in the women's suffrage movement and later emerged as an important writer.*

In what follows, I shall confine myself to a description of factory life in Lowell, Massachusetts, from 1832 to 1848, since, with that phase of Early Factory Labor in New England, I am the most familiar—because I was a part of it.

In 1832, Lowell was little more than a factory village. Five "corporations" were started, and the cotton mills belonging to them were building. Help was in great demand and stories were told all over the country of the new factory place, and the high wages that were offered to all classes of workpeople; stories that reached the ears of mechanics' and farmers' sons and gave new life to lonely and dependent women in distant towns and farmhouses. . . . Troops of young girls came from different parts of New England, and from Canada, and men were employed to collect them at so much a head, and deliver them at the factories. . . .

At the time the Lowell cotton mills were started the caste of the factory girl was the lowest among the employments of women. In England and in France, particularly, great injustice had been done to her real character. She was represented as subjected to influences that must destroy her purity and self-respect. In the eyes of her overseer she was but a brute, a slave, to be beaten, pinched and pushed about. It was to overcome this prejudice that such high wages had been offered to women that they might be induced to become mill-girls, in spite of the opprobrium that still clung to this degrading occupation. . . .

The early mill-girls were of different ages. Some were not over ten years old; a few were in middle life, but the majority were between the ages of sixteen and twenty-five. The very young girls were called "doffers." They "doffed," or took off, the full bobbins from the spinning frames, and replaced them with empty ones. These mites worked about fifteen minutes every hour and the rest of the time was their own. When the overseer was kind they were allowed to read, knit, or go outside the mill-yard to play. They were paid two dollars a week. The working hours of all the girls extended from five o'clock in the morning until seven in the evening, with one half-hour each, for breakfast and dinner. Even the doffers were forced to be on duty nearly fourteen hours a day. This was the greatest hardship in the lives of these children. Several years later a ten-hour law was passed, but not until long after some of these little doffers were old enough to appear before the legislative committee on the subject, and plead, by their presence, for a reduction of the hours of labor.

Those of the mill-girls who had homes generally worked from eight to ten months in the year; the rest of the time was spent with parents or friends. A few taught school during the summer months. Their life in the factory was made pleasant to them. In those days there was no need of advocating the doctrine of the proper relation between employer and employed. *Help was too valuable to be ill-treated.* . . .

The most prevailing incentive to labor was to secure the means of education for some *male* member of the family. To make a *gentleman* of a brother or a son, to give him a college education, was the dominant thought in the minds of a great many of the better class of mill-girls. I have known more than one to give every cent of her wages, month after month, to her brother, that he might get the education necessary to enter some profession. I have known a mother to work years in this way for her boy. I have known women to educate young men by their earnings, who were not sons or relatives. There are many men now living who were helped to an education by the wages of the early mill-girls.

It is well to digress here a little, and speak of the influence the possession of money had on the characters of some of these women. We can hardly realize what a change the cotton factory made in the status of the working women. Hitherto a woman had always been a money *saving* rather than a money earning, member of the community. Her labor could command but small return. If she worked out as servant, or "help," her wages were from 50 cents to $1 .00 a week; or, if she went from house to house by the day to spin and weave, or do tailoress work, she could get but 75 cents a week and her meals. As teacher, her services were not in demand, and the arts, the professions, and even the trades and industries, were nearly all closed to her.

As late as 1840 there were only seven vocations outside the home into which the women of New England had entered. At this time woman had no property rights. A widow could be left without her share of her husband's (or the family) property, an " incumbrance" to his estate. A father could make his will without reference to his daughter's share of the inheritance. He usually left her a home on the farm as long as she remained single. A woman was not supposed to be capable of spending her own, or of using other people's money. In Massachusetts, before 1840, a woman could not, legally, be treasurer of her own sewing society, unless some man were responsible for her. The law took no cognizance of woman as a money-spender. She was a ward, an appendage, a relict. Thus it happened that if a woman did not choose to marry, or, when left a widow, to remarry, she had no choice but to enter one of the few employments open to her, or to become a burden on the charity of some relative. . . .

One of the first strikes that ever took place in this country was in Lowell in 1836. When it was announced that the wages were to be cut down, great indignation was felt, and it was decided to strike or "turn out" en masse. This was done. The mills were shut down, and the girls went from their several corporations in procession to the grove on Chapel Hill, and listened to incendiary speeches from some early labor reformers.

One of the girls stood on a pump and gave vent to the feelings of her companions in a neat speech, declaring that it was their duty to resist all attempts at cutting down the wages. This was the first time a woman had spoken in public in Lowell, and the event caused surprise and consternation among her audience.

It is hardly necessary to say that, so far as practical results are concerned, this strike did no good. The corporation would not come to terms. The girls were soon tired of holding out, and they went back to their work at the reduced rate of wages. The ill-success of this early attempt at resistance on the part of the wage element seems to have made a precedent for the issue of many succeeding strikes.

Source: Harriet H. Robinson, "Early Factory Labor in New England." In Massachusetts Bureau of Statistics of Labor, *Fourteenth Annual Report*. Boston: Wright & Potter, 1883, 380–82, 387–88, 391–92.

CONDITIONS IN THE MINES

Improved conditions in Britain's mines came, in large measure, through the efforts of the Children's Employment Commission (Mines) Report released in 1842 and published in the parliamentary record the following year. Undertaken by a royal commission of inquiry headed by Lord Anthony Ashley-Cooper, seventh Earl of Shaftesbury, the report followed up on earlier efforts at factory reform and led directly to the Mines and Collieries Act of 1842 that placed serious and enforceable limits on the employment of women and children in the mines of the United Kingdom.

From the whole of the evidence which has been collected under the present Commission . . . relative to the EMPLOYMENT and the PHYSICAL CONDITION of the Children and Young Persons . . . who are engaged in Trade and Manufactures, we find:

1. That instances occur in which children begin to work as early as three and four years of age; not infrequently at five, and between five and six; while, in general, regular employment commences between seven and eight; the great majority of the children having begun to work before they are nine years old . . .

2. That in all cases the persons that employ mere Infants and the very youngest children are the parents themselves, who put their children to work at some processes of manufacture under their own eye, in their own houses; but children begin to work together in numbers, in larger or smaller manufactories, at all ages, from five years old and upwards . . .

4. That in a very large proportion of these Trades and Manufactures female children are employed equally with boys, and at the same tender ages: in some indeed the number of girls exceeds that of boys. . . .

6. That in the great majority of the Trades and Manufactures the youngest children as well as the young persons are hired and paid by the workmen, and are entirely under their control; the employers exercising no sort of superintendence over them, and apparently knowing nothing whatever about them. . . .

9. That in some Trades, those especially requiring skilled workmen, . . . apprentices are bound by legal indentures, usually at the age of fourteen, and for a term of seven years, the age being rarely younger . . . but by far the greater number are bound without any prescribed legal forms, and in almost all these cases they are required to serve their masters, at whatever age they may commence their apprenticeship, until they attain the age of twenty-one, in some instances in employment in which there is nothing deserving the name of skill to be acquired, and in other instances in employment in which they are taught to make only one particular part of the article manufactured; so that at the end of their servitude they are altogether unable to make any one article of their trade in a complete state.

10. That a large proportion of these apprentices consist of orphans, or are the children of widows, or belong to the very poorest families, and frequently are apprenticed by boards of guardians [i.e., officials regulating poor relief].

11. That the term of servitude of these apprentices may, and sometimes does commence as early as seven years of age, and is often passed under circumstances of great hardship and ill-usage, and under the condition that, during the greater part, if not the whole, of their term, they receive nothing for their labor beyond food and clothing. . . .

17. That in all the districts the privies are very commonly in a disgusting state of filth, and in great numbers of instances there is no separate accommodation for the males and females; but in almost all the buildings recently constructed a greater attention has been paid to the health and the decent comfort of the workpeople than in those of older date. . . .

19. That in some few instances the regular hours of work do not exceed ten, exclusive of the time allowed for meals; sometimes they are eleven, but more commonly twelve; and in great numbers of instances the employment is continued for fifteen, sixteen, and even eighteen hours consecutively.

20. That in almost every instance the children work as long as the adults; being sometimes kept at work sixteen, and even eighteen hours without any intermission.

21. That in the case of young women employed in the millinery and dress making business in the metropolis, and in some of the large provincial cities, even in what are considered the best regulated establishments, during the busy season, occupying in London about four months in the year, the regular hours of work are fifteen; but on emergencies, which frequently recur, these hours are extended to eighteen; and in many establishments the hours of

work during the season are unlimited, the young women never getting more than six, often not more than four, sometimes only three, and occasionally not, more than two hours for rest and sleep out of the twenty-four, and very frequently they work all night; there being in fact no other limit to the duration of their labor than their physical inability to work longer. . . .

23. That in some processes of Manufacture, as in winding for lace machines, the children have no regular and certain time whatever for sleep or recreation, being liable to be called upon at any period during sixteen, twenty, or twenty-two hours out of the twenty-four, while they have frequently to go from one place of work to another, often at considerable distances, at all hours of the night, and in all seasons. . . .

27. That in the cases in which the children are the servants of the workmen, and under their sole control, the master apparently knowing nothing about their treatment, and certainly taking no charge of it, they are almost always roughly, very often harshly, and sometimes cruelly used; . . . the treatment of them is oppressive and brutal to the last degree. . . .

29. . . . that accidents—such as hands contused, fingers cut off, jammed between wheel- cogs, or drawn in between rollers, and arms caught in straps— are, however, in some establishments, by no means uncommon; that sometimes the straps, wheels, etc., are so crowded and exposed that the utmost care is required on the part of the workpeople to escape injury; and that, in by far the greater number of instances, accidents might be prevented, if proper attention were paid to the disposition and fencing of the machinery. . . .

31. . . . that, from the early ages at which the great majority [of children] commence work, from their long hours of work, and from the insufficiency of their food and clothing, their "bodily health " is seriously and generally injured; they are for the most part stunted in growth, their aspect being pale, delicate, and sickly, and they present altogether the appearance of a race which has suffered general physical deterioration.

32. That the diseases which are most prevalent amongst them, and to which they are more subject than children of their age and station unemployed in labor, are disordered states of the nutritive organs, curvature and distortion of the spine, deformity of the limbs, and diseases of the lungs, ending in atrophy and consumption. . . .

From the whole of the evidence collected under the present Commission relative to the MORAL CONDITION of the Children and Young Persons included within its terms, whether employed In COLLIERIES and Mines or in TRADES and MANUFACTURES, we find:

1. That there are few classes of these children and young persons "working together in numbers," of whom a large portion are not in a lamentably low moral condition.

2. That this low moral condition is evinced by a general ignorance of moral duties and sanctions, and by an absence of moral and religious restraint, shown among some classes chiefly by coarseness of manners, and the use of profane and indecent language; but in other classes by the practice of gross immorality, which is prevalent to a great extent, in both sexes, at very early ages.

3. . . . their low moral condition . . . often having its very origin in the degradation of the parents, who, themselves brought up without virtuous habit, can set no good example to their children, nor have any beneficial control over their conduct.

4. That the parents, urged by poverty or improvidence, generally seek employment for the children as soon as they can earn the lowest amount of wages; paying but little regard to the probable injury of their children's health by early labor, and still less regard to the certain injury of their minds by early removal from school . . .

5. That the girls are prevented, by their early removal from home and from the day-schools, to be employed in labor, from learning needlework, and from acquiring those habits of cleanliness, neatness, and order, without which they cannot, when they grow up to womanhood, and have the charge of families of their own, economize their husbands' earnings, or give to their homes any degree of comfort; and this general want of the qualifications of a housewife in the women of this class is stated by clergymen, teachers, medical men, employers, and other witnesses, to be one great and universally-prevailing cause of distress and crime among the working classes. . . .

7. . . . the children and young persons generally, of both sexes, not only work together in the same room, but being often in closer proximity to each other than they are in the factories of cotton, wool, silk, and flax; and all classes of witnesses concur in attributing to this circumstance a highly demoralizing influence. . . .

12. That the means of secular and religious instruction, on the efficiency of which depends the counteraction of all these evil tendencies, are so grievously defective, that, in all the districts, great numbers of children and young persons are growing up without any religious, moral, or intellectual training; nothing being done to form them to habits of order, sobriety, honesty, and forethought, or even to restrain them from vice and crime.

13. That neither in the new Colliery and Mining towns which have suddenly collected together large bodies of the people in new localities, nor in the towns which have suddenly sprung up under the successful pursuit of some new branch of Trade and Manufacture, is any provision made for Education by the establishment of Schools with properly qualified teachers . . . ; nor in general is there any provision whatever for the extension of educational and religious institutions corresponding with the extension of the population.

14. That there is not a single district in which the means of instruction are adequate to the wants of the people, while in some districts the deficiency is so great that clergymen, and other witnesses, state that the schools actually in existence are insufficient for the education of one- third of the population.

15. That, were schools ever so abundant and excellent, they would be wholly beyond the reach of a large portion of the children employed in labor, on account of the early ages at which they are put to work.

16. That great numbers of children and young persons attend no day-school before they commence work; that even those who do go for a brief period to a day-school are very commonly removed to be put to labor at five, six, seven, and eight years old; and that the instances are extremely rare in which they attend an evening-school after regular employment has once begun. . . .

18. That, in all the districts, many children and young persons, whether employed in the mines of coal and iron, or in trades and manufactures, never go to any school, and some never have been at any school. . . .

23. That in all the districts, great numbers of those children who, had been in regular attendance in Sunday-schools for a period of from five to nine years, were found, on examination, to be incapable of reading an easy book, or of spelling the commonest word; and they were not only altogether ignorant of Christian principles, doctrines, and precepts, but they knew nothing whatever of any of the events of Scripture history, nor anything even of the names most commonly occurring in the Scriptures. . . .

32. That there are parents who not only anxiously endeavor to afford their children, even at the expense of some personal sacrifice and self-denial, good and sufficient food and clothing, but also the best education within their reach, and who themselves superintend, as well as they are able, their children's education and conduct; but this attention to their moral condition is rare. . . .

35. That from the whole body of evidence it appears, however, that there are at present in existence no means adequate to effect any material and general improvement in the Physical and Moral Condition of the Children and Young Persons employed in labor.

. . . It was no part of the duty prescribed to us by the terms of Your Majesty's Commission to suggest remedies for any grievances or evils which we might find to exist, because it was deemed necessary to obtain the fullest information as to the real condition of the persons included in the inquiry, before the consideration of remedies could be entertained with any prospect of advantage. This information we have now collected; and the picture which, in the faithful performance of this duty, we have been obliged to present of the physical and moral condition of a large portion of the working classes appears to us to require the serious consideration of Your Majesty's Government and of the Legislature.

. . . Westminster, January 30th, 1843.

Source: *British Parliamentary Papers*, 1843, vol. 13, #430. Children's Employment Commission, 195–220.

DEFENDING THE FACTORY SYSTEM

Andrew Ure (1778–1857) publicly advocated maintaining the existing factory system in opposition to any attempt to improve conditions through legislation. Born in Scotland, Ure became a medical doctor and chemist. His standing as a professor and public intellectual of international renown (he was also a Fellow of the Royal Society) made him effective in opposing reform. On behalf of industrial interests, he visited several model English textile mills in 1834. His conclusion that reformers exaggerated the mistreatment of workers was published in The Philosophy of Manufactures *the following year.*

When the wandering savage becomes a citizen, he renounces many of his dangerous pleasures in return for tranquility and protection. He can no longer gratify at his will a revengeful spirit upon his foes, nor seize with violence a neighbour's possessions. In like manner, when the handicraftsman exchanges hard work with fluctuating employment and pay, for continuous labour of a lighter kind with steady wages, he must necessarily renounce his old prerogative of stopping when he pleases, because he would thereby throw the whole establishment into disorder. Of the amount of the injury resulting from the violation of tile rules of automatic labour he can hardly ever be a proper judge; just as mankind at large can never fully estimate the evils consequent upon an infraction of God's moral law. Yet the factory operative, little versant in the great operations of political economy, currency, and trade, and actuated too often by an invidious feeling towards the capitalist who animates his otherwise torpid talents, is easily persuaded by artful demagogues, that his sacrifice of time and skill is beyond the portion of his recompense, or that fewer hours of industry would be an ample equivalent for his wages. This notion seems to have taken an early and inveterate hold of the factory mind, and to have been riveted from time to time by the leaders of those secret combinations, so readily formed among a peculiar class of men, concentrated in masses within a narrow range of country.

Instead of repining as they have done at the prosperity of their employers, and concerting odious measures to blast it, they should, on every principle of gratitude and self-interest, have rejoiced at the success resulting from their labours, and by regularity and skill have recommended themselves to monied men desirous of engaging in a profitable concern, and of procuring qualified hands to conduct it. Thus good workmen would have advanced their condition to that of overlookers, managers, and partners in new mills, and have increased at the same time the demand for their companions' labour in the market. It is only by an undisturbed progression of this kind that the rate of wages can be permanently raised or upheld. Had it not been for the violent collisions and interruptions resulting from erroneous views among the operatives, the factory system would have been developed still more rapidly and beneficially for all concerned than it has been, and would have exhibited still more frequently gratifying examples of skillful workmen becoming opulent proprietors. Every misunderstanding either repels capital altogether, or diverts it from flowing, for a time, in the channels of a trade liable to strikes. . . .

No master would wish to have any wayward children to work within the walls of his factory, who do not mind their business without beating, and he therefore usually fines or turns away any spinners who are known to maltreat their assistants. Hence, ill usage of any kind is a very rare occurrence. I have visited many factories, both in Manchester and in the surrounding districts, during a period of several months, entering the spinning rooms, unexpectedly, and often alone, at different times of the day, and I never saw a single instance of corporal chastisement inflicted on a child, nor indeed did I ever see children in ill-humour. They seemed to be always cheerful and alert, taking pleasure in the light play of their muscles,—enjoying the mobility natural to their age. The scene of industry, so far from exciting sad emotions in my mind, was always exhilarating. It was delightful to observe the nimbleness with which they pieced the broken ends, as the mule carriage began to recede from the fixed roller-beam, and to see them at leisure, after a few seconds' exercise of their tiny fingers, to amuse themselves in any attitude they chose, till the stretch and winding-on were once more completed. The work of these lively elves seemed to resemble a sport, in which habit gave them a pleasing dexterity. Conscious of their skill, they were delighted to show it off to any stranger. As to exhaustion by the day's work, they evinced no trace of it on emerging from the mill in the evening; for they immediately began to skip about any neighbouring play-ground, and to commence their little amusements with the same alacrity as boys issuing from a school. It is moreover my firm conviction, that if children are not ill-used by bad parents or guardians, but receive in food and raiment the full benefit of what they earn, they would thrive better when employed in our modern factories, than if left at home in apartments too often ill-aired, damp, and cold.

Source: Andrew Ure, *The Philosophy of Manufactures or an Exposition of the Scientific, Moral, and Commercial Economy of the Factory System of Great Britain.* London: Charles Knight, 1835, 278–80, 300–301.

LIVING AND WORKING IN MANCHESTER

Friedrich Engels (1820–1895) was a Prussian-born manufacturer, journalist, political philosopher, and activist who spent much of his life in England. He published The Condition of the Working-Class in England *in 1845 based on first-hand observation of the lives of laborers in the slums of British cities. Already acquainted with Karl Marx, together they wrote* The Communist Manifesto *in 1848 to rally the working classes to the cause of revolution, which the conditions outlined in this excerpt seem to justify.*

In Lancashire, and especially in Manchester, English manufacture finds at once its starting-point and its centre. The Manchester Exchange is the thermometer for all the fluctuations of trade. The modern art of manufacture has reached its perfection in Manchester. In the cotton industry of South Lancashire, the application of the forces of Nature, the superseding of hand-labour by machinery (especially by the power-loom and the self-acting mule) and the division of labour, are seen at the highest point. . . . The degradation to which the application of steam-power, machinery and the division of labour reduce the working-man, and the attempts of the proletariat to rise above this abasement, must likewise be carried to the highest point and with the fullest consciousness. . . .

The whole assemblage of buildings commonly called Manchester, and contains about four hundred thousand inhabitants, rather more than less. The town itself is peculiarly built, so that a person may live in it for years, and go in and out daily without coming into contact with a working-person's quarter or even with workers, that is, so long as he confines himself to his business or to pleasure walks. This arises chiefly from the fact, that by unconscious tacit agreement, as well as with outspoken conscious determination, the working-people's quarters are sharply separated from the sections of the city reserved for the middle class. . . . With the exception of this commercial district, all Manchester proper, all Salford and Hulme, a greater part of Pendleton and Chorlton, two-thirds of Ardwick, and single stretches of Cheetham Hill and Broughton are all unmixed working-people's quarters, stretching like a girdle, averaging a mile and a half in breadth, around the commercial district. Outside, beyond this girdle, lives the upper and middle bourgeoisie, the middle bourgeoisie in regularly laid out streets in the vicinity of the working quarters . . .; the upper bourgeoisie in remoter villas with gardens . . . in free wholesome country air, in fine, comfortable homes, passed once every half or quarter hour by omnibuses going into the city. . . .

Going from the Old Church to Long Millgate . . . are remnants of the old pre-manufacturing Manchester, whose former inhabitants have removed with their descendants into better-built districts, and have left the houses, which were not good enough for them, to a working-class population strongly mixed with Irish blood. Here one is in an almost undisguised working-men's quarter, for even the shops and beerhouses hardly take the trouble to exhibit a trifling degree of cleanliness. . . .

Right and left a multitude of covered passages lead from the main street into numerous courts, and he who turns in thither gets into a filth and disgusting grime, the equal of which is not to be found—especially in the courts which lead down to the Irk, and which contain unqualifiedly the most horrible dwellings which I have yet beheld. In one of these courts where stands directly at the entrance, at the end of the covered passage, a privy without a door, so dirty that the inhabitants can pass into and out of the court only be passing through foul pools of stagnant urine and excrement. This is the first court on the Irk above Ducie Bridge—in case anyone should care to look into it. Below it on the river there are several tanneries which fill the whole neighborhood with the stench of animal putrefaction. Below Ducie Bridge the only entrance to most of the houses is by means of narrow, dirty stairs and over heaps of refuse and filth. The first court below Ducie Bridge, known as Allen's Court, was in such a state at the time of the cholera that the sanitary police ordered it evacuated, swept, and disinfected with chloride of lime. . . .

At the bottom flows, or rather stagnates, the Irk, a narrow, coal-black, foul-smelling stream, full of *debris* and refuse, which it deposits on the shallower right bank. In dry weather, a long string of the most disgusting, blackish-green, slime pools are left standing on this bank, from the depths of which bubbles of miasmatic gas constantly arise and give forth a stench unendurable even on the bridge forty of fifty feet above the surface of the stream. But besides this, the stream itself is checked every few paces by high weirs, behind which slime and refuse accumulate and rot in thick masses. Above the bridge are tanneries, bonemills, and gasworks, from which all drains and refuse find their way into the Irk, which receives further the contents of all the neighbouring sewers and privies. It may be easily imagined, therefore, what sort of residue the steam deposits. Below the bridge you look upon the piles of *debris*, the refuse, filth, and offal from the courts on the steep left bank; here each house is packed close behind its neighbor and a piece of each is visible, all black, smoky, crumbling, ancient, with broken panes and window-frames.

Source: Friedrich Engels, *The Condition of the Working-Class in England in 1844*. London: Swan Sonnenschein & Co., 1892 [1845], 42, 45–46, 48–50.

THE ENLIGHTENMENT'S FOCUS ON EDUCATION
AND THE USEFULNESS OF KNOWLEDGE

Frederick II (1712–1786), King of Prussia, came to the throne at 28. He was a brilliant military leader, significantly expanding Prussian territory and influence while nationalizing and improving the effectiveness of the Prussian state (and the army that it supported). Powerfully influenced by the Enlightenment, Frederick II founded and supported learned societies like the Berlin Academy to spread both practical and philosophical ideas. His address to that body delivered in 1772 demonstrates that even a so-called absolute monarchy felt it necessary to instruct the population in the need for education and the importance of the useful knowledge spread by the Enlightenment.

Some unenlightened or hypocritical persons [ed.: Jean-Jacques Rousseau] have ventured to profess their hostility to the arts and sciences. If they have been allowed to slander that which does most honor to humanity, we must be all the more entitled to defend it, for that is the duty of all who love society and who are grateful for what they owe to literature. Unfortunately, paradox often makes a greater impression on the public than truth; it is then that we must disabuse the public and refute the authors of such nonsense, not with insults but with sound reason. I am ashamed to state in this Academy that people have had the effrontery to ask whether the sciences are useful or harmful to society, a subject on which no one should entertain the slightest doubt. If we have any superiority over animals, it is certainly not in our bodily faculties, but in the greater understanding which nature has given us; and what distinguishes one man from another is genius and learning. Where lies the infinite difference between a civilized people and barbarians if not in the fact that the former are enlightened, while the others vegetate in brutish ignorance? . . .

Man in himself is little enough; he is born with faculties more or less ripe for development. But they require cultivation; his knowledge must increase if his ideas are to broaden. . . . The greatest mind, without knowledge, is only a rough diamond that will acquire value only after it has been cut by the hands of a skilled jeweler. What minds have been thus lost to society, what great men of every kind stifled in the bud, whether through ignorance, or through the abject state in which they found themselves placed!

The true benefit of the State, its advantage and glory demand therefore that the people in it should be as well educated and enlightened as possible, in order to furnish it, in every field, with a number of trained subjects capable of acquitting themselves expertly in the different tasks entrusted to them. . . .

Although it is unnecessary to demonstrate to this illustrious audience and in this Academy that the arts and sciences bring both utility and fame to the peoples who possess them, it will perhaps not be without use to convince some less enlightened persons of the same thing, to arm them against the effects which some vile sophists might have on their minds. Let them compare a Canadian savage with any citizen of a civilized country of Europe, and all the advantage will be with the latter. How can one prefer crude nature to nature perfected, lack of means of subsistence to a life of ease, rudeness to politeness, the security of politeness enjoyed under the protection of the laws to the law of the jungle and to anarchy, which destroys the fortunes and conditions of families?

Society, a community of men, could not do without either the arts of the sciences. Thanks to surveying and hydraulics, riparian regions are protected from flooding; without these arts, fertile lands would become unhealthy marshes, and would deprive numerous families of their livelihood. The higher land could do without surveyors to measure out and divide the fields. The physical sciences, firmly established by experiment, help to perfect agriculture and, in particular, horticulture. Botany, applied to the study of medicinal herbs, and chemistry, which can extract their essences, serve at least to fortify our hope during our illnesses, even if their property cannot cure us. Anatomy guides and directs the surgeon's hand in those painful but necessary operations that save our life at the expense of an amputated limb.

The mechanical sciences are useful in every field: if a load is to be raised or transported, they will move it. If we are to dig into the bowels of the earth to extract metals, the science of mechanics, with ingenious machines, pumps out the quarries and frees the miner from the super-abundance of water which would cost him his life or his work. If we need mills to grind the most familiar and most basic form of food, the science of mechanics perfects them. It is the science of mechanics that helps craftsmen by improving the various types of craft at which they work. Every kind of machine lies within its province. And how many machines are needed in all the various fields! The craft of shipbuilding constitutes perhaps one of the greatest efforts of imagination; but how much knowledge the pilot must possess to steer his ship and brave wind and wave! He needs to have studied astronomy, to have good charts, an exact knowledge of geography and arithmetical skill, in order to ascertain the distance he has travelled and the point at which he is, and in this respect he will be helped in future by the chronometers which have just been perfected in England. The arts and sciences go hand in hand: we owe them everything, they are the benefactors of mankind.

Source: Frederick II, "Discourse on the Usefulness of the Arts and Sciences in a State" (1772). In S. Eliot and K. Whitlock, eds., *The Enlightenment, Texts I*. Milton Keynes: Open University Press, 1992, 66–67. © The Open University; used by permission.

RESISTING MECHANIZATION: THE LUDDITES

The Luddite movement began in 1811 in the heavily industrialized English Midlands. Workers whose livelihoods were threatened by mechanization and whose standard of living was already under assault from wartime inflation attempted to convince their employers to raise their wages and to stop using new machines. The first document attempted to lay out the workers' grievances in the hope that employers would act to help them. The second document, a Declaration *ostensibly from the Framework Knitters gathered at Ned Ludd's office in the Sherwood Forest and dated January 1, 1812, claimed that discussion was no longer enough: government legal repression was itself illegal because the manufacturers had misled Parliament. The* Declaration *also proclaimed that machines that contravened the customs of the knitting trade would be destroyed. In the Midlands, the Luddite movement destroyed 1,000 frames (4 percent of England's total) valued at £6,000–10,000. Heavy-handed government repression ensured that workers could protest their displacement by the machine only with the greatest difficulty.*

The Labourer is worthy of his Hire

At a General Meeting of Plain Silk Framework-knitters, held at the Fox and Owl Inn, December 9th, 1811, to take into consideration the increasing Grievances under which they labour, it was unanimously Resolved, that every means in their power should be employed to stop the progress of future Impositions upon their Manufacture, and that a Statement of their Case be once more submitted to their Employers, with an application for immediate Redress.

Gentlemen Hosiers,

GALLED by the pressure of unprecedented times, we cannot any longer remain indifferent to our common interest as men. As a body of ingenious artizans, employed on materials of great value; pent up in a close shop fourteen or sixteen hours a day; (A confinement prejudicial to many constitutions), having under our constant care machine confessedly difficult, from the construction of its principles, to preserve in good condition, and allowed to be one of the first productions of British genius; devoting our time and abilities alone, to adorn the rich and great, we conceive ourselves entitled to a higher station in society; and . . . considering our manufacture is consumed alone by the opulent, it ought to produce a competence adequate to the just wants of our families.

About thirty years ago, a Silk Stocking-maker obtained a decent subsistence; but since that time we have had to contend with two great drawbacks upon our necessary comforts, the one is imposition upon our manufacture, the other a tripled augmentation in the price of nearly every article we consume. . . . The average earnings of plain silk hands are indeed too well known to you, to be a very small pittance for the maintenance of a wife and two or three children; they do not exceed 10s. 6d. per week: if some average 13s. per week, this will do very little for a family. Three shillings at least must go for house-rent and taxes—one shilling for coal—one shilling and sixpence for soap and candles, for himself and family; and if he has a wife and three children he must have one stone and a half of flour, which is at least six shillings more; here we see the poor fellow has left three shillings and sixpence to provide all other necessaries of life.

. . . The imperious dictates of human nature impel us to raise up a manly voice in our own behalf: governed by every principle of right towards you, acknowledging that due deference to your superior station, yet loudly calling your attention to our present case. . . . Hedged in by a combination act, we cannot say to you as a public body, that we demand an advance of wages, but we can say that JUSTICE DEMANDS that we should receive remuneration for extra labour: this is all we want. . . .

Gentlemen, there is every reason in the world to prove that a remuneration ought and must take place. Several Hosiers in this town have openly avowed its necessity. The high price of provision is on our side, reason, honer, morality, philanthropy, necessity, justice, your own interest, as being accountable to the Almighty, the practicality of the case, the combination act, and the general suffrage of mankind; all declare that we ought to be remunerated for extra labour.

Gentlemen, being invited by some of you to state our grievances, we have used great plainness on the subject; well knowing that this will prvail, when acts of violence would render us detestable to mankind. . . .

Source: Kevin Binfield, ed., *Writings of the Luddites*. Baltimore: Johns Hopkins University Press, 2004, 80–84.

By the Framework Knitters.

A Declaration.

Whereas by the charter granted by our late Sovereign Lord Charles the Second by the Grace of God [King] of Great Britain France and Ireland, the Framework knitters are empowered to break and destroy all Frames and Engines that fabricate Articles in a fraudulent and deceitful manner and to destroy all Framework knitters Goods whatsoever that are so made And Whereas a number of deceitful unprincipled and intriguing persons did attain an Act to be passed in the Twenty Eighth Year of our present Sovereign Lord George the Third whereby it was enacted that persons entering by force into any

House Shop or Place to break or destroy Frames should be adjudged guilty of Felony And as we are fully convinced that such Act was obtained in the most fraudulent interested and Electioneering manner And that the Honorable the Parliament of Great Britain was deceived the motives and intentions of the persons was obtained such Act We therefore the Framework knitters do hereby declare the aforesaid Act to be Null and Void to all intents and purposes whatsoever As by the passing of this Act villainous and imposing persons are enabled to made fraudulent and deceitful manufactures to the discredit and utter ruin of our Trade. And Whereas we declare that the aforementioned charter is as much in force as through no such Act had been passed. And We do hereby declare to all Hosiers Lace Manufacturers and proprietors of Frames that We will break and destroy all manner of Frames whatsoever that make the following spurious Articles and Frames whatsoever that do not pay the regular prices heretofore agreed to the Masters and Workmen—All point Net Frames making single press, and Frames not working by the rack and rent and not paying the price regulated in 1810—Warp Frames working single Yarn or two course hole—not working by the rack, not paying the rent and prices regulated in 1809. Whereas all plain Silk Frames not Work according to the Gage—Frames not marking the Work according to quality Whereas all Frames of whatsoever description the Workmen of whom are not paid in the Corrent Coin of the Realm will invariably be destroyed. Whereas it hath been represented to the Framework knitters that Gangs of banditti have infested various parts of the Country under the pretence of being employed in breaking of Frames and hath committed divers Robberies upon our Friends and Neighbours I do hereby offer a reward of one thousand pounds to any person that will give any Information at my Office. I have Gave two thousand Pounds as secret money any person that will give any Information of those villainous and false rumours of the Frame Breakers (anyone that will come forward may depend upon the greatest Secresy and the same reward.

Given under my hand this 1st day of January 1812.

God protect the Trade.   Ned Lud's Office
                                                         Sherwood Forest.

Source: Kevin Binfield, ed., *Writings of the Luddites*. Baltimore: Johns Hopkins University Press, 2004, 90–91.

ROBERT OWEN ON EDUCATION AND THE EVILS OF CHILD LABOR

Robert Owen (1771–1858) was a Welshman whose experience managing cotton mills in Lancashire led him to implement a very different approach to managing labor when he was put in charge of his father-in-law's mill at New Lanark, Scotland. The large profits earned under his management helped demonstrate that the thoroughgoing exploitation of workers, especially of children, was not necessary to the success of the factory system. At the same time, Owen's concern with education and the welfare of society in general were important counterpoints to greedy, abusive mill owners. This passage is from A New View of Society, or Essays on the Principle of the Formation of Human Character and the Application of the Principle to Practice *written in 1813.*

According to the last returns under the Population Act, the poor and working classes of Great Britain and Ireland have been found to exceed twelve millions of persons, or nearly three-fourths of the population of the British Islands.

The characters of these persons are now permitted to be very generally formed without proper guidance or direction, and, in many cases, under circumstances which *must* train them to the extreme of vice and misery; and of course render them the worst and most dangerous subjects in the empire; while the far greater part of the remainder of the community are educated upon the most mistaken principles of human nature, such, indeed, as cannot fail to produce a general conduct throughout society, totally unworthy of the character of rational beings. . . .

In the year 1784, the late Mr. Dale of Glasgow [Owen's father-in-law] founded a spinning and weaving manufactory near the falls of the Clyde, in the county of Lanark in Scotland; and about that period cotton mills were first introduced into the northern part of the kingdom.

It was the power which could be obtained from the falls of water which induced Mr. Dale to erect his mills in this situation, for in other respects it was not well chosen: the country around was uncultivated; the inhabitants were poor, and few in number; and the roads in the neighborhood were so bad that the falls of Clyde now so celebrated were then unknown to strangers.

It was therefore necessary to collect a new population to supply the infant establishment with laborers. This however was no light task; for all the regularly trained Scotch peasantry disdained the idea of working from early till late, day after day, within cotton mills. Two modes only to obtain these laborers occurred: the one, to procure children from the various public charities in the country; and the other to induce families to settle around the works.

To accommodate the first, a large house was erected, which ultimately contained about five hundred children, who were procured chiefly from workhouses and charities in Edinburgh.

These children were to be fed, clothed, and educated; and these duties Mr. Dale performed with the benevolence which he was known to possess.

To obtain the second, a village was built, and the houses were let at a low rent to such families as could be induced to accept employment in the mills: but such was the general dislike to that to that occupation at the time, that, with a few exceptions, the persons must destitute of friends, employment, and character, were alone found willing to try the experiment; and of these a sufficient number to supply a constant increase of the manufactory could not be obtained. . . .

The benevolent proprietor spared no expense which could give comfort to the poor children which it contained. The rooms provided for them were spacious, always clean, and well ventilated; the food was of the best quality, and most abundant; the clothes were neat and useful; a surgeon was kept in constant pay to direct how to prevent as well as cure disease; and the best instructors which the country afforded were appointed to teach such branches of education as were deemed likely to be useful to children in their situation; and kind, well disposed persons were appointed to superintend all the proceedings. Nothing, in short, at first sight seemed wanting to render it a most complete charity.

But to defray the expense of these well devised arrangements, and support the establishment generally, it was absolutely necessary that the children should be employed within the mills from six o'clock in the morning to seven in the evening summer and winter; and after these hours their education commenced. The directors of the public charities from mistaken economy, would not consent to send the children under their care to the cotton mills, unless the children were received by the proprietors at the ages of six, seven, and eight. And Mr. Dale was under the necessity of accepting them at those ages, or stopping the manufactory which he had commenced.

It is not to be supposed that children so young could remain, with the interval of meals only, from six in the morning until seven in the evening, in constant employment on their feet within cotton mills, and afterwards acquire much proficiency in education. And so it proved; for the greater part of them became dwarfs in body and mind, and many of them deformed. Their labor through the day, and their education at night, became so irksome, that numbers of them continually ran away, and almost all looked forward with impatience and anxiety to the expiration of their apprenticeship of seven, eight, and nine years, which generally expired when they were from thirteen to fifteen years old. At this period of life, unaccustomed to provide for themselves, and unacquainted with the world, they usually went to Edinburgh or Glasgow, where boys and girls were soon assailed by the innumerable temptations which all large towns present; and many of them fell sacrifices to those temptations.

Thus were Mr. Dale's arrangements and kind solicitude for the comfort and happiness of these children rendered in their ultimate effect almost nugatory. They were sent to be employed, and without their labor he could not support them; but, while under his care, he did all that any individual circumstanced as he was could do for his fellow-creatures.

The error proceeded from the children being sent from the workhouses at an age far too young for employment; they ought to have been detained four years longer, and education; and then all the evils which followed would have been prevented. . . .

[After Owen took over] the system of receiving apprentices from public charities was abolished; permanent settlers with large families were encouraged, and comfortable houses were built for their accommodation.

The practice of employing children in the mills, of six, seven, and eight years of age, was discontinued, and their parents advised to allow them to acquire health and education until they were ten years old. (It may be remarked, that even this age is too early to keep them at constant employment in manufactories, from six in the morning to seven in the evening. Far better would it be for the children, their parents, and for society, that the first should not commence employment until they attain the age of twelve, when their education might be finished, and their bodies would be more competent to undergo the fatigue and exertions required of them. When parents can be trained to afford this additional time to their children without inconvenience, they will, of course adopt the practice now recommended.)

The children were taught reading, writing, and arithmetic, during five years, that is, from five to ten, in the village school, without expense to their parents; and all the modern improvements in education have been adopted, or are in process of adoption: some facilities in teaching arithmetic have been also introduced, which were peculiar to this school, and found very advantageous. They may therefore be taught and well trained before they engage in any regular employment. Another important consideration is, that all their instruction is rendered a pleasure and delight to them; they are much more anxious for the hour of school time to arrive, than end: they therefore make a rapid progress; and it may be safely asserted, that if they shall not be trained for form such characters as may be the most wished and desired, not one particle of the fault will proceed from the children; but the cause will rest in the want of a true knowledge of human nature, in those who have the management of them and their parents.

Source: Robert Owen, *A New View of Society: or Essays on the Principle of the Formation of Human Character and the Application of the Principle to Practice*. London: Richard Taylor and Co., 1813, 5, 35–36, 38–40, 49–51.

ADAM SMITH ON THE DIVISION OF LABOR

Adam Smith (1723–1790) was a Scotsman who became a professor at Glasgow University. He traveled widely before becoming a customs official. His Theory of Moral Sentiments *(1759) was influential in moral philosophy and in the emergence of the field of political economy, but his major work was undoubtedly* An Inquiry into the Nature and Causes of the Wealth of Nations *published in 1776. Smith articulated enormously important ideas about the complementary role of the market and the state in the economy. These two excerpts demonstrate that the division of labor had both positive and negative attributes.*

The greatest improvement in the productive powers of labour, and the greater part of the skill, dexterity, and judgment with which it is anywhere directed, or applied, seem to have been the effects of the division of labour.

The effects of the division of labour, in the general business of society, will be more easily understood, by considering in what manner it operates in some particular manufactures. It is commonly supposed to be carried furthest in some very trifling ones; not perhaps that it really is carried further in them than in others of more importance: but in those trifling manufactures which are destined to supply the small wants of but a small number of people, the whole number of workmen must necessarily be small; and those employed in every different branch of the work can often be collected into the same workhouse, and placed at once under the view of the spectator. In those great manufactures, on the contrary, which are destined to supply the great wants of the great body of the people, every different branch of the work employs so great a number of workmen, that it is impossible to collect them all into the same workhouse. We can seldom see more, at one time, than those employed in one single branch. Though in such manufactures, therefore, the work may really be divided into a much greater number of parts, than in those of a more trifling nature, the division is not near so obvious, and has accordingly been much less observed.

To take an example, therefore, from a very trifling manufacture; but one in which the division of labour has been very often taken notice of, the trade of the pin-maker; a workman not educated to this business (which the division of labour has rendered a distinct trade), nor acquainted with the use of the machinery employed in it (to the invention of which the same division of labour has probably given occasion), could scarce, perhaps, with his utmost industry, make one pin in a day, and certainly could not make twenty. But in the way in which this business is now carried on, not only the whole work is a peculiar trade, but it is divided into a number of branches, of which the greater part are likewise peculiar trades. One man draws out the wire, another straights it, a third cuts it, a fourth points it, a fifth grinds it at the top for receiving the head; to make the head requires two or three distinct operations; to put it on, is a peculiar business, to whiten the pins is another; it is even a trade by itself to put them into the paper; and the important business of making a pin is, in this manner, divided into about eighteen distinct operations, which, in some manufactories, are all performed by distinct hands, though in others the same man will sometimes perform two or three of them. I have seen a small manufactory of this kind where ten men only were employed, and where some of them consequently performed two or three distinct operations. But though they were very poor, and therefore but indifferently accommodated with the necessary machinery, they could, when they exerted themselves, make among them about twelve pounds of pins in a day. There are in a pound upwards of four thousand pins of a middling size. Those ten persons, therefore, could make among them upwards of forty-eight thousand pins in a day. Each person, therefore, making a tenth part of forty-eight thousand pins, might be considered as making four thousand eight hundred pins in a day. But if they had all wrought separately and independently, and without any of them having been educated to this peculiar business, they certainly could not each of them have made twenty, perhaps not one pin in a day; that is, certainly, not the two hundred and fortieth, perhaps not the four thousand eight hundredth part of what they are at present capable of performing, in consequence of a proper division and combination of their different operations.

In every other art and manufacture, the effects of the division of labour are similar to what they are in this very trifling one; though, in many of them, the labour can neither be so much subdivided, nor reduced to so great a simplicity of operation. The division of labour, however, so far as it can be introduced, occasions, in every art, a proportionable increase of the productive powers of labour. The separation of different trades and employments from one another, seems to have taken place, in consequence of this advantage. This separation too is generally carried furthest in those countries which enjoy the highest degree of industry and improvement; what is the work of one man in a rude state of society, being generally that of several in an improved one. In every improved society, the farmer is generally nothing but a farmer; the manufacturer, nothing but a manufacturer. The labour too which is necessary to produce any one complete manufacture, is almost always divided among a great number of hands. . . .

This great increase of the quantity of work which, in consequence of the division of labour, the same number of people are capable of performing, is owing to three different circumstances; first to the increase of dexterity in every particular workman; secondly, to the saving of the time which is commonly lost in passing from one species of work to another; and lastly, to the invention of a great number of machines which facilitate and abridge labour, and enable one man to do the work of many. . . . (Book I, Chapter 1).

In the progress of the division of labour, the employment of the far greater part of those who live by labour, that is, of the great body of the people, comes to be confined to a few very simple operations, frequently to one or two. But the understandings of the greater part of men are necessarily formed by their ordinary employments. The man whose whole life is spent in performing a few simple operations, of which the effects are perhaps always the same, or very nearly the same, has no occasion to exert his understanding or to exercise his invention in finding out expedients for removing difficulties which never occur. He naturally loses, therefore, the habit of such exertion, and generally becomes as stupid and ignorant as it is possible for a human creature to become. The torpor of his mind renders him not only incapable of relishing or bearing a part in any rational conversation, but of conceiving any generous, noble, or tender sentiment, and consequently of forming any just judgment concerning many even of the ordinary duties of private life. Of the great and extensive interests of his country he is altogether incapable of judging, and unless very particular pains have been taken to render him otherwise, he is equally incapable of defending his country in war. The uniformity of his stationary life naturally corrupts the courage of his mind, and makes him regard with abhorrence the irregular, uncertain, and adventurous life of a soldier. It corrupts even the activity of his body, and renders him incapable of exerting his strength with vigour and perseverance in any other employment than that to which he has been bred. His dexterity at his own particular trade seems, in this manner, to be acquired at the expence of his intellectual, social, and martial virtues. But in every improved and civilized society this is the state into which the labouring poor, that is, the great body of the people, must necessarily fall, unless government takes some pains to prevent it. (Book V, Chapter 1).

Source: Adam Smith, *An Inquiry into the Nature and Causes of the Wealth of Nations*, ed. Edwin Canaan, 5th ed. London: Meuthen, 1904 [1776].

Key Questions

QUESTION 1: WHY WAS ENGLAND FIRST TO INDUSTRIALIZE?

The depth of the link between England as starting point of modern industrialization and the idea of an industrial revolution has been hotly debated since the dawn of the 19th century. As David Landes noted, the term "industrial revolution" was first used in 1799 when a French envoy to Berlin observed that his nation had begun such a transformation. Clarifying the connection between place and process is essential to understanding the Industrial Revolution both as an historical phenomenon and its lessons for contemporary economic development.

This frequently asked question also reminds readers that although England was the first country to industrialize, other nations were not far behind. To acknowledge the nature and causes of the wide gap that emerged between Britain and its closest competitors in the first half of the 19th century is one of the vital issues in understanding what was "revolutionary" about the British Industrial Revolution. The question of "Why was England first?" illuminates not only the internal foundations of England's Industrial Revolution, but the competitive context of this groundbreaking event.

Since the aftermath of World War II, the question of why England was the first country to experience an industrial revolution has been intimately linked to the history of technology. In 1948, T. S. Ashton explained the Industrial Revolution as when a "wave of gadgets swept over England" beginning around 1760. A generation later, David Landes fleshed out this interpretation based on the superiority of British technology in *The Unbound Prometheus: Technological*

Change and Industrial Development in Western Europe from 1750 to the Present
(1969). Landes's account has dominated understandings of this question ever
since.

A great deal of attention has been focused on how those gadgets were invented and made. Studies of innovators and manufacturing pioneers have
been complemented by examination of the role of workers and the working
classes in facilitating or inhibiting industrialization. At the same time, scholars have explored the impact of key institutions like the framework of property rights, the tax system, and the financial system capped by the Bank of
England. Taken together, these studies pointed to the unique features of British industrialization.

Although Landes's work compared England to the rest of western Europe,
his focus was clearly on the role of technology in the three key industries of
textiles, coal, and iron. Thanks to a flood of studies exploring developments
in Britain, it became only natural for other scholars to explore the comparative dimensions. Contemporary industrial developments in France, Belgium,
the German lands, and the United States received concerted attention as did
parts of Europe and other areas of the world that only industrialized later.
These studies contextualized British industrialization by highlighting what
was truly unique and what was European or even western about the Industrial
Revolution. These studies found that it was less British scientific prowess than
skill at implementing innovations that marked English technological advance
as different from the continent.

The logical next step for testing arguments about the key factors in the
British Industrial Revolution was to determine their impact. Changes in England's Gross National Product (GNP) had been measured and linked to the
chief industrial districts with changes over time noted in minute detail, but
most assertions about the standard of living for diverse groups or for the
country as a whole were not based on adequate data. C. Knick Harley and
Nicholas Crafts, among a host of others, spent a decade examining the available quantitative evidence to delineate the effect of transformative industrial
growth on the standard of living in general and of diverse groups. The data
suggested that the British standard of living did not improve during the first
half-century of the Industrial Revolution. What they found ignited a major
controversy. Their findings were challenged and their numbers checked and
rechecked. Problems with the statistics were explored and their limitations
exposed and factored into the analysis. When all was said and done, it was
clear that the British standard of living did not start to improve until the
1820s at the earliest with the 1830s as more likely. For more than two full
generations, the working classes, and even the British people as a whole, did
not benefit from the Industrial Revolution. Who did profit and how that

balance of power could be maintained are deeply uncomfortable questions for proponents of the British model of industrialization. The conclusion about the standard of living is one of the most important yet unresolved issues with regard to the question of why England was first. The consequences of being first on the long-delayed improvements in the standard of living is another vital subject that has not been fully dealt with by either historians or economists.

The issue of why England was first to industrialize is also closely tied to current interest in the contributions of colonialism and especially slavery to the Industrial Revolution. This subject will be considered in detail in Question 3, but it is also relevant to this issue. If Britain's empire, based on slavery and the slave trade, furnished the profits and resources that drove industrialization, then the issue of exploitation, not just of the working classes but throughout the Atlantic world must take center stage in answers to the question of why England was first.

England's uniqueness is unquestioned. This island nation not only managed to turn its economic advantages into an industrial revolution, it managed to do it first and to maintain that position for more than a century. That feat was based on technological advances, but other factors such as geography, institutions, the role of the state, entrepreneurialism, and colonialism also contributed in significant—and hotly debated—ways. The distinguishing features of its society and scientific culture enabled England to lead the world in developing a manufacturing economy. Identifying which factors and features were critical and differentiated England from its competitors goes a long way to understanding how an industrial revolution could occur. The answer to why England was first remains relevant to contemporary policy studies focused on economic development.

Why was England first to industrialize? Many factors went into English leadership of the Industrial Revolution: it cannot be narrowed down to a single issue. Technology? Scientific culture? Resource endowments, especially iron and coal? Geography? Colonialism and slavery? State policies? Entrepreneurship? Labor discipline? Supply of capital? This question seeks to help readers understand which aspects of England's economy and society were essential to its competitive advantage, so while the question is fundamentally about England, it is also profoundly comparative. At the same time, although these essays are historical in nature, they also provide insight into present-day questions of economic development. The answers to this question are not framed as the only reasons for English leadership, but rather as the most important explanatory factor or factors.

Étienne Stockland's analysis of the question is an updated version of the dominant interpretation, namely, that it was technology above all that enabled

England to become the first industrial nation. Stockland wrote this essay while conducting research for his doctoral dissertation on the environmental and economic history of livestock. He focuses on the south of France and on the 18th century. Stockland is an advanced graduate student in the History Department at Columbia University.

The second essay is written by Jeff Horn who is Professor of History at Manhattan College. He too is a historian of France and the author of five previous books on the French and Industrial Revolutions that explore technology, trade, colonialism, politics, and the role of the state. He takes a more explicitly comparative approach to the question by considering what impeded Britain's competitors while emphasizing the role of contingency in England's ability to touch off and maintain the Industrial Revolution.

ANSWER: ÉTIENNE STOCKLAND, BRITAIN INDUSTRIALIZED FIRST BECAUSE OF TECHNOLOGY

Technological innovation was why Britain was the first country to experience an industrial revolution. Between c. 1750 and 1850, a host of mechanical inventions were developed that had a revolutionary impact on the production of manufactured goods, especially textiles and metals. Remarkable upsurges in productivity and drastic reductions in the amount of labor needed to produce yarn and iron among many other things followed from the mechanization of industry. These mechanical innovations first found widespread industrial applications in Great Britain. Why did other economically developed countries in the 18th and early 19th centuries like France, the Netherlands, China, or India lag behind Britain in this process of technological change? The question has been hotly debated since the end of the 18th century, when the industrial basis of the British economy took shape. A variety of economic, social, and geographical factors sustained British technological prowess to permit that state to commence an industrial revolution.

High Wages

British wages in the 18th century were exceptionally high by comparison with other countries in Europe and Asia. Foreign travelers marveled at the high living standards of British laborers, who were better nourished and clothed than their counterparts on the European continent. For British entrepreneurs, however, the high cost of labor was an impediment that increased prices and made their goods less competitive in domestic and international markets. The high costs of labor in Britain acted as a powerful incentive to develop machines that could reduce the amount of labor-time required for each output unit. As Adam Smith (1723–1790) wrote in *The Wealth of Nations* (1776), the purpose of industrial machinery was to "increase the productive power of labor, or to enable the same number of laborers to perform a much greater quantity of work." The textile industry was the first to reap the benefits of mechanization. By mechanizing hand techniques for carding and spinning cotton, machines like James Hargreaves's (1720–1778) spinning jenny, Richard Arkwright's (1732–1792) water frame, and Samuel Crompton's (1753–1827) spinning mule significantly reduced the amount of time and labor required to produce yarn. This labor savings based on technological advance gave British textiles an unrivaled competitive advantage on the global market. Mechanical innovations were later introduced into other, less glamorous, industries like printing, pin making, food processing, glass manufacturing, and metalworking. To avoid high wages, technological advances enabled productivity growth in a broad range of economic sectors thanks to the steady mechanization of tasks previously performed by manual labor.

Cheap Energy

What made these mechanical innovations even more productive was that they were increasingly powered by inorganic sources of energy. The steam engines developed by Thomas Newcomen (1664–1729) and James Watt (1736–1819) converted heat released by burning coal into energy that could be harnessed for mechanical work. The first steam-powered factories were established in the late 1770s. Technical improvements to the steam engine in the first half of the 19th century expanded the industrial application of steam rather rapidly in many sectors. These inventions allowed Britain to make the first transition to what economic historian Edward Anthony Wrigley has called a "mineral-based energy economy." By the beginning of the 19th century, British industry consumed five times as much coal as the entire European continent. Tremendous productive gains in manufacturing followed from the substitution of fossil fuels for less efficient and more costly organic sources of energy such as wood, human, or animal power. Political economist Andrew Ure (1778–1857) remarked in his *Philosophy of Manufactures* (1835) that if horses had not been supplanted by steam engines in powering mechanized cotton mills, "at the present day, they would devour all the profits of the manufacturer."

Why was Britain the first country to make such extensive use of mineral energy for industrial purposes, when other countries such as France, the Netherlands, and China either possessed or had access to significant coal reserves? Geography played a key role. The major deposits of high-quality coal in Britain—in Lancashire, Wales, and Northumberland—were conveniently located near waterways or the sea that allowed for easy transportation inland, to coastal cities, or abroad. The construction of a dense network of canals beginning in the 18th century further reduced the costs of transporting coal to diverse sites of industrial production. Britain's natural endowments and geography, combined with an increasingly efficient transportation infrastructure, provided manufacturers with ready access to cheap coal that incentivized a technologically driven transition to steam-powered factory production.

Scientific Culture

If Britain's high-wage, cheap energy economy provided powerful incentives for the development of fossil fuel–powered, labor-saving technology, its unique intellectual and social environment provided a favorable context for such innovations. A distinctive scientific culture characterized by frequent exchanges among natural philosophers, entrepreneurs, and artisans acted as a breeding ground for technical innovation. The proliferation of vectors of intellectual interaction between these groups lay behind what historian Joel Mokyr called the "Industrial Enlightenment." Somewhat informal societies like the Manchester Literary and Philosophical Society or the more organized Lunar Society of Birmingham and what became known as the Royal Society of Arts in London provided a meeting ground for scientists, entrepreneurs, and artisans. These gatherings acted as a bridge between laboratory and workshop. Public scientific lectures like the Mechanics Institutes, eagerly attended by men of commercial and artisanal backgrounds, demonstrated how the laws of physics could be usefully applied to industry. Numerous periodicals, books, and pamphlets disseminated a wide variety of useful scientific and technological knowledge to diverse audiences. Through these various channels, British laborers and entrepreneurs acquired a high degree of technological literacy and a growing appetite for mechanical innovations. The associations between mechanically minded scientists and technologically savvy artisans and entrepreneurs were the foundation of a knowledge economy out of which the technological marvels of the British Industrial Revolution emerged.

Conclusion

Britain was the first country to industrialize because of its success in developing and perfecting technology that greatly enhanced productive capacity in a range of economic sectors. High wages and cheap coal provided incentives for this type of technological innovation. Yet a favorable intellectual and social environment for the production, dissemination, and implementation of useful knowledge was necessary for these incentives to be translated into concrete material gains. Unique economic, geographical, and social factors lay behind the rapid spate of technological innovations developed between c. 1750 and 1850 that allowed Britain to achieve a relatively short-lived position of global dominance by the mid-19th century.

ANSWER: JEFF HORN, BRITAIN BECAME THE FIRST INDUSTRIAL NATION BECAUSE OF GEOGRAPHY AND LUCK

Great Britain emerged as the first industrial nation in the second half of the 18th century. British leadership took advantage of impressive technological creativity, increasingly heavy-handed control of the working classes, major financial resources and stability, and phenomenal contributions from colonialism. That leadership was hardly uncontested and many of these factors had more to do with Britain's ability to sustain industrialization rather than to get it started in the first place. Across the channel, France was not only a commercial and military rival, but also a major industrial contender. Based on its own competitive advantages, France might have been able to overtake or overshadow Britain in the initial stages of industrialization if it had not been for the support provided by geography and luck.

English-language commentators frequently forget the fact that France was the largest industrial producer in the world during the 18th century (though not per capita). In terms of basic science and in certain areas of industrial technology, France and other areas on the continent were the unquestioned front-runners. Many commentators also overlook a number of important trends, namely, that French foreign trade surpassed Britain's over the course of the 18th century and was increasing at a faster rate. With guilds, tolls, and other economic impediments under assault from Enlightened government officials and a vast internal market three times the size of Britain's, France might have usurped Britain's industrial leadership had just a few events turned out differently. Contingency cannot be left out of explanations of why Britain was the first industrial nation.

Geography comprised a major set of pieces of the puzzle. Geography provided a number of enormous advantages to Britain that were essential to that island nation's ability to commence an industrial revolution. Resources comprised a significant part of the British competitive edge. England had plenty of highly fertile farmland to support a large and growing population of people who did not work the land and allow them to eat as well or better than their rivals on the continent. Large stocks of animals provided food and fertilizer, but also leather and wool. In addition, Britain possessed high-quality supplies of coal and iron so essential to early industrialization as well as lead, tin, kaolin, and other clays. These resources constituted a near optimal basis for an industrial revolution based on textiles, iron, and coal.

Britain's low mountains, numerous fast-running streams, pattern of rivers, jagged coastline, superb harbors, and separation from the continent also provided unrivaled geographic advantages. England is compact and relatively easily traversed, encouraging the construction of turnpikes and canals. Streams provided numerous potential sources of water power and the interlocking river systems of the Thames, Trent, Severn, and Wash covered most of the country. In combination with the craggy shoreline, this meant that nowhere in England is more than 70 miles from the Atlantic or 30 miles from a navigable river with access to the sea. Abundant harbors and estuaries scattered around the country provided safe havens where ships were protected from the tempestuous Atlantic as well as jumping off points for sea-borne commerce.

The ease and extent of transportation by water was perhaps the greatest geographical advantage enjoyed by Britain. Rivers and canals enabled goods to be exchanged quickly and relatively cheaply across the length and breadth of the country. Widespread access to the sea provided an even more inexpensive means of transporting goods. No other nation with the resources to commence industrialization possessed this massive cost advantage to engage in long-distance trade. Before the onset of industrialization, British road transport costs were about 1 shilling per ton-mile. On inland waterways, transport cost a little more than 20 percent of that figure with coastal shipping averaging significantly less than that. Transporting goods by land was far slower and more expensive than by water. A very high percentage of Britain's cost advantage in long-distance trade stemmed from transportation. Another substantial wedge resulted from superior access to energy sources such as coal whose rock bottom price derived from low transport costs. Geography was essential to British industrial leadership.

The English Channel also formed a moat that protected the Hanoverian state from the vicissitudes of continental warfare. Without this defensive barrier, it is hard to imagine how England could have avoided invasion and defeat in 1688, 1715, 1745, 1755–1761, 1778–1781, 1793–1794, 1797–1798, and 1800–1812. To take one example, even if England could have stopped a Napoleonic invasion in 1805, the loss of life and property would likely have been enormous and the war effort and/or recovery would have diverted precious resources from productive use. Conquest might also have shifted state policy away from supporting industrialization. Britain used continental wars and France's distraction to conquer new territories in India and to acquire much of France's empire in the western hemisphere. These acquisitions were essential, even necessary contributors to British industrialization. Had France not been distracted by the Revolution and its attempt to dominate Europe under Napoleon, that nation might well have matched or even surpassed Britain's industrial achievements.

Britain's powerful defensive position also allowed the Hanoverian state to concentrate its military efforts abroad and on the navy. Britain did not have to tie up resources in an expensive standing army capable of contending with the European great powers. What money was spent on land forces could be used to keep control of the Scots and Irish and dominate the working classes, aiding entrepreneurs and providing monopoly control over markets and resources. Lower overall military expenditures and diminished threat levels encouraged and enabled British political stability, an essential factor in Great Britain's ability to industrialize first.

Geography enabled England to develop a true national market more than 150 years before the continental countries. These industrial followers had to use dense webs of railroads to imitate the economic opportunities that geography gave to Britain. A national market depressed market prices for food and other commodities, permitting greater consumption and lower transaction costs. As a competitive advantage, geography was hard to match, much less beat.

Yet luck cannot be discounted in understanding why Great Britain was able to take advantage of its opportunities and commence an industrial revolution. It is always a chancy thing to play "What if?" but sometimes a counterfactual scenario can illuminate complex processes or situations. England and France fought a series of eight wars between 1688 and 1815 for the mastery of Europe. The turning point was the Seven Years War (1756–1763) in which England acquired a dominant position in India and the Americas. Defeat left France bankrupt, impoverished, and bereft of the political and economic position that might have enabled it to challenge Britain as it commenced industrialization. Why did France lose? Czar Peter III's accession to the throne of Russia in 1762 saved Prussia from defeat and Hanover from conquest, and prevented French continental hegemony. Had Empress Elizabeth lived another six months or Peter III been unwilling to give up Russian conquests in order to win favor with Prussia, France's overseas losses might have been balanced by European gains. The playing field could have been far more even, allowing France's great resources, wealth, and population to permit it to challenge Britain for the industrial mastery of Europe. Other possibilities could be created, but the point is that British industrialization was conditional (not accidental), rather than determined as the literature so often seems to suggest.

This essay seeks to highlight the profound significance of geography and contingency in British industrial leadership. Technological innovation, political stability, colonialism, control of the working classes, along with several other factors cannot and should not be discounted in trying to understand why and how Britain was able to industrialize. But the question being explored here is slightly different, namely, why was Britain first? To answer that question, it is necessary to go beyond standard accounts to consider the geographical basis of the economy and the factors that restrained Britain's competitors. Geography was the single greatest factor in allowing Britain to be first, but luck also played a significant role.

CLOSING

Why was England first? Technology certainly played an important role. Étienne Stockland makes a convincing case for technology's significance, though he also pays close attention to the prior existence of a high-wage economy and to England's tremendous endowment of cheap energy resources. For Stockland, these two factors facilitated the productivity of England's scientific culture. Horn also emphasizes England's wealth of coal and sites appropriate for waterwheels, but he puts it in more general terms under the heading of "geography." He focuses greater attention on how geography protected the island nation from invasion and allowed it to concentrate on economic development in ways that its continental competitors could not. As an island, England could also focus on acquiring and profiting from its empire in ways that France and other European states could only dream of.

English economic leadership also depended on contingency. Many accounts of the English industrial revolution suggest that with its resource and capital endowments, institutions, leadership, profitable empire, and technological creativity, the Hanoverian state was destined to be the first industrial nation. Such quasi-deterministic interpretations are rejected implicitly by Stockland and explicitly by Horn, in part because they are historians of political economy and write primarily about France, England's chief political, military, economic, and technological competitor. It is essential to recall the multiple pathways and accidents of history that enabled some individuals, groups, societies, and states to take advantage of their economic opportunities while preventing others from doing the same. There is a difference between being able to commence an industrial revolution and being the first to do so. The gap that developed in the 19th century between England and its competitors stemmed, in large measure, from the Hanoverian state's position as industrial pioneer. That is one of the most important reasons why it matters why England was the first.

DOING MORE

Online

"The Industrial Revolution Begins in England (1760–1850)." Available online at http://webs.bcp.org/sites/vcleary/ModernWorldHistoryTextbook/Industrial Revolution/IRbegins.html.

Temin, Peter. "Two Views of the British Industrial Revolution." 1995. Available online at https://dspace.mit.edu/bitstream/handle/1721.1/64205/twoviewsofbritis 00temi.pdf?sequence=1.

Voigtländer, Nico, and Hans-Joachim Voth. "Why England? Demographic Factors, Structural Change and Physical Capital Accumulation during the Industrial Revolution." *Journal of Economic Growth*. 2006. DOI 10.1007/s10887–006–9007–6. Available online at http://www.anderson.ucla.edu/faculty/nico.v/Research /WhyEngland_JEG.pdf.

Print

Ashton, Thomas S. *The Industrial Revolution, 1760–1830*. London: Oxford University Press, 1948.

Broadberry, Stephen, and Kevin H. O'Rourke, eds. *The Cambridge Economic History of Modern Europe*, vol. 1, *1700–1870*. Cambridge: Cambridge University Press, 2010.

Crafts, N. F. R. *British Economic Growth during the Industrial Revolution*. Oxford: Clarendon Press, 1985.

Crafts, N. F. R., and C. Knick Harley. "Output Growth and the British Industrial Revolution: A Restatement of the Crafts-Harley View." *Economic History Review* 45 (1992): 703–30.

Horn, Jeff, Leonard N. Rosenband, and Merritt Roe Smith, eds. *Reconceptualizing the Industrial Revolution*. Cambridge, MA: MIT Press, 2010.

Landes, David S. *The Unbound Prometheus: Technological Change and Industrial Development in Western Europe from 1750 to the Present*. Cambridge: Cambridge University Press, 1969.

Landes, David S. "The Fable of the Dead Horse; or, The Industrial Revolution Revisited." In *The British Industrial Revolution: An Economic Perspective*, 2nd ed., edited by Joel Mokyr. Boulder, CO: Westview Press, 1999.

QUESTION 2: WAS THE EXPLOITATION OF THE WORKING CLASSES NECESSARY TO HAVE AN INDUSTRIAL REVOLUTION?

Men, women, and children made the goods that generated an Industrial Revolution. Did they do so willingly or did they have to be forced to do so? And if they had to be forced, was it done in a manner that can be described as exploitation? How did entrepreneurs and managers get their workforce to do dangerous, unpleasant tasks for up to 14 hours a day, six days a week? If exploitation was necessary to the Industrial Revolution in England, was it required everywhere or just there? These secondary questions provide nuance and depth to understanding the importance of the original dilemma.

A very significant proportion of the laborers who spun the thread, put warp to weft, forged the iron, and mined the coal that made the English Industrial Revolution had no choice in the matter. Parish apprentices, other children either sent by or working with their parents, and women were either unpaid or received only a pitiful fraction of the already low compensation of an adult male. Immigrants from Scotland and Ireland also worked for rock-bottom wages. The dangers of a deep pit or experimental or poorly made machines; the environmental threats of laboring in enclosed spaces full of the dust and chaff of wool, cotton, and linen fibers; along with the loss of leisure, education, and health resulting from workdays that stretched from before dawn to after dusk even in summer, six days a week, were the lot of many, probably most, of the first generations of factory workers. This question examines whether such conditions were deliberate, necessary, and exploitative.

This question is and has always been controversial. Even at the dawn of industrialization, workers did not simply or easily accept the working conditions. They banded together into coalitions, destroyed machines, and sought to exert control over their work environment in numerous ways. Such behavior explains why entrepreneurs relied so heavily on workers who were not there by choice. Workers also "voted with their feet": they sought alternative employment, migrated within the British Isles, or emigrated elsewhere. For them, the issue was clearly one of exploitation and what they could do about it.

Entrepreneurs and managers, of course, viewed the matter quite differently. They claimed that they could not increase wages, lower hours, or improve conditions if they wished to stay in business, much less make a profit. Laborers, entrepreneurs asserted, still had too much control over the workplace and did not produce as much as they should. Their emphasis was, unquestionably, the necessity of squeezing as much profit as possible from the labor force to maximize their investments, to encourage the development of industrial society that might lead to a "revolution."

In hopes of fostering an industrial revolution and avoiding a political revolution, state decision makers in England generally sided with entrepreneurs in any conflict between management and labor. The Hanoverian state eliminated the right of workers to organize or engage in collective bargaining and refused to limit hours or mandate minimum standards for health or safety until England had become the "workshop of the world" and the un-questioned industrial powerhouse. When workers attempted to use their superior numbers to get more money, better conditions, or fewer hours, the state made sure that their efforts were stillborn, intervening with force when necessary. Only after 1830 and then in a limited way did the state intervene to stop the worst of what the working classes experienced as exploitation. In the 20th century, the degree of state intervention on behalf of either workers or entrepreneurs depended mostly on the politics of the party in power.

The debate about the necessity of poor working conditions and paying the lowest possible wages to those who labored in the factories and mines of the Industrial Revolution raged across the 19th and into the 20th century. This was no simple scholarly debate; rather, the answer to this question has tremendous political and policy implications not only for industrialized countries but also for the developing world. What constitutes exploitation and how it was or can be established and maintained remains a fundamentally political question.

Historians and economists have approached the issue of exploitation of the working classes and its necessity to rapid industrialization in a variety of—often highly politicized—ways. In approaches to the Industrial Revolution, E. P. Thompson and an outstanding cohort of other labor historians like Eric Hobsbawm who were influenced greatly by Marxism delineated the conditions that workers endured and demonstrated that the working classes had not simply accepted their treatment. Following in these footsteps but also taking advantage of developments in the interlinked but separate histories of women and of children, the position of these groups has received a great deal of recent attention that demonstrates how bad their working conditions and pay scales were. The downward revisions to understandings of the standard of living for the working classes during the first two generations of industrialization have also bolstered the case that the working classes were exploited during the Industrial Revolution.

Others scholars have argued—more or less explicitly—that if workers did not emigrate and if they were able to purchase increasing amounts of consumer goods, then they could not really have been exploited. Jan de Vries's evocation of an "Industrious Revolution" in which the laboring classes worked harder (and longer) in order to be able to purchase manufactured trinkets or foodstuffs like coffee, chocolate, sugar, and tea can be understood as rejecting the notion of working-class experience as inherently exploitative. Comparison of the standard of living of workers to those in England's closest competitors shows that wages were often higher and consumption beyond the barest necessities greater there than elsewhere.

Historians of business and management have reconstructed the accounting for certain firms and sectors providing insight into the degree of profit that could and sometimes did accrue to the owners of successful enterprises. How profits were achieved and the contributions made by skimping on maintenance, safety, and wages while extending the work day and expectations of output must be understood in order to evaluate the "necessity" of the treatment of the working classes during the first 50 years of the Industrial Revolution.

In addition to greater attention to the histories of women and children in the Industrial Revolution, the issue of exploitation has been widened by greater attention to the empire and the profits amassed from colonies dependent on slavery. Although most scholars consider this a separate issue from the necessity of working-class exploitation, attention to the global dimensions of the economic developments that gave rise to the English Industrial Revolution provides new insight into the nature of industrialization in the 18th and 19th centuries.

Was the Industrial Revolution fundamentally exploitative of the English working classes? Did it have to be? Although contemporary documentary evidence of poor working conditions and extremely long hours for relatively low pay is overwhelming, these difficult circumstances do not automatically or inescapably imply the existence of exploitation. The necessity of these circumstances to an industrial revolution is a more hotly debated question. Could adequate profits have been earned if the laboring classes worked shorter hours, in a better work environment, for more money? Would those more modest profits have provided sufficient capital and the incentive to entrepreneurs to have touched off and sustained an industrial revolution? These questions suggest that the issue of whether the exploitation of the working classes was necessary to the Industrial Revolution requires clear definition of terms and judgment of the sources.

Sergio Castellanos-Gamboa takes a more quantitative approach that owes much to economics to conclude that things got better for the workers beginning around 1815 and quickening a generation later, but that the answer is harder to determine for earlier periods because of inadequacies of the data. He is in his third year in the PhD program of the Business School at Bangor University in the United Kingdom. Castellanos-Gamboa is working on the post-1945 evolution of consumer credit in Britain.

Jeff Horn emphasizes exactly that earlier period because it was then that the Industrial Revolution was most desperate for workers and profits. He also stresses the lived experience of the workers when examining the issue of exploitation. Horn is professor of history at Manhattan College and has written or edited five previous books that focus heavily on labor relations to understand the unique elements of European industrialization.

ANSWER: SERGIO CASTELLANOS-GAMBOA, THE EXPLOITATION OF THE WORKING CLASSES WAS NOT NECESSARY TO AN INDUSTRIAL REVOLUTION

To address this issue, the definition of labor exploitation is the appropriate starting point. Social scientists usually seek to understand and explain the world as objectively as possible. Defining terms helps to understand the nature of the argument and any conclusions drawn. Labor exploitation has been understood primarily through the lens of either socialism or neoclassical economics. Karl Marx analyzed the relationship between labor and capital. He argued that labor exploitation happens when workers cannot better their lives over the long term: they earn only enough to subsist so they can keep working. For most neoclassical economists, labor exploitation occurs only when wages are less than the marginal productivity of labor. That means that workers should be paid an amount equivalent to their contribution to overall production, which would generally occur in perfect, competitive labor markets.

Both definitions, nonetheless, include two important components. The first one, the value of labor, is not easy to measure. The final price of a good contains information about the whole production process, in which the added value of labor is an important part. The second element, the issue of fairness, is even more challenging. What is workers' fair share of the value of production? To judge whether labor exploitation occurred, this essay will explore the evolution of wages for the working classes along with working conditions and the standard of living both before and during the Industrial Revolution.

Although there were significant increases in wages during the Industrial Revolution compared to preindustrial times, other factors have to be taken into account when analyzing labor exploitation. First of all, real wages do not seem to have increased before the onset of the Napoleonic wars at the very end of the 18th century. Second, some evidence suggests that living standards at best stagnated during the first decades of industrialization, while evidence about an increase in working hours is mixed. Nor is there sufficient evidence that workers had to develop new work habits or become subject to a new time discipline.

Labor Productivity, Wages, Living Standards, and Working Conditions

Economic historian Gregory Clark argues that a more efficient and therefore a more productive economy was the main reason for the huge economic growth touched off by the Industrial Revolution. A notable increase in labor productivity during this period was the main driver of this growth. Therefore, if neoclassical economics is correct, we should expect wages to increase in a similar fashion. In particular, we would expect real wages to increase, showing an improvement in the working classes' purchasing power. Moreover, empirical evidence should exist that living standards were better for the new working classes than before the Industrial Revolution, justifying an increase in the hours worked.

Recent estimations of the evolution of wages for artisans and laborers in the building trades in England show an increase in real wages of about 60 percent between 1760 and 1860, with most of the increase happening after 1820. Other estimates put the increase at around 30 percent in the same period. These lower estimates mean that wages increased less than the improvement in output per worker, which demonstrates that some of the profits derived from that increase in labor productivity did not go to the workers. Proponents of an "Industrious Revolution" find that real wages for England and other countries show little evidence of an increase in purchasing power for workers' wages, and note that there was actually some deterioration before 1820. They focus, however, on evidence of growing consumer demand for a broader range of products among the working classes.

Marx's collaborator Friedrich Engels argued in 1844 that preindustrial workers were far better off than their successors who toiled in the factories because they achieved better living standards with fewer hours worked. Clark recognizes that during its first decades, the Industrial Revolution was not accompanied by a noticeable improvement of living conditions for the working classes, but emphasizes that this trend changed around the same time that real wages increased, i.e., after 1820 at the earliest and more likely around 1850. From that date to the beginning of the 20th century, conditions for workers improved and they started to earn salaries well above the subsistence level, opening the path for the emergence of a new middle class.

There seems to be mixed evidence of the evolution of the number of hours worked. In Birmingham and the Black Country, there is no evidence of a drastic change in the hours worked or the working conditions during the first half of the 19th century. However, more generally, there appears to have been a significant increase in the hours worked. This situation suggests a number of possibilities as to why workers might increase their supply of labor. For example, was there an "Industrious Revolution" that led them to exchange leisure for labor in order to earn the money to purchase a broader range of new consumer products? To answer that question is beyond the scope of this essay, but even if an "Industrious Revolution" occurred that led workers to labor longer hours, there does not seem to be evidence that the change in the working conditions should be labeled as labor exploitation.

Conclusion

The Industrial Revolution is a very powerful example that our understanding of the past is not absolute and can still be improved in different ways. Making use of new historical sources that shed new light is one way to do so. Another means of bettering historical understandings is to implement more sophisticated methodologies to assess more accurately previous theories.

The question of whether exploitation of the working classes was necessary to have an Industrial Revolution is very challenging. First of all, we must define what we mean by labor exploitation. Second, we have to analyze critically the information available regarding real wages, labor productivity, and living standards as well as qualitative data related to working conditions in factories, workshops, and mines. Finally, we have to find an appropriate measure to determine fair remuneration per time unit of labor for the working classes. Because of these complicated factors, the debate is still a vivid one.

There is evidence that the increase in economic efficiency and therefore economic growth was driven by an increase in labor productivity. Real wages seem to have increased steadily, but only after the end of the Napoleonic wars in 1815. The issue that remains controversial relates to the working classes' living standards across the whole period. Although people had access to a broader range of consumer products, considerable data suggests that they had to increase the hours they worked to acquire them, therefore reducing leisure time and very likely their living standards, at least during the first half of the 19th century.

To consider labor exploitation's potential link to the outbreak of an industrial revolution, we have to dig further into the qualitative data regarding the actual conditions under which workers were hired. In Britain, the relationship between employers and employees seems to have changed after the conclusion of the first Industrial Revolution around 1850 in favor of workers, with a reduced working day and more holidays. Nonetheless, although evidence for the exploitation of the working classes is not strong, some of the harsh working conditions imposed on the labor force did not seem to be a necessary condition for the Industrial Revolution to happen.

ANSWER: JEFF HORN, THE EXPLOITATION OF THE WORKING CLASSES WAS NECESSARY TO HAVE AN INDUSTRIAL REVOLUTION

Arguments claiming that such exploitation was not required for industrialization tend to start their considerations of the evidence in 1800 or 1820 rather than in 1760 or 1780 when the Industrial Revolution began. They ignore how difficult it was to find people willing to work in the first factories and they ignore the extraordinary lengths that industrial entrepreneurs went to in order to ensure a supply of docile labor. Without the exploitation of the working classes in the first generations of the Industrial Revolution, the British tinkerers who solved the practical problems involved in industrialization would not have had the time or profit cushion to work out their ideas. Nor would they have had the incentive to persevere through the inevitable hard times if they could not skim profits from the wages and working conditions of their laborers. To execute a relatively rapid transformation that yielded British industrial domination, the exploitation of the working classes to maximize entrepreneurial profits was absolutely necessary.

Until the Industrial Revolution had been underway for about 50 years, the lives of those who labored in factories suffered from their participation in the industrialization process. Research has demonstrated conclusively that the working classes' standard of living, their measure of well-being, began to improve only after 1830, a trend that accelerated after 1850. Living standards fell in the generation from 1760 to 1780, rose marginally until the early 1790s, and then declined once again until around 1820. The standard of living only began to improve in the 1820s, with most of the improvement coming after 1830. From 1760 to 1820, the standard of living fell about 16 percent before increasing by over 40 percent between 1820 and 1850. For the British economy as a whole, real family income, which measures the amount of goods and services that can be purchased, increased about 30 percent in the entire period, but the first three generations of factory workers experienced a declining standard of living.

How that increase in income was achieved also matters enormously. Higher family income stemmed from a surge in the number of hours worked on the part of men, women, and children alike. In 1760, the average employed British adult worked nearly 50 hours a week. In 1850, British adults labored more than 61 hours a week with many factory workers and miners putting in up to 84 hours a week. Despite legislation limiting their hours and potential places in employment, by that same date, 36 percent of children aged 10–14 worked full time for wages outside the home.

Factories and mines were also deeply unpleasant places to labor—an important feature of the exploitation of the British working classes. Early industrial machinery was dangerous, cutting off fingers, toes, and limbs: steam engines were prone to explode, scattering shrapnel. Mine shafts collapsed or asphyxiated miners. Pollution, extremes of heat and cold, lack of ventilation, and many other unhealthy factors had a strong impact on the life span and health of workers. Manchester, in the county of Lancashire, the industrial heart of England, witnessed some of the worst exploitation of the working classes. With a life-span of only 17 years because of exceptionally high rates of infant mortality, workers in Manchester could look forward to a mere 43 percent of the life-span of the average British person. In 1850, the average Briton was physically shorter, less healthy, less literate, and worked much longer hours than in 1760. They were also subjected to far harsher discipline as managers and foremen sought to train people to be as tireless and efficient as the machines they tended. Money is not everything: these considerations of health and welfare greatly outweigh an increased ability to consume in determining whether the working classes were exploited.

Factory labor was only a last resort: workers did not voluntarily submit to their own exploitation. The first factories tended to be located in areas that were both relatively impoverished and densely populated. They offered wages that were about 20 percent higher than nonfactory jobs to entice workers who clearly did not want to submit to industrial discipline. A lack of alternatives other than emigration or starvation drove some into the factories. Jobs also attracted some to the factories from Ireland and the Highlands of Scotland: these workers hoped to earn enough money to return home as soon as possible.

The factories also relied fundamentally on those with no other options. Women were offered jobs in the mills, factories, and mines, but never for wages even remotely equivalent to men's. In Manchester, the highest paid woman factory worker made only a quarter of the highest paid male and the average woman earned nearly 40 percent less than the average man. Children earned a mere one-sixth to one-eighth of an adult laborer (in proportion to their gender). With few other choices, women and children comprised the bulk of industrial labor. In 1818, over half of the workers in English cotton factories were adult women. Children made up another third of the labor force. Scottish factories were even more dependent on the labor of women and children. Many children accompanied their parent(s) into the factories or mines, but many more were sent there as "apprentices." Parents committed children up to the age of 21 to work for their parish (local religious community) in exchange for money or other support, paid to the parents, not the child doing the work. A child could also be apprenticed to a master or entrepreneur for up to seven years. Thus, a substantial number of young people under the age of 21 had to work 12–14 hours a day, six days a week, living in barracks, lofts, or dormitories, often hundreds of miles from home. Without recourse to parish apprentices, women, and children, entrepreneurs like Richard Arkwright and Josiah Wedgwood who elaborated the factory system could not have found workers. Treating those workers poorly and underpaying them drastically was essential to the profits that underlay the rapid spread of the factory system. The heavy reliance on underpaid, underage, and unfree workers demonstrates the exploitative nature of the labor system in the first generations of the British Industrial Revolution.

The necessity of exploitation to the British Industrial Revolution was also demonstrated by the actions of the Hanoverian state. Legal repression in myriad forms was complemented by military repression whenever workers resisted their exploitation. Workers were legally prohibited from combining or joining forces in any way, while entrepreneurs were encouraged to form trusts to set wages and prices. Particularly during the age of the French Revolution and Napoleon (1789–1815), the average British person lost many of their customary rights and protections while new repressive laws restricted individual liberties. The ability of British entrepreneurs to get the state to make machine-breaking into a crime carrying the death penalty in 1812 during the Luddite movement is representative of how the legal system protected the economic interests of factory owners by disciplining the working classes.

The factual evidence that the English working classes were exploited is overwhelming. Although some entrepreneurs or apologists like Andrew Ure attempted to defend the treatment of the working classes, their efforts should be seen as justifications for a system that earned huge profits for elites at the expense of the health and welfare of the working classes. The emigration of significant numbers of people from the British Isles in search of opportunity demonstrates how dire the situation was and the lengths that people would go to in order to avoid factory work. As attitudes shifted in the 1820s and 1830s, the British state eventually began to investigate the treatment of workers. The testimony of workers, entrepreneurs, and state employees charged with oversight and inspection is incontrovertible in demonstrating the abuses of the system and the reliance on exploitation to maximize profits. That initial attempts at government regulation of the worst of industrial abuses took decades to become effective as entrepreneurs thwarted both the spirit and the letter of the new laws in the name of keeping their profits as high as possible reveals the ongoing exploitation of the British working classes.

CLOSING

Whether the exploitation of the working classes was necessary to the Industrial Revolution looks very different depending on which period is given priority. If the emphasis is 1760–1800 or even 1820, then it is much harder to make the case that the working classes were not exploited, though the issue of necessity remains an open question. For the period after 1820 or 1830, whether the working classes experienced exploitation is more debatable. However, the necessity of poor treatment of the working classes is undermined by the example of entrepreneurs like Robert Owen and the ongoing profitability after legislative protections were finally passed and made effective in the 1830s and 1840s.

Sergio Castellanos-Gamboa takes a more business-friendly, quantitative approach to determining whether exploitation took place. He points to the economic relationship between productivity and wages as the best means of investigating the issue of exploitation and whether it was needed to generate an industrial revolution. Jeff Horn also deploys statistics, but his approach centers on how working people actually lived. Given the well-known shortcomings of the data collected in this era, all statistics should be taken with a rather large grain of salt. The necessity of exploitation is a sensitive subject that requires further analysis using both quantitative and qualitative data. Readers are encouraged to consider this question equally from the perspective of entrepreneurs and managers and from that of the working classes, as well as considering what might have been best in the short and in the long run for society as a whole.

DOING MORE

Online

Burnette, Joyce. "Women Workers in the British Industrial Revolution." Available online at https://eh.net/encyclopedia/women-workers-in-the-british-industrial -revolution/.

Nye, John V. C. "Standards of Living and Modern Economic Growth." Available online at http://www.econlib.org/library/Enc/StandardsofLivingandModern EconomicGrowth.html.

Tuttle, Carolyn. "Child Labor during the British Industrial Revolution." Available online at https://eh.net/encyclopedia/child-labor-during-the-british-industrial -revolution/.

Print

Clark, Gregory. "The Condition of the Working-Class in England, 1209–2004." *Journal of Political Economy* 113, no. 6 (2005): 1307–40.

De Vries, Jan. *The Industrious Revolution: Consumer Behavior and the Household Economy, 1650 to the Present*. Cambridge: Cambridge University Press, 2008.

Floud, Roderick, and Paul Johnson, eds. *The Cambridge Economic History of Modern Britain*, vol. 1, *Industrialisation, 1700–1860*. Cambridge: Cambridge University Press, 2004.

Hobsbawm, Eric. *Industry and Empire: The Birth of the Industrial Revolution*. London: Penguin, 1969.

Horn, Jeff. *The Path Not Taken: French Industrialization in the Age of Revolution, 1750–1830*. Cambridge, MA: MIT Press, 2006.

Humphries, Jane. *Childhood and Child Labour in the British Industrial Revolution.* Cambridge: Cambridge University Press, 2011.

Thompson, E. P. *The Making of the English Working Class.* New York: Vintage Books, 1966 [1963].

QUESTION 3: COULD AN INDUSTRIAL REVOLUTION HAVE TAKEN PLACE WITHOUT EUROPEAN COLONIALISM AND IMPERIALISM?

Confronting the global history of the Industrial Revolution has emerged as vital to understanding this complicated subject. By forcing us to go beyond evocations of the national or even transnational or regional histories of industrialization to examine the importance of European colonialism and imperialism as necessary precursors to industrial transformation, this question underscores the growing importance of the emerging global economy. Although Europe's global commitments and industrialization are usually dealt with separately, this question emphasizes the fact that they were actually intimately linked.

Furnishing raw materials, goods, and markets, Europe's colonies and global trade ties were essential to generating the capital and consumer demand that enabled industrialization to occur. Emphasis on colonies and imperialism dependent on the slave trade and slavery also raises the issue of exploitation and its link to the Industrial Revolution in a new key. This question also focuses attention on the role of the state: Mercantilist trade policies and dedication to war making appear as critical components of government action that enabled and supported industrialization. The acquisition of Europe's largest empire and the most valuable global trade ties by England also goes a long way in explaining why that nation was the first to experience an industrial revolution.

Trade, especially exchange with the colonies, has always been an important part of the story of early-modern economic development. Since a growing percentage of 18th-century English and French commerce was tied to Atlantic trade, colonialism and imperialism were included in the discussion, though usually as objects rather than subjects, particularly in the literature written by Europeans. Scholars' delineation of the changing contours of commercial interaction between Europe and its colonies and later with other global trading partners was crucial to understanding how trade, especially trade with the colonies, sustained the manufacturing economy.

With regard to the colonies, the role of European governments in fostering industrialization has been misunderstood. Many scholars have accepted Adam Smith's attack on mercantilism for slowing down or preventing economic growth as actual English policy rather than a critique of his contemporary practice. The English observed fundamentally mercantilist trade policies until the middle of the 19th century, especially when it came to its colonies. By protecting markets and supplies of raw materials, supporting the British merchant marine, establishing monopolies and encouraging private investors to seek opportunities abroad, mercantilism was an effective state means of fostering growth in manufacturing. Instead of undermining the possibility of an industrial revolution, English mercantilism seems to have supported or perhaps enabled industrialization, especially in the 18th and early 19th centuries. Even the loss of 13 North American colonies, in large measure because of mercantilist trade policies, did not challenge the basic course or effectiveness of British state action during the first generations of the Industrial Revolution.

In the last 30 years, however, investigations of trade have placed greater emphasis on the contributions provided by Europe's colonies and imperial trade ties. Growing attention to globalization and the emergence of a true global economy has shifted the terms of the discussion. In particular, the influence of slavery in enabling Europe to industrialize at the expense of other parts of the world has come to the fore. European colonialism and imperialism are now indelibly part of the story of the Industrial Revolution in ways that these subjects had never been before.

The current contours of this question owe much to the work of Joseph Inikori. His masterful study of the contributions of slavery and the slave trade to the Industrial Revolution has been a revelation. With Africans generating no less than 69 percent (in 1651–1670 and again in 1848–1850) and up to 83 percent (in 1761–1780) of the value of British Atlantic commerce, it is impossible to ignore the importance of slavery and the slave trade in the accumulation of capital that made an industrial revolution possible. In the wake of Inikori's findings, which ensure greater focus on the issue of exploitation—primarily of slaves rather than workers—the ever-present dark side of colonialism has received additional attention. Kenneth Pomeranz provided an additional piece of the global puzzle by arguing that it was domination of the resources and markets of North and South America that permitted Europe to leapfrog China on the path to an industrial revolution. By posing this "what if" question, Pomeranz concentrated attention on the political economy of global power relations rather than on solely European concerns or more formal economic issues. Clearly, in these accounts, the slaves who made the western hemisphere such a profitable possession seem to have been necessary for an industrial revolution. The empire might even have served as a model for how the state and entrepreneurs could control rebellious workers at home. But the complicated challenge to the existing literature posed by Inikori and Pomeranz is still not fully integrated into most accounts of industrialization.

This question also underscores the need to consider the role of stocks of capital in industrialization both more critically and more creatively. How much was needed to enable an industrial revolution? Could it have been acquired elsewhere? Could England, in particular, with its relatively small size and population, have found an alternative? How long might it have taken? Would the delay have permitted England's competitors to steal a march? Put another way, the essential question is: What was the tipping point in terms of capital stocks in allowing or even encouraging industrialization? An essentially technical economic analysis ought to be complemented by an answer that takes cultural attitudes into account. What level of reserves was necessary to permit investors to support new ways of manufacturing? Did the benefits of colonialism and imperialism provide governing elites with the experience and confidence to encourage entrepreneurs and control the working classes? Such questions are becoming much more prominent in financial considerations of the Industrial Revolution.

Colonialism and imperialism obviously played a major role in the British Industrial Revolution. The exact nature of that role and whether the contributions of colonialism and empire were necessary to the transformation of manufacturing that occurred between 1750 and 1850 are much more uncertain. The greatly enhanced attention given to the inputs of Africans in the Atlantic world has shifted the terms of this question so that scholarly consensus is in flux. What is absolutely clear is that the foundations of European industrial revolutions must take global trade and colonies into account.

Europe did not industrialize by itself. Manufacturing relied on markets, resources, and profits from around the globe in order to transform society. In the 18th and early 19th centuries, Europeans depended on the Atlantic world for these inputs more than any other global region. In that era and in that place, European colonialism was inextricably linked to slavery and the slave trade, which recalls forcibly the issue of exploitation. This question also calls for analysis of exactly how much capital—either per capita or in total—is necessary to begin and sustain an industrial revolution.

Sophie Muller's essay is focused squarely on the Atlantic world. Based on a variety of factors including mercantilism, she concludes that colonialism in the so-called New World was necessary to the British Industrial Revolution. Muller is completing her doctorate in history at the Graduate Center of the City University of New York. Her dissertation is entitled "Poster Boys: Paternalism, Working-Class Boyhood, and Masculinity in Victorian and Edwardian London." She teaches part-time at John Jay College of Criminal Justice and the Cooper Union.

The second essay is by Jeff Horn, who recognizes the importance of colonialism and imperialism to the Industrial Revolution but argues comparatively that the profits, markets, and resources garnered through colonialism were necessary but not sufficient to explain Britain's industrial transformation. Horn is professor of history at Manhattan College and the author of five previous books. His most recent monograph, *Economic Development in Early Modern France: The Privilege of Liberty, 1650–1820* (Cambridge University Press, 2015) explores these same issues of trade and empire.

ANSWER: SOPHIE MULLER, COLONIALISM AND IMPERIALISM IN THE NEW WORLD WERE ESSENTIAL TO THE BRITISH INDUSTRIAL REVOLUTION

In the late 18th century, Britain was the first country to undergo the Industrial Revolution, in large part due to the resource advantage and increased markets provided by colonization of the New World. The Industrial Revolution ultimately marked a shift from handicraft goods to rapidly produced, machine-made goods utilizing unskilled labor. Although many economies around the world industrialized after 1780, one of the central questions is: Why did Britain industrialize first? Most commonly, new technologies and mechanical innovation have been seen as the root. While the invention of machines to assist production was essential to efficiency in output, it was Britain's New World colonialism and Atlantic commercial networks that expanded the supply of resources and markets necessary for industrial growth. Britain established long-term economic connections to the New World that yielded a competitive advantage in resources, new captive markets, an increased share of global markets, and a spark for domestic transformation. Without colonialism and imperialism in the New World, Britain could not have started and maintained an industrial revolution.

Britain was certainly not the only, or the first, western European country to conquer an overseas empire in the New World. Spain and Portugal received significant profits from the removal of precious metals like gold and silver from their Caribbean and Latin American colonies beginning in the early 16th century. The conversion of Caribbean and South American territories to first tobacco and then sugar plantations maintained or even increased the commercial advantage of New World colonialism for western Europe. While Britain profited from colonies of exploitation in Central and South America as well as the Caribbean, it was the addition of settlement colonies in North America during the 17th century that were critical to Britain's long-term commercial success.

Spain and Portugal gained significantly in the short term from the resources flowing out of their New World territories, but struggled to open up markets for the consumption of goods sold by European merchants. These countries received short-term riches but gained little long-term commercial benefit. Instead, it was the British, Dutch, and French who ultimately succeeded in fostering multilateral flows of goods around the Atlantic, through both formal networks of joint-stock companies as well as informal networks of private traders, privateers, and pirates. However, the strength and disruptive capacity of British informal networks, as well as political and military upheavals on the continent, diverted French and Dutch resources, facilitating British colonial dominance. By the start of the Industrial Revolution, Great Britain had surpassed the Netherlands as the mercantile and commercial capital of Europe. Even after the loss of the 13 colonies, Britain had amassed the most valuable territorial empire in the western hemisphere and was continuing to expand global trade networks utilizing New World advantages. This dominance was in part responsible for the continuance of Britain's economic empire even after U.S. independence in 1783.

The New World's colonial resources paved the way for Britain's Industrial Revolution in a number of ways. The most straightforward of these advantages was that New World territorial conquests increased Britain's access to natural resources, the core of the mercantilist economy. Resources like precious metals, sugar, and tobacco were utilized by Britain to increase domestic consumption and enhanced Britain's position in trade with the continent as well as enabling increased trade with China and India. As China was in the process of demonetarizing from paper money to metal coins, the only way to secure high-value luxury items like silks and porcelain was in exchange for New World silver. The physical geography of Europe's North American colonies, often referred to as "ghost acreage," also provided an answer to the Malthusian problem of population growth overtaking agricultural resources. While it was the sugar- and tobacco-producing colonies that provided the initial economic windfall, trade networks established with the settlement colonies of New England were also a critical investment that later supported British industrialization. While the New England territories were not immediately profitable in raw materials, they were an important part of Britain's Atlantic World trade. New England provided food and goods that supported Britain's sugar-producing colonies in the Caribbean and South America so that they could specialize in plantation production. In return, raw materials and precious metals flowed back to New England and then across the Atlantic in exchange for British manufactured goods. This multilateral trade strengthened Britain's global position in markets and generated significant profits: the New England colonies were essential to the strength of the network.

Britain also gained long-term commercial advantages from the protectionist economic policies put in place within the empire well before industrialization. Navigation Acts passed in 1651 and renewed in 1662, 1663, 1670, and 1673, lasting at least partly through the mid-19th century, reflected the mercantilist desire to keep imperial resources within the empire and out of the hands of foreigners, especially European competitors. While not benefitting from the lower market price advantage of "free trade," the requirement that all New World resources pass through British ports entrenched a trade monopoly across the Atlantic. North American colonies consumed British manufactured goods and in return supplied food and resources to Britain's sugar-producing colonies, whose resources then flowed back to Britain for trade or production. Britain gained considerable financial advantages from this controlled trade. These entrenched networks survived the end of the Navigation Acts and the independence of the 13 colonies. The continuation of this connection over the long term had something to do with continued high demand for British consumer goods in the newly independent American states. However, markets do not tell the whole story.

British investors had long-standing financial relationships with Chesapeake tobacco plantation owners. Even after the American Revolution, these plantation owners remained conduits through which American tobacco made its way into continental European markets. These British merchants also benefited from the distraction of European military conflicts after 1792. While no longer obligated to trade, Britain remained America's primary trading partner continuing the exchange of New World resources for British manufactured goods. At the beginning of the 19th century, Britain continued to be the conduit through which America conducted most of its overseas trade. The importance of Britain's unequal trade relationship with newly independent and increasingly wealthy America during the early stages of the Industrial Revolution should not be understated. This network yielded not only increasing export/import income, but also allowed for an increasing flow of American cotton in the 19th century, enhancing and continuing Britain's industrial supremacy in textiles.

Overseas colonial conquests and resource advantages also supported Britain's domestic production. Growing resource extraction from the Americas increased the population of port cities, resulting in the rise in demand for coal as an urban fuel source. The conquest and protection of colonies, as well as internal European conflicts, were costly, but increased demand for coal and iron to manufacture arms thus supported industrial development. Investment in joint-stock companies and career opportunities from overseas trade amplified the flow of capital to the British aristocracy and provided new opportunities for manufacturing and factory investment, which would be the foundation of the emerging middle class.

While there was a confluence of factors resulting in Britain being the first nation to industrialize, at the core of economic advantage and opportunity were the resources and commercial networks opened up by conquest and long-term investment in the New World. Resources from the Americas eased and permitted global trade for Europeans while encouraging the development of new markets and commercial relationships. Without these trade opportunities and resource advantages—in other words, without colonialism and imperialism—it would have been impossible for Britain to specialize its manufacturing ahead of other leaders in trade and innovation. Based on mercantilist principles, Britain established long-term commercial relationships with the 13 colonies that resulted in a highly profitable import/export and investment relationship with America that survived independence. British manufacturing for economic exchange as well as military demand, the latter in part to maintain colonial holdings, helped fuel domestic industrial production, setting off what would become a century of industrial dominance.

ANSWER: JEFF HORN, BRITISH COLONIALISM WAS A NECESSARY BUT NOT SUFFICIENT CAUSE OF THE INDUSTRIAL REVOLUTION

European colonialism provided the resources and profits that underlay the Industrial Revolution. Britain, however, did not have to be a major colonial power. That nation could have initiated industrialization by trading with the colonies of other European powers. An open exchange of manufactures for colonial goods might have accomplished the same things, but it seems unlikely that it would have allowed Britain to be the *first* industrial nation. Such counterfactual conjectures can be used to highlight the essential factors in a complicated process.

England was far from the first European colonial power. Spain and Portugal established colonies and trading stations in several places in the western hemisphere, Africa, and Asia that enabled them to tap into these areas' wealth for their own benefit. The advantages of colonialism were so clear that states in competition with the Iberian powers, most notably the Dutch, French, and English, immediately disputed their control and, in the 17th century, both conquered some of Spain's or Portugal's colonies and established others on their own. It was also in the 17th century that the foundations of plantation agriculture in the so-called New World using slave labor were laid, as that region's easily exploitable mineral wealth was exhausted.

The path England took in the 17th century led to an industrial revolution in the 18th. To acquire or establish colonies required the mobilization of scarce resources that often had a quite slow return on investment. Competition with powerful continental military powers like Spain and France or naval powerhouses like the Dutch forced the English state to develop greater authority and to implement monopolistic trade policies that would later become associated with mercantilism. State action could have focused on defense, trade, and supporting the development of those English industries, crafts, and productions that were or could become internationally competitive.

When England began to industrialize in the third quarter of the 18th century, its empire consisted primarily of Bengal in India and scattered outposts along the western coastline of Africa, various Caribbean islands of which Jamaica was the largest and most important, and a large number of colonies on the mainland of North America like Canada, Florida, and what came to be known as the 13 colonies. Although Bengal generated considerable profits for the British East India Company and the 13 colonies yielded quantities of tobacco, indigo, and rice that did not duplicate what Great Britain itself produced, the vast bulk of British trade was in tropical and semitropical commodities such as sugar, cotton, chocolate, coffee, and rice from the Caribbean basin. These commodities were re-exported to Europe or exchanged for luxury goods from Asia. Millions of Africans were traded for European manufactures and then brought as slaves to the western hemisphere to grow these commodities. This global trading network was essential to British industrialization.

Atlantic trade spawned huge profits for Europeans. Britain's exports, re-exports, imports, and service grew from an average annual value of £20,084,000 in 1651–1670 to £105,546,000 in 1781–1800 reaching an amazing £231,046,000 in 1848–1850. About 40 percent of this total was produced by Britain. According to historian Joseph Inikori, African labor generated more than half of this wealth, reaching a high point of 83 percent of British Atlantic commerce in 1761–1780. Not only was Atlantic trade growing rapidly, but the exchange also intensely favored Europe. Annual profit from British trade with the 13 North American colonies was £2.64 million out of an already depressed official total of £9.5 million. Thus, 28 percent of the volume of trade was European profit.

The effects of this rapid expansion of highly profitable trade were profound. Growing trade encouraged technological innovation. Integrating different territories into a global trading system brought new opportunities that fostered commercial and industrial diversification. Perhaps more importantly, demand for manufactured goods was no longer limited to the size of the domestic or even regional market. Commercial profits were often invested in industrial concerns, and improved forms of business practice including joint-stock companies and the London stock market were developed to cope with the tremendous profits. Within Britain itself, entrepreneurs found numerous ways and means of exercising their skills, and access to addictive commodities and fashionable luxury goods led some workers to labor more hours in order to afford coffee, chocolate, or a silk scarf. To carry this expanded trade, Britain's merchant fleet emerged as the largest in the world, more than tripling in tonnage over the course of the 18th century.

The mercantilist policies developed to manage this trade were based on colonialism, but they did not have to be. Managing foreign trade to keep a positive balance led the British government to favor producers at both the top and bottom of the market who could acquire and maintain markets abroad. The British government successfully favored domestic producers at the expense of consumers. As a policy approach, free trade was barely considered, much less implemented before the middle of the 19th century.

The possibility that Britain could have garnered the profits and products it needed to industrialize without colonialism is provided by trade with the newly independent United States after 1783. Despite losing political control of these former colonies, trade burgeoned, reaching almost £30 million in 1800, more than 300 percent higher than when the Declaration of Independence was promulgated. Profitable though it was, the benefit from U.S. trade was small potatoes compared to that from the slave trade. It is important to note that British colonists purchased only a small percent of the human beings that the British brought to the western hemisphere. The colonies of other European powers absorbed the vast bulk of them. Also, while the East India Company acquired vast swaths of land, not all of Britain's chartered companies were colonialist. Indeed, the Muscovy and Levant companies were highly profitable despite not governing any territory. Mercantilist trade policies supported and encouraged colonialism, but territorial expansion was not always necessary to their success. The probability of slower growth because of fewer protected markets, greater competition, and lowered margins did not preclude British industrialization, but making the breakthrough to an industrial revolution would have been far more difficult and, at the earliest, it would have come a generation or two later. The huge profits generated by the empire, as opposed to colonial trade, came only in the 19th century, when the British Industrial Revolution was already well underway.

The great exception to this counterfactual hypothesis is Ireland. Until 1801, Ireland was a colony of first England and then Great Britain. The needs of the Irish economy were thoroughly subordinated to Britain's to avoid or minimize competition. This protected market and source of raw materials was essential to British economic competitiveness and showed English and Scottish elites the profit possibilities of colonialism. It is hard to imagine how Britain could have had an industrial revolution in the 18th and 19th centuries without firm control of Ireland.

Historian Kenneth Pomeranz argues that it was privileged access to the resources and markets of the Americas that enabled Europe to industrialize before China. A huge proportion of the economic value of the western hemisphere in the 18th century was provided by African slavery. Britain did not have to control territory in order to participate in these benefits. In fact, by concentrating on developing new technologies to improve production as well as innovative goods to sell, without incurring the massive expenses of a long series of colonial wars fought around the globe, Britain might possibly have become an even more efficient international competitor. In short, colonialism in the Atlantic world was both necessary and sufficient to European industrialization. British colonialism, however, was a necessary but not sufficient cause of the Industrial Revolution.

CLOSING

In the 18th and early 19th centuries European colonialism and imperialism centered on the Atlantic world. Following in the footsteps of Portugal and Spain, England, France, and the Netherlands established outposts and trade ties in and to various places in Africa and the Americas during the 17th century. Slavery and the slave trade enabled the development of these links and colonies. This trade provided products, especially tropical commodities; consumed a high proportion of Europe's export of manufactured goods; and spawned a high percentage of these nations' commercial profits. It cannot be doubted that various national industrial revolutions, especially Britain's, benefited greatly from European domination of these trade relationships.

Both authors agree that colonialism and imperialism were essential contributors to the British Industrial Revolution and that the Atlantic world was the key to growing European domination of global trade. Where they differ is on the meaning of those contributions. Muller argues that the economic advantages provided by the "New World" to Britain were necessary to the Industrial Revolution by exploring the growth of markets and the provision of resources including with the independent United States. By deploying counterfactuals as well as thinking comparatively about the emergence of trade relations in the Atlantic world, Horn believes that through trade Britain could have accrued the same or similar benefits that it received through colonialism and imperialism. Without colonies, Britain could still have industrialized, though the process might have taken longer to get underway. The essays of Muller and Horn indirectly support the thesis of Kenneth Pomeranz that domination of the Americas was the key advantage that Europe had in the race with China to industrialize. Colonialism and imperialism were state policies that spurred European competitiveness and enabled an industrial revolution.

DOING MORE

Online

Harley, C. Knick. "Slavery, the British Atlantic Economy and the Industrial Revolution." University of Oxford Discussion Papers in Economic and Social History 113, April 2013. Available online at https://www.nuff.ox.ac.uk/economics/history/paper113/harley113.pdf.

Stuchtey, Benedikt. "Colonialism and Imperialism, 1450–1950." Available online at http://ieg-ego.eu/en/threads/backgrounds/colonialism-and-imperialism/benedikt-stuchtey-colonialism-and-imperialism-1450–1950.

The Transatlantic Slave Trade Database. Available online at http://www.slavevoyages.org/.

Print

Davis, David Brion. *Inhuman Bondage: The Rise and Fall of Slavery in the New World.* New York: Oxford University Press, 2008.

Hont, Istvan. *Jealousy of Trade: International Competition and the Nation-State in Historical Perspective.* Cambridge, MA: Belknap Press, 2005.

Inikori, Joseph E. *Africans and the Industrial Revolution in England: A Study in International Trade and Economic Development.* Cambridge: Cambridge University Press, 2002.

Morgan, Kenneth. *Slavery, Atlantic Trade and the British Economy, 1660–1800.* Cambridge: Cambridge University Press, 2000.

Pomeranz, Kenneth. *The Great Divergence: China, Europe, and the Making of the Modern World Economy.* Princeton, NJ: Princeton University Press, 2000.

Voth, Hans-Joachim, and Peter Temin. *Prometheus Shackled: Goldsmith Banks and England's Financial Revolution after 1700.* Oxford: Oxford University Press, 2013.

Wallerstein, Immanuel. *The Modern World-System III: The Second Era of Great Expansion of the Capitalist World-Economy, 1730s–1840s.* Berkeley: University of California Press, 2011.

Selected Annotated Bibliography

ONLINE SOURCES

Simply typing a term into a search engine on the Internet is likely to get you sponsored links, Wikipedia, or unreliable material. It is a far better research strategy to start with a recognized portal or a known scholar with a recognizable, appropriate institutional affiliation and use them to find material that is reliable, accurate, and appropriately cited. If you must use Wikipedia, follow the links to sites that have experts making sure that the information is accurate. Google Books has a vast collection of materials related to the Industrial Revolution, but separating the wheat from the chaff is difficult. It is better to find references beforehand to something that might be available on Google Books than to start searching there. Although there is a great deal of excellent material available on the Web—and more every day—much of it, even on sites that purport to be for educators or students, is rife with errors and amounts to little more than a brief introduction. Regarding the Industrial Revolution, as with any other topic, Internet resources must be used with great care and should start with the sites listed below.

http://echo.gmu.edu/
The Roy Rosenzweig Center for History and New Media (http://chnm.gmu.edu/) is an excellent starting point for most historical research. Its links are checked regularly to make sure that they are working. This institution also works with experts in many fields related to the study of the past to make sure controversial subjects are linked appropriately. The digital address above is to ECHO (Exploring and Collecting

History Online), a directory of 5,000 plus Web sites dedicated to science, technology, and industry. Start here for general sites on the Industrial Revolution.

http://www.econlib.org/index.html
The Library of Economics and Liberty has an encyclopedia that is interesting and provocative as well as some primary sources, a few books, and several guides to help find materials. Much of the material and information found on or through this site has a particular political viewpoint: it can still be valuable, but it should be used with caution and never uncritically.

http://eh.net/
EH-Net is maintained by a number of highly respected scholarly organizations related to economic history, broadly speaking. It has several useful resources. The Encyclopedia is reputable and useful, though it is hardly comprehensive. The Databases and How Much Is That? section provide useful information about economic history, especially related to questions of change or exchanges over time.

http://legacy.fordham.edu/Halsall/mod/modsbook14.asp
Fordham University's Internet Modern History Sourcebook's collection of primary sources on the Industrial Revolution is an excellent place for students and scholars to find accessible, well-edited, and reliable documents. It is quite stable, which means you can link to it, though things have shifted on occasion. Other subjects like 18th-century Britain will also have relevant documents, so browsing often repays your effort.

http://invention.si.edu/
The Lemelson Center for the Study of Invention and Innovation at the Smithsonian Institution is a good place to consider issues related to invention in U.S. history. It provides more technical material on science and technology than almost any other site.

http://ebooks.library.cornell.edu/m/moa/
The Making of America collection at the Cornell University Library is a well-curated means of accessing primary sources about early industrialization in the United States, with particular emphasis on science and technology.

https://memory.loc.gov/ammem/index.html
The American Memory project at the Library of Congress is a superb place to look for primary sources including images on subjects related to U.S. industrialization. The general collection contains much of interest for those exploring industrialization in other places.

http://www.nationalarchives.gov.uk/
The British National Archives provides access to a considerable collection of primary sources and images. The Find Guides can help you navigate its enormous holdings.

Although focused on the United Kingdom, this repository has documents related to industrialization around the globe, especially in former and current British colonies.

http://www.lib.utexas.edu/maps/
The Perry-Castañeda Library Map Collection at the University of Texas Library is a phenomenal collection of historical maps covering the entire world. The maps are available in a variety of formats and include many maps specific to resources, transportation, and demography that are directly relevant to the Industrial Revolution.

http://www.spinningtheweb.org.uk/
This is a rich collection of materials related to textile history in Northwest England where the Industrial Revolution began. As with all good local history sites, there is material here found nowhere else.

http://www.victorianweb.org/
The Victorian Web has an eclectic collection of primary and secondary source materials. Many topics cannot be explored here, but those that are present are usually useful and reliable. It is not always updated and there are some dead links. Not the best place to start, but a reasonable repository of documents, interpretations, and links.

PRINT SOURCES

Economic History

Daunton, Martin J. *Progress and Poverty: An Economic and Social History of Britain 1700–1850*. Oxford: Oxford University Press, 1995.
This book is the most insightful socioeconomic account of this critical century and a half. Well written, it presents a convincing version of why and how the Industrial Revolution occurred when and where it did. For a general text, it is highly recommended.

De Vries, Jan. *The Industrious Revolution: Consumer Behavior and the Household Economy, 1650 to the Present*. Cambridge: Cambridge University Press, 2008.
This highly controversial book has received a great deal of attention for its provocative yet problematic linked arguments about the willingness of laborers to work longer and harder in order to consume more as well as for its emphasis on the role of this aspect of demand in enabling the occurrence of the Industrial Revolution.

Floud, Roderick, and Paul Johnson, eds. *The Cambridge Economic History of Modern Britain*, vol. 1, *Industrialisation, 1700–1860*. Cambridge: Cambridge University Press, 2004.
This book is one of the key interpretations of the British Industrial Revolution. For economic history, this work by acknowledged experts in the field ought to be

consulted. Although a little less wide ranging than previous versions, in the subjects it does treat, Floud and Johnson set the standard.

Mokyr, Joel. *The Enlightened Economy: An Economic History of Britain 1700–1850.* New Haven, CT: Yale University Press, 2009.
Mokyr, one of the finest economic historians alive, turns his focus to the role of the knowledge economy in fostering the Industrial Revolution. The book emphasizes the role of culture in economic development.

Pollard, Sidney. *The Genesis of Modern Management: A Study of the Industrial Revolution in Great Britain.* Cambridge, MA: Harvard University Press, 1965.
This path-breaking book links contemporary business practice to the age of the Industrial Revolution. There is still no better place to learn about the role of management in fostering the British Industrial Revolution.

Wrigley, E. A. *Energy and the English Industrial Revolution.* Cambridge: Cambridge University Press, 2010.
By demonstrating the role of energy in the Industrial Revolution, Wrigley has made a profound argument about the nature of economic development. Although the origins of some of his statistics give pause, as does whether they can be compared in the way he asserts, this brief volume presents a powerful and provocative interpretation of the British Industrial Revolution.

General Studies of the British Industrial Revolution

Griffin, Emma. *A Short History of the British Industrial Revolution.* Houndsmills, UK: Palgrave, 2010.
Griffin's lively and idiosyncratic account is easy to read and covers the basics with considerable verve and sufficient evidence. She attacks the views that it was British education and/or technology that drove the Industrial Revolution.

King, Steven, and Geoffrey Timmins. *Making Sense of the Industrial Revolution: English Economy and Society 1700–1850.* Manchester: Manchester University Press, 2001.
Organized thematically, King and Timmins take on certain issues of daily life that are rarely found in other volumes. This book is a useful complement to more economically oriented approaches.

Mantoux, Paul. *The Industrial Revolution in the Eighteenth Century: An Outline of the Beginnings of the Modern Factory System in England,* rev. ed. New York: Harper & Row, 1961.
This classic still provides the best glimpse of the dirt and grit of the early textile mills and how difficult it was to establish the factory system. The people who made the Industrial Revolution—entrepreneurs, inventors, managers, foremen, and workers—mattered enormously to Mantoux. This account is still unmatched for what it does.

The Global Origins of the Industrial Revolution

Allen, Robert C. *The British Industrial Revolution in Global Perspective*. Cambridge: Cambridge University Press, 2009.
Allen's concise, well-argued volume seeks to explain British leadership by emphasizing wages, agriculture, and cheap engines. Other scholars may not agree with his arguments, but they have to respond to them.

Inikori, Joseph E. *Africans and the Industrial Revolution in England: A Study in International Trade and Economic Development*. Cambridge: Cambridge University Press, 2002.
Without question, Inikori's challenge to scholars of the Industrial Revolution has been one of the most profound of the last generation. His powerful argument about the exploitative nature of the British Industrial Revolution and its reliance on slavery has not been adequately dealt with by the scholarship.

Pomeranz, Kenneth. *The Great Divergence: China, Europe, and the Making of the Modern World Economy*. Princeton, NJ: Princeton University Press, 2000.
Pomeranz's provocative assertion that the origins of economic "divergence" between China and Europe were based on the West's exploitation of other parts of the world undermines the complacency of insular scholars of Europe and the United States.

The Industrial Revolution Outside Britain

Broadberry, Stephen, and Kevin H. O'Rourke, eds. *The Cambridge Economic History of Modern Europe*, vol. 1, *1700–1870*. Cambridge: Cambridge University Press, 2010.
This short book is a more general European approach to understanding economic change and the place of the British Industrial Revolution in its continental context. It contains 11 chapters by noted experts.

Horn, Jeff, Leonard N. Rosenband, and Merritt Roe Smith, eds. *Reconceptualizing the Industrial Revolution*. Cambridge, MA: MIT Press, 2010.
This book contains 15 clearly written chapters that explore the Industrial Revolution in national context. Multiple chapters consider the British experience and two explore the United States, while others examine various European countries along with Japan, India, China, and Brazil. The bibliography also provides useful references.

Hounshell, David A. *From the American System to Mass Production, 1800–1932: The Development of Manufacturing Technology in the United States*. Baltimore: Johns Hopkins University Press, 1984.
This ground-breaking examination of the process of technological change spawned a host of imitators and competitors and is still one of the most highly readable accounts of U.S. industrialization.

Smith, Merritt Roe. *Harpers Ferry Armory and the New Technology: The Challenge of Change*. Ithaca, NY: Cornell University Press, 1977.
This classic examination of the workings of the Harpers Ferry armory and its place in the story of American industrialization is still rewarding.

Labor

Burnette, Joyce. *Gender, Work and Wages in Industrial Revolution Britain*. Cambridge: Cambridge University Press, 2008.
This powerfully argued book is controversial, but has stimulated important debate. Burnette asserts that differences in jobs and pay resulted from genuine disparities in productivity and were therefore a response to market forces.

Humphries, Jane. *Childhood and Child Labour in the British Industrial Revolution*. Cambridge: Cambridge University Press, 2011.
The best of a large number of similar books, Humphries compiled an unmatched set of autobiographies of young workers, which underlay an account of the Industrial Revolution that brings together economic statistics and intimate detail in a unique way.

Thompson, E. P. *The Making of the English Working Class*. New York: Vintage Books, 1966 [1963].
This magisterial account set the agenda for studies of the people who made Industrial Revolution for a generation. Reading this book will give a real sense of the problems and challenges faced by the working classes during the later stages of the British Industrial Revolution as well as their relationships with management and the state.

Primary Sources

Cole, G. D. H., and A. W. Filson, eds. *British Working Class Movements: Select Documents 1789–1875*. New York: St. Martin's Press, 1967.
This is an older collection, but it brings together a wonderful set of documents about how workers attempted to deal with mechanization, new technologies, growing managerial control, and the oppression of the state.

Pollard, Sidney, and Colin Holmes, eds. *Documents in European Economic History: Industrial Power and National Rivalry, 1870–1914*. New York: St. Martin's Press, 1968.
This venerable collection is particularly strong in demonstrating the role of management in the Industrial Revolution, both in Britain and elsewhere.

Science and Technology

Jacob, Margaret C. *Scientific Culture and the Making of the Industrial West*. Oxford: Oxford University Press, 1997.

This concise account investigates the role of culture in yielding scientific and technological advances in a comparative fashion.

Landes, David S. *The Unbound Prometheus: Technological Change and Industrial Development in Western Europe from 1750 to the Present.* Cambridge: Cambridge University Press, 1969.
Landes's interpretation, with its emphasis on the role of technology, is at the heart of most modern studies of the Industrial Revolution. Although the analysis also covers the continent, the British paradigm is at the basis of Landes's influential account of economic development.

MacLeod, Christine. *Heroes of Invention: Technology, Liberalism and British Identity 1750–1914.* Cambridge: Cambridge University Press, 2007.
This book explores how inventors and invention came to be central to British conceptions of themselves. MacLeod also makes clear both the myths and realities involved in this process and the significance for the emergence of liberal society.

Mokyr, Joel. *The Level of Riches: Technological Creativity and Economic Progress.* Oxford: Oxford University Press, 1991.
This short volume is full of insight into the relationship of technological improvement and economic development. It is clear and is still one of the best books on why some inventions matter more than others and that how people use an invention sometimes matters as much or more than its technical superiority.

Index

About the Author and Contributors

THE AUTHOR

JEFF HORN is Professor of History at Manhattan College. He is the author or editor of five previous books including *Economic Development in Early Modern France: The Privilege of Liberty, 1650–1850* (Cambridge University Press, 2015). He is working on the biography of a terrorist in the age of the French Revolution and will soon embark on writing a global history textbook *A People's History of the World* to be published by Oxford University Press.

THE CONTRIBUTORS

SERGIO CASTELLANOS-GAMBOA is a third-year PhD candidate at Bangor University, UK. His main areas of research interests include consumer finance, economic history, and financial macroeconomics. His current research aims at analyzing the evolution of consumer credit in Britain after World War II.

SOPHIE MULLER is a PhD Candidate in History at the Graduate Center, CUNY. She is a scholar of Victorian and Edwardian Britain with a specialization in childhood, masculinity, and class. She is completing her dissertation titled "Poster Boys: Paternalism, Working-Class Boyhood, and Masculinity in Victorian and Edwardian London." She also adjuncts at John Jay College of Criminal Justice and the Cooper Union.

ÉTIENNE STOCKLAND is a doctoral candidate in the History Department at Columbia University. His current research project is on the environmental and economic history of livestock in the South of France during the 18th century.